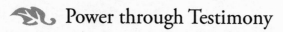 Power through Testimony

Edited by Brieg Capitaine
and Karine Vanthuyne

Power through Testimony

Reframing Residential Schools in the Age of Reconciliation

UBCPress · Vancouver · Toronto

26 25 24 23 22 21 20 19 18 17   5 4 3 2 1

Printed in Canada on FSC-certified ancient-forest-free paper (100% post-consumer recycled) that is processed chlorine- and acid-free.

Library and Archives Canada Cataloguing in Publication

Power through testimony : reframing residential schools in the age of reconciliation/edited by Brieg Capitaine and Karine Vanthuyne.

Includes bibliographical references and index.
Issued in print and electronic formats.
ISBN 978-0-7748-3389-9 (hardcover). – ISBN 978-0-7748-3391-2 (PDF).
ISBN 978-0-7748-3392-9 (EPUB) . – ISBN 978-0-7748-3393-6 (kindle)

1. Native peoples – Canada – Residential schools. 2. Native students – Canada–Social conditions. 3. Truth and Reconciliation Commission of Canada. 4. Truth commissions – Social aspects – Canada. I. Capitaine, Brieg, author, editor. II. Vanthuyne, Karine, 1974–, author, editor

E96.5.P69 2017   371.829'97071   C2016-908106-0
                                                                                       C2016-908107-9

Canada

UBC Press gratefully acknowledges the financial support for our publishing program of the Government of Canada (through the Canada Book Fund), the Canada Council for the Arts, and the British Columbia Arts Council.

This book has been published with the help of a grant from the Canadian Federation for the Humanities and Social Sciences, through the Awards to Scholarly Publications Program, using funds provided by the Social Sciences and Humanities Research Council of Canada.

Printed and bound in Canada by Friesens
Set in Garamond by Marquis Interscript
Copy editor: Robert Lewis
Proofreader: Kristy Lynn Hankewitz
Indexer: Margaret de Boer
Cover designer: Martyn Schmoll

UBC Press
The University of British Columbia
2029 West Mall
Vancouver, BC V6T 1Z2
www.ubcpress.ca

Contents

Foreword

RONALD NIEZEN

FOR THOSE WHO HEAR of the testimony presented to Canada's Truth and Reconciliation Commission on Indian residential schools, it can be shocking to learn that the Government of Canada and the Anglican, Catholic, Presbyterian, and United Churches were responsible for a residential school policy that forcibly took tens of thousands of children from their families and incarcerated them in institutions with the intention of eliminating their distinct languages and ways of life. It can be especially troubling to learn about the prevalence of sexual abuse in these schools from those who, as children, were victimized by sexual sadists and about the lasting effects of their trauma into adulthood, within their families, and across generations. And for those who look further into the work of the TRC, it can be disturbing to learn that there was a lack of engagement in the process of recognition and reparation by the federal government for the harms of the schools, with minimal government participation in the TRC's events and obstruction of its access to official documents.

These are the kinds of experiences and issues that, rightfully, easily capture our attention. But as the chapters in this book show, there is much to be gained by looking beyond the most prominent harms and controversies, beyond the obvious sources of sympathy, and beyond the compelling ideas that readily provoke compassion and indignation in order to also inquire into those issues and ideas that tell us more about the bigger picture, about such things as the place of the TRC in the history of human rights and transitional justice or the powerful influence of the mandates of truth commissions on the narratives they receive (or solicit) and the histories they produce.

The emotionally powerful narratives of abuse in the schools tended to make this issue the foundation of the TRC, but it is important to recognize that the sexual abuse of children is endemic in all institutions in which individuals are given absolute control over the absolutely powerless. Even though it was a central theme in the testimony to the TRC, sexual abuse in institutional settings is a much wider issue than that of the abuse that took place in residential schools. This point is illustrated by the fact that the Catholic Church has been challenged with the prevalence of pedophilia in the priesthood on a nearly global scale, with Pope Francis recently admitting in an interview, published in *La Repubblica* in July 2014, that "pedophilia is a leprosy within the Church that even implicates bishops and cardinals." In *Restoring Dignity: Responding to Child Abuse in Canadian Institutions*, the Law Commission of Canada (2000) finds that sexual abuse is endemic in all institutions in which children are held, including orphanages, schools for the deaf, and so forth. And on occasion, those who had experienced abuse in related institutions appeared before the TRC to give testimony, including representatives of the Duplessis Orphans at the Montreal National Event. This aspect of the abuse of power relations targets children as vulnerable, not Indigenous peoples as subjects of assimilation policy. In a way, the pervasiveness of testimony about sexual abuse in Canada's TRC tells us more about the consequences of institutional failure on a grand scale than about assimilation-oriented Indigenous policy. If children are at high risk of sexual abuse in all circumstances in which adults have unchecked power over them, what are the sources of harm that are unique to residential schools?

One of the things that stands out when we look for the bigger picture implied by this question is a basic historical correlation: the unfolding recognition of the harms of residential schools corresponds remarkably with the phenomenon sometimes known as the "human rights revolution." The TRC is very much a part of a global phenomenon in which truth commissions have become a means toward social, constitutional, and political reform (some even apply the term "healing") in the aftermath of mass crime. Moreover, Indigenous and Inuit people's awareness that their rights were violated by the residential schools can be understood in the context of a growing acceptance of human rights as a pathway toward political autonomy on the margins of states. The claims of residential school survivors are in this sense closely connected to the emergence of the global Indigenous movement and to the more general emergence of human rights as a pathway toward the moral correction of states.

Canada's Truth and Reconciliation Commission is unique in the extent to which the harms of historical proportion for which the state was responsible were to a great extent unknown to the public at large. This is unheard of in other circumstances in which truth commissions have taken place. The public in South Africa did not have to be informed about the existence of apartheid; the people of Chile did not have to be given basic facts about the abuses of dictator Augusto Pinochet's regime; nor did the people of Guatemala have to be told about the existence of their civil war. In these circumstances, as with many others of a similar kind, there is a basic public consensus on the historical facts that are the focal point of the state's transition and the subject matter of the truth commission. In Canada, however, the existence of Indian residential schools in this sense was relatively remote from public attention or concern. This circumstance means that Canada's TRC is also unique in the extent to which it assumed the task of public education and of reforming the dominant historical narrative of the state.

Truth commissions, by their nature, are strictly limited in their ability to take on this task of historical reform. This limitation is particularly evident in the case of Canada's TRC. For one thing, the mandate of the commission restricted the range of inquiry through a narrow definition of the institutions known as Indian residential schools, excluding, for example, those that were run by provincial governments, those that incarcerated Métis children, who did not have federal recognition as "status" Indians, or even those that were attended by Innu and Inuit children in Labrador (now the subject of a class action lawsuit), which were excluded from the Indian Residential Schools Settlement Agreement on the grounds that they were not funded directly by the federal government. To these can be added a range of institutions that had a similar orientation to assimilation-through-education of Indigenous and Inuit children, including day schools and orphanages. That is, if the subject matter of the TRC was the forced removal and assimilation of Indigenous and Inuit children, this focus does not correspond to the narrow range of institutions that were the object of its inquiry, as formally defined in the Settlement Agreement.

The historical capacities of the TRC were also limited by the kind of testimony it received and solicited. This circumstance was related to the challenge it faced of overcoming public ignorance and apathy. The organizers and participants of the TRC were highly motivated in their efforts to cultivate awareness and sympathy, making this aspect of their work similar to the lobbying activities of those justice-oriented nongovernmental organizations that rely on donations and activist involvement and that seek to bring public attention to their chosen cause(s), sometimes attempting to overcome indifference by making the causes they represent easy to understand, by simplifying the sources of moral responsibility and the consequences of harm, and, above all, by making the harm stand out as repugnant, giving audiences a sense that they are being privileged to hear unspeakable truths.

The disadvantage of a commission that was oriented toward public engagement and the affirmation of survivor experience was that it largely excluded from view the ordinary ideas and experiences that were the foundation of the residential schools as a historical phenomenon. The repugnant behaviour that first captures our attention has a tendency to stand alone, to be the source of our indignation at the presentation of facts and the narration of experience. There is sad irony in the fact that many of the same ideals of progress, common humanity, and the realization of individual potential through education can be found both in the background of Indian residential schools and in the truth commission that sought to come to terms with the harms caused by these schools. If this is the case, what really went wrong? More to the point, how might these ideals go wrong again in other institutional settings? In an odd way, the focus on repugnant forms of harm and extreme suffering encourages a kind of complacency, which finds comfort in the idea that such obvious abuses are now visible to the world and could never happen again.

The fact that oversimplified messages arise almost naturally out of an effort to correct a condition of ignorance suggests that there is something important and unrecognized about the public reception of knowledge, particularly knowledge about rights and the harms of the state. What are the conditions that produce widespread public knowledge of a rights cause, as well as dissidence under circumstances in which acting on that knowledge is opposed by the state? Is there something inherent in new media that intensifies the memetic effects of communication, effects that at the same time diminish people's capacity to see beyond the enclosures of rediscovered identity and their own self-interest? To put this in more concrete terms, does the production of knowledge about residential school experiences encourage the creation of closed communities based on oversimplifications of complex realities? The emerging body of research on Canada's Truth and

Reconciliation Commission on Indian residential schools, in which this book has a central place, suggests that the legal structures that limit what is sayable and the media that communicate what is said within those limits each contribute to narrowness and distortions of opinion. This circumstance means that to achieve its central goal – reconciliation on a grand scale out of an ambitious production of knowledge – the TRC was challenged by more than government obstruction and a lack of public interest in the truths it sought to make known. It first had to overcome new forces of enclosure, of nonreconciliation, particularly the tendency for communities to form around ideas that provide security and a sense of belonging while overlooking the costs of intolerance.

Power through Testimony

Introduction

BRIEG CAPITAINE AND KARINE VANTHUYNE

> Brave survivors, through telling their stories, have stripped white supremacy of its legitimacy.

> – Phil Fontaine, grand chief of the Assembly of First Nations, in response to the Government of Canada's 2008 "Statement of Apology"

"THE RESIDENTIAL SCHOOL STORY is far from finished," historian John S. Milloy (1999, 355) prophetically announced in one of the first published analyses of the history of the Indian residential school system in Canada. Since the publication of Milloy's book in 1999, residential schools have become one of the most important topics in the field of Indigenous studies. In this volume, however, we do not examine this history per se but instead focus on how it is being revisited, reframed, broadcast, and received by a variety of Indigenous and non-Indigenous actors in the wake of the Indian Residential Schools Settlement Agreement in Canada. Do memories of residential schools, as they are now rearticulated, have the capacity to transform social relationships between Canadian society and Indigenous peoples? Can they put an end to the domination and inequality that has long characterized these relationships? Have these memories "stripped white supremacy of its legitimacy," as suggested in the comment above by former grand chief of the Assembly of First Nations Phil Fontaine?

Beginning in 1876, the Canadian government sought to educate Indigenous children and assimilate them into mainstream Canadian society by promoting, and then requiring, their attendance at church-run schools (Miller 1996; Chrisjohn and Young 1997; Milloy 1999). By separating children from their parents and communities, denigrating Indigenous ways of living and thinking, and practising punitive forms of discipline, the schools aimed to eradicate Indigenous languages and cultures. Although some children had positive experiences with caring teachers and good education, the system was chronically underfunded, mismanaged, inadequately staffed, and rife with disease, malnutrition, neglect, and death. It is estimated that of the approximately 150,000 children who attended these institutions, at least 4,000 died and that many more of them were victims of physical or sexual abuse (Walker 2014). Those who were not subject to extreme violence still suffered from severe loneliness, fear, and cultural oppression. The last residential school closed in 1996.

Until the 1990s, as sociologist Eric Woods explains in this volume, the residential school system was predominantly represented as a benevolent policy of assimilation through education that was implemented by the Canadian government for the well-being of First Nations children and all "Indian tribes," more broadly (Milloy 1999, 6). Beginning in the 1960s, some bureaucrats and journalists attempted to raise public or governmental awareness of the injustices of the residential school system, but their levels of authority were not significant enough to impact dominant representations. However, this prominent image of the schools was shattered when Indigenous organizations and their academic allies, mainly non-Indigenous anthropologists (Haig-Brown 1988) and historians (Milloy 1999; Miller 1996), began to publicly reveal the extent to which the schools had been abusive. At the same time, the testimonies of former residential school students, many of whom came to collectively self-identify as survivors on the basis of shared experiences of mistreatment, became ever more audible thanks to the proceedings of the Royal Commission on Aboriginal Peoples. This inquiry, which took place between 1991 and 1996, eventually led to an important shift in authorship of the residential school story. Survivors' voices, which had until then not been heard as publicly accepted truth (Million 2013, 93) or which remained constrained by courts' procedures (Blackburn 2012), became historical facts. The residential school no longer symbolized a crime against individual students. Rather, as the voices of survivors entered the public sphere, the residential school system gradually came to be understood as a targeted program of assimilation deliberately organized by the state and religious institutions, the destructive effects of which are still being felt in Indigenous communities. *Breaking the Silence: An Interpretive Study of Residential School Impact and Healing as Illustrated by the Stories of First Nations Individuals* (Assembly of First Nations 1994) is an example of how the story of residential schools became the story of its survivors. Released by the Assembly of First Nations in the midst of increasing numbers of sexual abuse trials initiated by survivors and implicating residential school staff, it made explicit that survivors' "own interpretive frame would now be the frame from which they would tell the story" (Million 2013, 95).

The Royal Commission on Aboriginal Peoples was established in 1991 by the federal government in response to inherent antagonisms in state-Indigenous relations that had become acutely visible at the standoff in Oka, Quebec, in the summer of 1990.[1] It culminated in 1996 in a five-volume final report (RCAP 1996). The report covered a vast range of issues, including 440 recommendations that, all in all, called for the renewal of the legal and political relationship between Indigenous peoples and non-Indigenous peoples as well as between Indigenous peoples and the federal and provincial governments in Canada on the basis of the recognition of Indigenous nationhood (Turner 2013). Although most of these recommendations were tabled, ignored, or deferred, one issue, that of the confinement and abuse of Indigenous children in the Indian residential school system, was immediately addressed, since it made "the demands of Aboriginal redress amenable to a neoliberalising agenda" (Henderson 2013, 71).[2] In 1998 the Government of Canada's minister of Indian affairs offered a "Statement of Reconciliation" that expressed regret for "past actions that resulted in weakening the identity of Aboriginal Peoples, suppressing their languages and cultures, and outlawing spiritual practices" (Canada 1998, 2). It also announced a $350 million healing fund to address, through community-based initiatives, the lingering issues faced by those who were physically or sexually abused in the schools (Llewellyn 2002). Litigation by survivors, which grew from 6,000 to 12,000 cases between the years 2000 and 2004 (McKiggan 2007), doubled, nonetheless, due to the government's failure to recognize the residential school system as fundamentally wrong and its refusal to acknowledge the cultural harms caused by the schools (Jung 2011). In response to this wave of legal claims, the government proposed and implemented an Alternative Dispute Resolution Process as a means to redirect claims from the litigation process, reduce costs and timeframes, and facilitate healing and reconciliation (Regan 2010). However, this process too was quickly criticized for being overly complex, excluding claims related to cultural damages, failing to include healing elements, and ignoring the broader implications of the residential schools (Aboriginal Healing Foundation 2002; Llewellyn 2002; Regan 2010; Jung 2011). Survivors' dissatisfaction with the government's Alternative Dispute Resolution Process was demonstrated by their unwillingness to comply: a 2005 government document reveals that of 13,500 claimants, merely 1,200 applied for the process (Funk-Unrau and Snyder 2007). Many survivors opted instead for a $2.3 billion lawsuit, which was eventually given the green light to proceed to trial when the court ruled that the process did not represent a preferable means for settling the dispute (Regan 2010). In response to the numerous concerns raised about the Alternative Dispute Resolution Process, the government signed a Political Agreement in 2005, committing to negotiate a more adequate settlement process for former residential school students (ibid.; Jung 2011). However, news from the Ministry of Justice that the government did not intend to allow for their extensive involvement in the implementation of a compensation plan sparked further action (Barnsley 2005). Thus, in the wake of the Political Agreement, the Assembly of First Nations, led by then grand chief Phil Fontaine, launched a class action lawsuit against the government on behalf of all survivors and victims of the Indian residential school system.

In 2006 the Government of Canada and the churches that had once administrated the schools finally agreed with the Assembly of First Nations and regional Inuit representatives to an out-of-court settlement (Regan 2010). The Indian Residential Schools Settlement Agreement, the largest settlement of a class action lawsuit in Canadian history, involved (1) a healing fund and a commemoration fund, (2) a Common Experience Payment to every living survivor who attended an Indian residential school, (3) an Independent Assessment Process for individual claims related to physical and sexual abuse, and (4) a truth and reconciliation commission (IRSSA 2006).

On June 11, 2008, several days after the Truth and Reconciliation Commission officially began its work, Prime Minister Stephen Harper delivered an apology on behalf of the Canadian population to former residential school students. His speech, delivered in the House of Commons, was generally well received by Indigenous peoples, who found it to be a long-overdue show of public and political recognition of the extent of the harms done (Regan 2010). Unlike the "Statement of Reconciliation" (Canada 1998), Harper's apology went beyond a narrow acknowledgment of the role of the state in setting up and running residential schools. It also recognized that the residential school system was based on a racist ideology that not only led to sexual and physical abuse but also caused long-lasting emotional damage. Moreover, the apology was addressed not solely to former students of residential schools but also to their families, their communities, and the Indigenous community writ large. This apology, claims anthropologist Eva Mackey (2013), was nonetheless framed in such a way as to limit the definition of the wrongdoing that was its subject. As a result, it dismissed responsibility for land theft and broken treaties. Many responses from Indigenous leaders, she continues, therefore "push[ed] at the boundaries of the apology" (ibid., 57) as a way of reminding the settler state about the importance of acknowledging these material issues if true reconciliation was to happen in Canada.

Embroiled in the court proceedings around the scandals over child sexual abuse that began to come to light in the 1980s, religious institutions, whose power had by then considerably diminished, often had no choice but to publicly apologize. In 1986 the United Church presented its apologies to First Nations, although without explicitly mentioning residential schools. In 1991 the Reverend Doug Crosby presented apologies to First Nations people for what may have happened to them in the residential schools, as well as for the very existence of the schools, thereby acknowledging the imperialist undertaking in which the Catholic Church had taken part. The Royal Commission on Aboriginal Peoples then incited the Anglican and Presbyterian Churches to also present apologies in 1993 and 1994, respectively.

Power through Testimony looks at how residential schools are remembered and restoried in the wake of the Settlement Agreement and related official apologies. Focusing on the memorialization of the residential school system as a symbolic action is a new approach, as the first studies of the agreement, conducted at around the time of its implementation, for the most part took an institutional or legal approach. These early studies of the agreement focused on the socio-political conditions that surrounded its creation (Kelly 2008; Stanton 2011), mandate (Jung 2011; Nagy and Sehdev 2012), limitations (Alfred 2009; Flisfeder 2010; James 2010; Snyder 2010; Czyzewski 2011; Kershaw and Harkey 2011), or potential (Regan 2010; Hughes 2012; Stanton 2012). As is the case with many other studies of policies and programs implemented to address historical injustices (Ensalaco 1994;

Lemarchand 1994; Klosterman 1998), these first studies of the Settlement Agreement, for the most part, examined it from the point of view of its effectiveness. They did not appreciate the power of actors' stories and discourses to transform social relations.

This book focuses on that power, following the analytical framework developed by sociologist Tanya Goodman in her study of South Africa's Truth and Reconciliation Commission. In that study, Goodman (2009, 26) defines testimonies "as public acts of storytelling from a ritual and performative point of view." Her way of looking at public truth-telling processes is grounded in a horizontal conception of society that puts symbolic action and the meanings that actors give to social facts at the centre of social life. It builds on a number of sociologists' (Lamont 2000; Eyerman 2001; Alexander 2006) claims that communicative and symbolic dimensions are central to challenges of power structures emanating from victims of injustices.

Our approach, therefore, overcomes the normative conception of justice that informs most classical approaches to studying so-called transitional justice processes. Here, we examine how actors involved in the implementation of the Settlement Agreement, and the TRC in particular, have produced a new story about the Indian residential school system and how this symbolic action has succeeded, or not, in forging new attitudes and practices toward Indigenous peoples. The rules of most of the legal and political actions in which Indigenous actors have invested energy in order to practice their fundamental right to self-determination essentially remain set by the settler state (Tully 2002; Niezen 2004; Capitaine 2014). This situation has led many Indigenous intellectuals to privilege, instead, a more critical and symbolic approach to decolonization (Corntassel 2008; Million 2011, 2013). These authors insist on the power of restorying, or producing "counter-narratives of diplomacy, law, and peacemaking practices – as told by Indigenous Peoples themselves" (Corntassel, Chaw-win-is, and T'lakwadzi 2009, 138), as a key way of transforming power relations between settlers and Indigenous actors. We follow that perspective in this book.

Through a set of original contributions based on field research or text analysis conducted between 2010 and 2013, we highlight how the residential schools era has been resignified through the work of the TRC and the other reparation programs of the Settlement Agreement more largely. From our perspective, the TRC, like the Common Experience Payment and the Independent Assessment Process, is an actor that – through the events it organized, the forms and procedures it compelled, the data, testimonies, and artifacts it collected, and the actions it took – has defined what the Indian residential school system should officially mean. In taking this view, we follow in the footsteps of key scholars in the field of memory studies who have looked at crucial events, such as the fall of the Berlin Wall (Olick and Robbins 1998), as triggers of social recall and (non)acknowledgment of past wrongs. As we show, not only has the implementation of the Settlement Agreement prompted various forms of recollection of the residential school system; it has also encouraged Indigenous actors to denunciate other and ongoing colonial harms, as well as diverse forms of recognition and denial of such harms within the larger Canadian society.

What follows, therefore, is not an evaluation of what the TRC, the Common Experience Payment, and the Independent Assessment Process had accomplished, as per their mandate. We are not measuring to what extent these reparation programs met their goals as defined in the Settlement Agreement. Like anthropologist Ronald Niezen's (2013, xii) event ethnography of the TRC, we instead examine the agreement's reparation programs as institutions-in-the-making with key societal effects. Our contributions therefore address the following questions: What discourses and counter-discourses have Settlement Agreement reparation programs produced? What kind of performances have they encouraged? Which modes of identification have they activated? And how have these various processes or representations of the residential school system impacted participants and nonparticipants alike? Have they changed how settler colonialism is addressed in Canada?

The contributors to Part 1, "The Truth and Reconciliation Commission in Action," examine these questions by exploring the changing representational dynamics of the residential school system through time, as well as the current contribution of survivors to these dynamics. In so doing, they discuss the extent to which the residential school story that the TRC produced can contribute to liberating Indigenous selves and nations from still-dominant Eurocentric systems of assimilation. Whereas sociologist Eric Woods proposes a sweeping history of the transformation of public representations of residential schools in Canada since their establishment, sociologist Brieg Capitaine focuses on how the TRC has more particularly participated in the schools' resignification as sites of trauma. Cultural studies scholar Robyn Green then examines more precisely how expressions of love at the TRC may take on contradictory meanings from diverging positions. The section concludes with a conversation between Métis human kinetics scholar Janice Cindy Gaudet and Cree traditional knowledge keeper and

Mushkegowuk grand chief Lawrence Martin about shame and the role of Cree and Métis legends in healing.

Contributors to Part 2, "Conflicting Memories and Paths of Action," situate the public representation of residential schools that the TRC has produced within larger histories and personal experiences of colonization and dispossession. They underline the new forms of exclusion that this reading of the Indian residential school system is generating by highlighting the contrasting meanings that forced residential schooling takes on from divergent positions. Whereas anthropologist Simone Poliandri outlines how "being survivors" has become an additional form of individual and collective form of identification among the Mi'kmaw of Nova Scotia, anthropologist Arie Molema sketches the exclusions and remainders of memories that the Settlement Agreement, as the legal institution that now recognizes who a survivor is, has produced among the Inuit of Labrador. Anthropologist Karine Vanthuyne then discusses the competing narratives of forced residential schooling she has encountered among the Cree of Eeyou Istchee.

Contributors to Part 3, "(Un)reckoning with Historical Abuses," explore how former school staff, and church organizations more largely, received the residential school story that the TRC produced. Legal scholar Jula Hughes shows how, in their reporting on the work of the TRC as its events unfolded, Anglican, Catholic, and United Church journals, despite addressing the residential school system and its legacy, usually failed to capture the systemic and institutional impacts of this system as part of a broader set of colonizing policies. Religious studies scholar Cheryl Gaver outlines resistance to the representation of the residential school system as tragedy among the Anglicans she surveyed in Northwest Territories and Yukon. At the root of such resistance, she identifies ignorance, indifference, positive personal experiences in the schools, and colliding worldviews.

Transitional Justice and Decolonization

The TRC, along with the Common Experience Payment and the Independent Assessment Process, has contributed to the formalization of the field of transitional justice. To what extent, some of us therefore wonder, is the implementation of a transitional justice program effective in addressing ongoing settler colonialism in Canada? Is it enabling a genuine transformation of Indigenous-settler relationships? How has the TRC contributed to the decolonization of the institutional logic that holds sway over the relationships between Indigenous peoples and Canadian society? Responses to these questions are varied: whereas some see the symbolic activity of the TRC as a path for increased agency and for the reclaiming of freedom by Indigenous peoples in Canada, others are more critical, pointing out the difficulty actors face in extending reparations beyond the legacy of the residential schools.

The term "transitional justice" emerged in the late 1980s in the context of Latin American countries' so-called transitions to democracy (Lefranc 2008). It has since been used by an increasing number of postconflict experts and scholars to describe and legitimize a global set of standardized policies and programs favouring restorative over retributive justice (Arthur 2009).[3] Retributive justice focuses on committed crimes, their perpetrators, and the evaluation of offenders' sentences, given the severity of their actions. Restorative justice focuses instead on the negative consequences of these crimes for victims and what needs to be accomplished to reverse or at least reduce these impacts. Grounded in a restorative justice approach, transitional justice and its different modalities – including truth and reconciliation commissions, reparation programs such as the Common Experience Payment and the Independent Assessment Process, and projects of commemoration – are therefore primarily focused on victims of abuse, not their perpetrators. Although promoters of transitional justice recognize that it is not possible to repair the deleterious impacts of crimes committed during prolonged episodes of political or institutional violence, they hope to contribute to the wider acknowledgment of such wrongdoings and their impacts through the implementation of transitional justice programs and, as a result, to restore the dignity of victims and promote their reconciliation with the wider society.

Through a critical analysis of the Settlement Agreement, political scientist Courtney Jung (2011) has highlighted some of the potential complexities involved in using a transitional justice framework to process Indigenous demands for justice in Canada. The framework of transitional justice, she reminds us, was originally devised to facilitate reconciliation in countries undergoing transitions from authoritarian regimes to democracy – not to renegotiate the terms of the Indigenous-settler relationship on the basis of the recognition of Indigenous nationhood, as recommended by the Royal Commission on Aboriginal Peoples. Despite the constitutional changes of 1982 that entrenched Indigenous rights, the same governmental system under which the residential school system operated continues – including the Indian Act, the Indian reserve system, and the status of Indigenous communities as constitutionally subordinated jurisdictions controlled by a government primarily accountable to outsiders (James 2010). Therefore, Jung warns that treating Indigenous demands for justice as a matter of human rights is an ethically loaded project, as it risks legitimating the status quo between the settler state and Indigenous peoples in Canada.

This preoccupation was compounded by the relatively weak mandate of the investigative arm of the Settlement Agreement, the TRC. This body lacked subpoena powers and was prohibited from naming any individual accused of misconduct in its report, activities, or events, unless their identity had already been established through legal proceedings or through admission or public disclosure by that individual. Political scientist Matt James (2012, 190) argues that a ban on naming "means that even the limited sanction of negative publicity for the architects and perpetrators of abuses – often important to the idea of transitional justice as conventionally understood – is unavailable to the Canadian Commission." Given such limitations, political scientist Rosemary Nagy (2013) wonders to what extent the TRC had the capacity to advance decolonization, which she defines, following historian Waziyatawin Angela Wilson and sociologist Michael Yellow Bird, as "overturning the colonial structure and realizing Indigenous liberation" (ibid., 59). Such a deep structural change, she argues, would require settlers' expansive interpretation of residential schools not merely as a policy gone wrong but also as part of a larger program of colonization. Nagy argues that for this to happen, settlers must take ownership of colonial violence, past and present, debunk deeply ingrained colonial attitudes and patterns of behaviour, and recognize the direct, historical relationship between their privilege and Indigenous relative deprivation. Was the TRC able to accomplish these highly important yet vastly complex tasks?

It is important to note that, as we explained above, the Settlement Agreement was not imposed by the settler state on Indigenous peoples but was the outcome of a court-supervised settlement to a class action lawsuit launched by survivors (Stanton 2011). It was negotiated by representatives of the state, the churches, and Indigenous organizations, and as James (2012, 189) explains, these negotiations were shaped "by the dissatisfaction of all the parties with the adversarial nature and slow pace of the conventional legal process on the one hand, and by the longstanding desire of victims for a broader societal focus on their experiences on the other." Following legal scholar Kim Stanton (2011), James (2012, 189) argues that although the precise role that individual survivors played in these negotiations is unclear, they remained "the driving force behind the settlement negotiations." He further explains that with respect to the inclusion in the agreement of a truth commission more specifically, the prolonged reluctance and resistance of the state and the churches to acknowledge survivors' claims of injustice committed in and as a result of the residential school system "made the struggle for a truth commission one about voice and respect. Residential school survivors demanded that Canada open up, listen, learn, and start taking responsibility for the damage caused. The Commission is their victory and tribute" (ibid., 184).

As one of several components of the Settlement Agreement, the TRC was designed to discuss residential schools in a more contextualized manner than the Common Experience Payment and the Independent Assessment Proces. Certainly, on the part of many survivors, especially those who shared the Assembly of First Nations' model for a truth commission,[4] there was a desire to implement public education on larger systemic and collective issues (Nagy 2013). As then grand chief of the Assembly of First Nations Phil Fontaine stated, "Canadians have to accept in the fullest way possible that the story of the residential school experience is also their story" (quoted in ibid., 58). To this end, the TRC's commissioners defined the goal of reconciliation as societal healing, grounded in interpersonal understanding and forgiveness. James (2012, 195) believes that the emphasis on "the emotional need for understanding and support of individual residential school survivors" and "the remarkable power of the decision to forgive" that this definition relies upon may at first seem to come at the cost of overlooking structural oppression and inequalities – as political scientist Mahmood Mamdani (2002) has ardently criticized in regard to South Africa's Truth and Reconciliation Commission. This is what many Indigenous scholars have also decried. For political scientist Taiaiake Alfred (2009, 181), for instance, reconciliation, as it has been framed in the Settlement Agreement, is "an emasculating concept, weak-kneed and easily accepting of half-hearted measures of a notion of justice that does nothing to help Indigenous peoples regain their dignity and strength." According to Alfred, it is impossible to advance decolonization from within colonial institutions whose establishment had the effect of reducing and weakening Indigenous peoples. What is instead needed is the development of a "restitution-reconciliation peace-building process" (ibid., 183). This approach would entail that Canadian society recognize in a concrete way the illegitimate appropriation of

Indigenous territory and negation of the Indigenous right to self-determination. Political scientist Jeff Corntassel and philosopher Cindy Holder concur. According to them, the TRC, like all other modern truth commissions, has participated in marginalizing, concealing, and rendering invisible the issue of political self-determination for Indigenous peoples. These authors argue that by focusing on the construction of a new, more inclusive nation, the TRC has engaged in a politics of distraction that has "shift[ed] the discourse away from restitution of indigenous homelands and resources and ground[ed] it instead in a political/legal rights-based process that plays into the affirmative repair policies of states and ultimately rewards colonial injustices" (Corntassel and Holder 2008, 472).

Yet James (2012, 196) shows that the TRC commissioners insisted on their intent to promote an affective understanding of reconciliation as a way to "undermine racist myths of Indigenous inferiority, expose the destructive impact of the residential schools and showcase the resilience of Indigenous cultures." Undermining settler ignorance was their way of enhancing Indigenous peoples' self-determination agendas. To what extent has this particular process of epistemological decolonization for the sake of promoting Indigenous nations' sovereignty among the larger public, and more particularly among the churches' clergy and congregations, been effective?

Jula Hughes's contribution to this volume suggests that the TRC's stress on interpersonal understanding and forgiveness may have instead promoted what she calls conciliatory mimicry among the churches that once administrated and staffed the residential school system. Hughes defines conciliatory mimicry as "a resort to making people and institutions almost, but not quite, the same" in order "to legitimate power and to maintain a comfortable balance between sameness and difference." Drawing on textual analysis of documentation produced by the TRC, she argues that as a response to its lack of subpoena powers, and consequential inability to compel the participation of alleged perpetrators, the TRC reframed the status of the churches so that rather than being seen as potentially guilty parties, they were seen as co-victims of the residential school "experience." This reframing, she demonstrates, not only narrowed the conceptual gap between victims and perpetrators but also significantly altered the content of their contribution to the TRC. She notes that in their reporting of the work of the TRC, Anglican, Catholic, and United Church journals tended to focus on positive experiences at the schools or to externalize negative experiences either by attributing them to schools run by another church or by focusing on student-to-student mistreatments or intergenerational legacies. Hughes therefore concludes that "the depiction of the reconciliation process of the TRC in church publications completely failed to capture the systemic and institutional impacts of the residential school system as part of a broader set of colonizing policies ... Indigenous material exclusion, political under-representation, and economic and human insecurity all remained largely hidden from view."

In the end, therefore, few people in the churches seem to be getting the message, to paraphrase the title of the chapter by Cheryl Gaver. Giving voice to survivors' experiences does not seem to suffice, as James (2012, 199) warns, as a means "to produce larger societal understandings of colonialism as a system, or even to situate residential schools as core institutions in a colonization agenda of land theft and political dispossession." Drawing on an extensive ethnographic survey of Anglican Church clergy and congregations in the Northwest Territories, Gaver identifies additional roadblocks to this process of epistemological decolonization: indifference and ignorance, knowledge based on personal experience, and colliding worldviews. She explains that "some people are simply not interested and never will be." Others have difficulty acknowledging their church's responsibility. Some know former students who had positive experiences, or they perceive forgiveness from harmed students to be long-coming despite all the efforts they have deployed to repent. However, Gaver finds that the most significant obstacle is that any conversation about "the invisible and intangible dimensions that impacted students in subtle ways, even when schools or staff were respectful of Indigenous cultures," is missing. Although colonialism has been reckoned with, coloniality is still being ignored.

As postcolonial theorist Walter Mignolo (2005) explains, "colonialism" refers to specific historical periods and places of imperial domination, whereas "coloniality" refers to the logical structure of colonial domination. "Coloniality, therefore, points toward and intends to unveil an embedded logic that enforces control, domination, and exploitation disguised in the language of salvation, progress, modernization, and being good for everyone" (ibid., 6). Unveiling this logic, continues Mignolo, names the experiences and views of the world and history of those whose humanity has been denied and, in so doing, decentres so-called modernity as the one and only frame of knowledge. This process of decentring has yet to happen among the larger Canadian public, but it is required for decolonization to take place in this country.

Remembering the Schools, Restorying the Relationship

The decolonization of Indigenous peoples in Canada does not, however, depend solely on the activity of governmental and religious institutions or on the activity of Indigenous leaders. If we are to understand the degree and scope of the effects of these processes of renegotiation of unequal power dynamics, attention must also be paid to the performative and symbolic nature of power (Alexander 2011).

To this end, Indigenous intellectuals attempted very early on to decolonize sites of knowledge production – in particular, sites of scientific knowledge production (Kovach 2009; Smith 2012). In addition, and more recently, these intellectuals have begun to see artistic, literary, and narrative expressions as vehicles for a powerful form of decolonization: "We need to recognize our own power to reposition these [colonial narratives], to reattach and play new meaning to old horror, to renarrate, to restory our attachments, and certainly to live them differently, to speak to power differently" (Million 2011, 328). In their chapter, Janice Cindy Gaudet and Lawrence Martin show how conversation has a challenging effect on systems of shame. It evokes empathetic reflexivity of its effects in personal lives and everyday relationships. In so doing, they remind us that the TRC not only opened up institutionalized spaces of testimony but also increased communication as intersubjectivity. By grounding their analysis in the intimate experience of shame, they show how conversation can be a concrete process of subjectivation, which in the form of irony or laughter can sometimes help to overcome the shame of being itself.

The approach proposed here involves envisaging power not in its material or structural dimension but in its symbolic dimension. In so doing, it reassesses the materialist critique of the TRC. For James (2012), even though the truth that emerged from the commission did not identify precise actors and institutions responsible for past injustices, which would potentially have cleared the way for real reparations, the TRC, by being victim-centred, acted as a symbolic reversal of the power relations and colonial knowledge assumptions that had been embodied in the schools and that continue to be woven into Canadian institutions and society today. It is no longer the authorities who are constructing historical accounts; rather, by speaking out at national or regional TRC events, the survivors constructed a new collective memory – one that runs counter to and questions the status quo of Canadian history.

Social science's interest in groups' collective memories has increased dramatically in recent decades, leading to the re-editing of the pioneering studies of sociologist Maurice Halbwachs (1925, 1968). In opposition to the psychological approach to memory of philosopher Henri Bergson (1896), Halbwachs defined individual recollections as the product of collective memories – that is, the collective representations of the past that social groups share. Many social scientists, as anthropologist Joël Candau (2005) explains, have criticized Halbwachs concept of collective memories for presupposing the existence of a collective consciousness "external and superior to individual minds" (Bastide 1970, 82; our translation). From this Durkheimian perspective, Candau continues, individuals are considered to be the passive repositories of a collective memory predetermined by the needs and interests of the groups to which they belong. However, other social scientists, such as political scientist Marie-Claire Lavabre (1998), anthropologists Maria G. Cattel and Jacob J. Climo (2002), and sociologists Jeffrey K. Olick, Vered Vinitzky-Seroussi, and Daniel Levy (2011), claim that Halbwachs was not so much "in favour of a supraordinate mind, but in favour of shared or collective thought arising from interactions among individuals as members of groups" (Cattel and Climo 2002, 4). They therefore highlight the value of some of his theoretical postulates, such as Halbwachs's (1992, 40) insistence on the role of shared memories in constituting group identities over time and his contention that "the past is not preserved but is reconstructed on the basis of the present." From this perspective, individuals remember as members of social groups – that is, as social beings with reference to social identities. Their memories are the product of a selective process of interpretation of the past that usually follows their groups' political ends. Thus, alongside victors' collective memories and identities, victims' countermemories emerge to question the status quo (Foucault 1997).

Since their apparition in the 1980s in the wake of Latin America's transition to democracy (Lefranc 2008), truth commissions have become key sites for the struggle to reckon with victims' countermemories of abusive pasts. Thanks to their use of a predominantly victim-centred approach, as we have argued above, truth commissions are considered by their sponsors to be a powerful means "to lift ... the lid of silence and denial from contentious and painful periods of history" (Hayner 2002, 25). But what is the status of countermemories produced through truth commissions? If memory work was once imagined as a practice oppositional to hegemonic power, to paraphrase performance studies scholar Jill Lane and anthropologist Marcial Godoy-Anativia (2010), in what ways has the institutionalization of such work transformed strategies of counterhistory production and truth telling among history's victims? Have residential school survivors embraced the official countermemory and associated identities that Canada's TRC has produced, or are they creating new ones?

In his chapter, Eric Taylor Woods discusses the long and difficult process of representation of the history of residential schools in the public sphere and finds that the ability of the TRC to engender a lasting countermemory, one collaboratively constructed with participants, rests in part on the social positioning of those who spoke up at its events. This countermemory needed to acquire the ring of truth, and the key element of this process was the social distance between those who spoke up and those who listened (Alexander 2012), as well the legitimacy of those who articulated this new memory. Brieg Capitaine shows that residential schools, when accorded the status of cultural trauma, become a reference point that delineates spatial and temporal frontiers. Spatially, a distinction is made between "us" and "the others"; temporally, boundaries are created between a mythical past, a present of deprivation, and a future marked by resistance and by a new collective identity. The "success" of the TRC in implanting this counter-memory derived not only from a narrative framework sufficiently large to make identification possible but also from the social proximity between Indigenous peoples, most of whom had a period in their personal trajectories when they experienced emptiness, violence, and in some cases, resilience. The singular experience of residential schools and the collective discourse around cultural collapse, but also the positivity and the resistance of survivors, all found an echo with the TRC's Indigenous audience.

In her chapter, Simone Poliandri shows that in the case of the Mi'kmaw, this countermemory – like the "survivor" identity that is attached to it – arouses a strong sense of identification and has generated new social, political, and legal struggles. Here, the figure of Nora Bernard, a Mi'kmaw survivor and former director of the Shubenacadie Indian Residential School Association, is central. The charismatic legitimacy of the actors plays an equally important role in the transmission of this memory. In this sense, Poliandri's contribution echoes Niezen's (2013) analysis of the TRC, which shows how the countermemory of residential schools that has been produced in its wake relies on a set of scientific knowledges and rationalist paradigms that exert an influence in return, primarily through the notion of historical trauma. The legal-rational legitimacy may thus also play a role in the transmission and the status of this countermemory.

Nevertheless, one of the by-products of the narrative constructed by the TRC is that it renders the experience uniform even as the telling of it, the giving of voice to it, signifies for the actors a concrete demonstration of their own subjectivity, reflexivity, and capacity to position themselves in the social space while not losing themselves therein. Moreover, in his chapter, Arie Molema shows that, because it emerges in part out of the mandate of the TRC and the methods of the Settlement Agreement, this countermemory cannot help but exclude certain victims and privilege a particular truth, as is often the case with truth commissions (Hayner 2002). Not all memories of forced schooling have been recognized, adjudicated, and valued the same by the Canadian settler state through its implementation of the agreement. Only survivors who attended an institution that has been formally recognized as a residential school in the agreement have received the Common Experience Payment and been considered eligible for the Independent Assessment Process. Favouring another approach, since it found "the exclusion of these students [from nonrecognized residential schools] a serious roadblock to meaningful and sincere reconciliation," the TRC (2012, 9) welcomed the participation of all former students, regardless of the institutions they had attended. Nonetheless, this policy did not prevent some nonrecognized students from feeling, once again, as though they were nobody's children (Cuffe 2012). As one woman told Molema, "The TRC thinks that because I speak the truth, I'm on the step to *healing*. No ... It takes a whole lot more than *talking* ... Three o'clock in the morning when everybody's asleep and I can't sleep. And I'm alone in the world. And the thoughts are going around in a circle."

Poliandri also discusses survivors from formally recognized schools whose experiences resisted the kind of verbalization the TRC prescribed. In the healing workshops that he attended in the Mi'kmaq communities where he conducted his research, Poliandri met people who remained silent most of the time, but when they did choose to speak, they voiced "pain – 'right here, deep inside my guts.'" To be sure, the pain that any kind of violence provokes usually "encompasses an irreducible nonverbal dimension that we cannot know – not at least in any normal mode of knowing – because it happens in a realm beyond language" (Morris 1997, 27). Yet some silences about experiences of violence are not intrinsic but are socially and politically produced. The Settlement Agreement, as a legally sanctioned collective memory of Canada's colonial past, commends what survivors and nonsurvivors alike ought to reckon as abusive or nonabusive, condemnable or noncondemnable, and related to or unrelated to their experience of residential schools and settler colonialism more largely. However, this situation does not mean that all survivors have embraced this memory of the schools and of the larger history of settler colonialism in Canada.

In this volume, Karine Vanthuyne shows that, although some of the Cree of Eeyou Istchee's narratives of mandated schooling focus on the mistreatment and loss of close family relations, others emphasize resistance to abuses and the useful acquisition of English literacy in order to take things over. She argues that the contrasts between these two kinds of accounts are grounded in diverging assessments of the well-being of the Cree following the ratification of the James Bay and Northern Quebec Agreement. Some Cree believe that their greater integration into the settler states of Canada and Quebec through this agreement has been beneficial since it has allowed their nation to regain its self-reliance. Others feel that it has meant the demise of their essentially nonmaterialistic way of relating to their social world. This disagreement echoes ongoing debates in Cree territory (Lapointe and Scott forthcoming) and beyond (Preston 2013) about the ability of Indigenous nations to maintain their cultural identity in the face of growing externally led developments on their homelands, such as hydroelectric dams, forestry industries, and mines.

Therefore, although the Settlement Agreement, as Canada's official, new collective memory of its colonial history, might have the power to shape how this past is currently and predominantly accounted for in this country, it does not restrict the terms of the conversations Indigenous actors have about it in Canada. Although this memory tends to ignore issues of land and governance to focus instead on institutionalized child abuse, what Indigenous peoples end up speaking about when they discuss the schools are these very issues. In this volume, Robyn Green shows how some survivors who testified at the TRC's events actually subverted the compartmentalization of colonial experiences that the Settlement Agreement has produced. By identifying the connection between residential schooling and dispossession, they gestured toward the realization of sovereignty, both political and territorial. Looking more specifically at the meaning that participants at TRC events gave to the term "love" and the activity of loving, Green argues that although their expressions of love are inscribed in a project of humanity that aspires to universality, they should not be strictly regarded as dismantling the potential for self-determination. Speaking about love, she claims, may also promote self-determination by acknowledging both survival and acts of wrongdoing enacted by the settler state.

Alfred and Corntassel (2005, 601) claim that "there is a danger in allowing colonization to be the only story of Indigenous lives. It must be recognized that colonialism is a narrative in which the Settler's power is the fundamental reference and assumption, inherently limiting Indigenous freedom and imposing a view of the world that is but an outcome or perspective on that power." For this reason, they stress the importance of restorying as a first step to remembering and revitalizing Indigenous collective and individual consciousness. Corntassel and social work scholars Chawwin-is and T'lakwadzi (2009, 139) explain that "a re-storying process for Indigenous Peoples entails questioning the imposition of colonial histories on our communities." We argue that, in the end, although it is premised on Canada's colonial narrative and therefore seems to constitute a politics of distraction (Corntassel and Holder 2008, 472), the Settlement Agreement has opened up a space in which the residential school story, and that of settler colonialism more largely, is not only remembered but also, more importantly, reframed.

NOTES

1 In the spring of 1990, Mohawks barricaded access to a few dozen acres that the small community of Oka sought to use for expansion of a golf course. The Mohawks claimed the land as a sacred burial ground and argued that it rightly belonged to them.

2 "In an era of ideological consensus about the properly 'modest' state," explains English studies scholar Jennifer Henderson (2013, 63), "the recognized wrongs of the past are often seen to be related ... to the spectre of the bloated interventionist state that reached too far, constrained or coerced, and thereby violated individual integrity." From a neoliberal perspective, what needs to be redressed, therefore, regarding Canada's colonial wrongdoings, are assaults on Indigenous subjects' individual rights to self-sufficiency, not violations of Indigenous nations' collective rights to self-determination – the latter of which would have been accomplished through implementation of the main recommendation of the Royal Commission on Aboriginal Peoples (1996), namely, a recognition of the right to Indigenous nationhood by the Canadian state (Turner 2013).

3 Our definition of "transitional justice" as favouring restorative over retributive justice follows historian Paige Arthur's (2009) conceptual history of this expression, not its genealogy by legal scholar Ruti G. Teitel (2003). Whereas Teitel traces the origins of modern transitional justice back to the First World War, and therefore includes retributive measures of justice within her definition of the term, Arthur argues against such "anachronism." Arthur claims

that a history of transitional justice can begin only with the invention of the phrase itself, which did not take place before 1992, according to her keyword searches in databases of international newspapers, law reviews, and social science journals. And since 1992, as Teitel herself argues, restorative measures of justice have been increasingly favoured over retributive measures of justice.

4 In her analysis of the genesis of the TRC, Nagy (2014, 200) states that "two different approaches to a truth commission were brought together during the settlement negotiations." The first approach, she explains, was promoted by the Assembly of First Nations and had a more legalistic focus on accountability and the public record. The other, she continues, was promoted by those who, in the course of the settlement negotiations in 2004, participated in the TRC Roundtable, which comprised survivors, Indigenous healers and leaders, and representatives of Protestant organizations. Their approach was focused more on grassroots and community. As the TRC completed its mandate, Nagy concludes, both visions of a truth commission continued to exist in tension.

REFERENCES

Aboriginal Healing Foundation. 2002. *The Healing Has Begun: An Operational Update from the Aboriginal Healing Foundation.* Ottawa: Aboriginal Healing Foundation.

Alexander, Jeffrey C. 2006. *The Civil Sphere.* New York: Oxford University Press.

–. 2011. *Performance and Power.* Cambridge, UK: Polity.

–. 2012. *Trauma: A Social Theory.* Cambridge, UK: Polity.

Alfred, Taiaiake. 2009. "Restitution Is the Real Pathway to Justice for Indigenous Peoples." In *Response, Responsibility, and Renewal: Canada's Truth and Reconciliation Journey,* ed. Gregory Younging, Jonathan Dewar, and Mike DeGagné, 179–87. Ottawa: Aboriginal Healing Foundation.

Alfred, Taiaiake, and Jeff Corntassel. 2005. "Being Indigenous: Resurgences against Contemporary Colonialism." *Government and Opposition* 40 (4): 597–614. http://dx.doi.org/10.1111/j.1477-7053.2005.00166.x.

Arthur, Paige. 2009. "How 'Transitions' Reshaped Human Rights: A Conceptual History of Transitional Justice." *Human Rights Quarterly* 31 (2): 321–67. http://dx.doi.org/10.1353/hrq.0.0069.

Assembly of First Nations. 1994. *Breaking the Silence: An Interpretive Study of Residential School Impact and Healing as Illustrated by the Stories of First Nations Individuals.* Ottawa: Assembly of First Nations.

Barnsley, P. 2005. "AFN Launches Class Action Lawsuit." *Windspeaker* 23 (6): 8–13.

Bastide, Roger. 1970. "Mémoire collective et sociologie du bricolage." *L'Année sociologique (1940/1948–),* 3rd series, 21: 65–108.

Benhabib, Seyla. 1996. *The Reluctant Modernism of Hannah Arendt.* Lanham, MD: Rowman and Littlefield.

Bergson, Henri. 1896. *Matière et mémoire: Essai sur la relation du corps à l'esprit.* Reprint, Paris: Presses universitaires de France, 2008.

Blackburn, Carole. 2012. "Culture Loss and Crumbling Skulls: The Problematic of Injury in Residential School Litigation." *Political and Legal Anthropology Review* 35 (2): 289–307. http://dx.doi.org/10.1111/j.1555-2934.2012.01204.x.

Canada. 1998. "Statement of Reconciliation." In *Gathering Strength: Canada's Aboriginal Action Plan,* 2–3. Ottawa: Minister of Indian Affairs and Northern Development. http://www.ahf.ca/downloads/gathering-strength.pdf.

Candau, Joël. 2005. *Anthropologie de la mémoire*. Paris: Armand Colin.

Capitaine, Brieg. 2014. "Les voies de la résistance autochtone à la colonisation." In *Des lendemains doux-amers: Espoirs et désenchantements du Tiers-Monde postcolonial*, ed. Maurice Demers and Patrick Dramé, 246–60. Montreal: Presses de l'Université de Montréal.

Cattel, Maria G., and Jacob J. Climo. 2002. "Introduction: Meaning in Social Memory and History." In *Social Memory and History: Anthropological Perspectives*, ed. Jacob J. Climo and Maria G. Cattel, 1–36. Walnut Creek, CA: Altamira.

Chrisjohn, Roland D., and Sherri Young. 1997. *The Circle Game: Shadows and Substance in the Indian Residential School Experience in Canada*. Penticton, BC: Thetus Books.

Corntassel, Jeff. 2008. "Toward Sustainable Self-Determination: Rethinking the Contemporary Indigenous-Rights Discourse." *Alternatives* 33 (1): 105–32. http://dx.doi.org/10.1177/030437540803300106.

Corntassel, Jeff, and Cindy Holder. 2008. "Who's Sorry Now? Government Apologies, Truth Commissions, and Indigenous Self-Determination in Australia, Canada, Guatemala, and Peru." *Human Rights Review* (Piscataway, New Jersey) 9 (4): 465–89. http://dx.doi.org/10.1007/s12142-008-0065-3.

Corntassel, Jeff, Chaw-win-is, and T'lakwadzi. 2009. "Indigenous Storytelling, Truth-telling, and Community Approaches to Reconciliation." *English Studies in Canada* 35 (1): 137–59. http://dx.doi.org/10.1353/esc.0.0163.

Cuffe, Sandra. 2012. "Nobody's Children: Métis Residential School Survivors Continue to Fight for Recognition." *Vancouver Media Co-op*, June 24. http://vancouver.mediacoop.ca/fr/story/nobodys-children/11481.

Czyzewski, Karina. 2011. "The Truth and Reconciliation Commission of Canada: Insights into the Goal of Transformative Education." *International Indigenous Policy Journal* 2 (3): 1–12. http://ir.lib.uwo.ca/cgi/viewcontent.cgi?article=1026&context=iipj.

Ensalaco, Mark. 1994. "Truth Commissions for Chile and El Salvador: A Report and Assessment." *Human Rights Quarterly* 16 (4): 656–75. http://dx.doi.org/10.2307/762563.

Eyerman, Ron. 2001. *Cultural Trauma: Slavery and the Formation of African American Identity*. Cambridge, UK: Cambridge University Press. http://dx.doi.org/10.1017/CBO9780511488788.

Flisfeder, M.A. 2010. "A Bridge to Reconcoliation: A Critique of the Indian Residential School Truth Commission." *International Indigenous Policy Journal* 1 (1): 1–25. http://ir.lib.uwo.ca/iipj/vol1/iss1/3.

Foucault, Michel. 1997. *"Il faut défendre la société": Cours au Collège de France, 1976*. Paris: Seuil/Gallimard.

Funk-Unrau, S., and A. Snyder. 2007. "Indian Residential School Survivors and State-Designed ADR: A Strategy for Co-optation?" *Conflict Resolution Quarterly* 24 (3): 285–304. http://dx.doi.org/10.1002/crq.175.

Goodman, Tanya. 2009. *Staging Solidarity: Truth and Reconciliation in a New South Africa*. Boulder: Paradigm Publishers.

Haig Brown, Celia. 1988. *Resistance and Renewal: Surviving the Indian Residential School*. Vancouver: Arsenal Pulp Press.

Halbwachs, Maurice. 1925. *Les cadres sociaux de la mémoire*. Reprint, Paris: Albin Michel, 1994.

–. 1968. *La mémoire collective*. 2nd ed. Paris: Presses universitaires de France.

–. 1992. *On Collective Memory*. Trans. Lewis A. Coser. Chicago: University of Chicago Press.

Hayner, Priscilla B. 2002. *Unspeakable Truths: Facing the Challenge of Truth Commissions.* New York: Routledge.

Henderson, Jennifer. 2013. "The Camp, the School, and the Child: Discursive Exchanges and Neoliberal Axioms in the Culture of Redress." In *Reconciling Canada: Critical Perspectives on the Culture of Redress,* ed. Jennifer Henderson and Pauline Wakeham, 63–83. Toronto: University of Toronto Press.

Hughes, Jula. 2012. "Instructive Past: Lessons from the Royal Commission on Aboriginal Peoples for the Canadian Truth and Reconciliation Commission on Indian Residential Schools." *Canadian Journal of Law and Society* 27 (1): 101–27. http://dx.doi.org/10.3138/cjls.27.1.101.

Indian Residential Schools Settlement Agreement (IRSSA). 2006. *Indian Residential Schools Settlement Agreement.* Ottawa: Government of Canada. http://www.residentialschool-settlement.ca/irs%20settlement%20agreement-%20english.pdf.

James, Matt. 2010. "Uncomfortable Comparisons: The Canadian Truth and Reconciliation Commission in Context." *Ethics Forum/Les ateliers de l'éthique* 5 (2): 23–35. https://papyrus.bib.umontreal.ca/xmlui/bitstream/handle/1866/4336/pdf_02_James.pdf?sequence=4

–. 2012. "A Carnival of Truth? Knowledge, Ignorance and the Canadian Truth and Reconciliation Commission." *International Journal of Transitional Justice* 6 (2): 182–204.

Jung, Courtney. 2011. "Canada and the Legacy of the Indian Residential Schools: Transitional Justice for Indigenous People in a Nontransitional Society." In *Identities in Transition: Challenges for Transitional Justice in Divided Societies,* ed. Paige Arthur, 217–50. Cambridge, UK: Cambridge University Press.

Kelly, Fred. 2008. "Confessions of a Born Again Pagan." In *From Truth to Reconciliation: Transforming the Legacy of Residential Schools,* ed. Marlene Brant Castellano, Linda Archibald, and Mike DeGagné, 11–40. Ottawa: Aboiriginal Healing Foundation. http://www.ahf.ca/downloads/from-truth-to-reconciliation-transforming-the-legacy-of-residential-schools.pdf.

Kershaw, Paul, and Tammy Harkey. 2011. "The Politics and Power in Caregiving for Identity: Insights for Indian Residential School Truth and Reconciliation." *Social Politics* 18 (4): 572–97. http://dx.doi.org/10.1093/sp/jxr015.

Klosterman, Theresa. 1998. "The Feasibility and Propriety of a Truth Commission in Cambodia: Too Little? Too Late?" *Arizona Journal of International and Comparative Law* 15 (3): 833–70.

Kovach, Margaret. 2009. *Indigenous Methodologies: Characteristics, Conversations and Contexts.* Toronto: University of Toronto Press.

Lamont, Michèle. 2000. *The Dignity of Working Men: Morality and the Boundaries of Race, Class, and Immigration.* Cambridge, MA: Havard University Press.

Lane, Jill, and Marcial Godoy-Anativia. 2010. "After Truth: Editorial Remarks." *E-Misférica* 7 (2): 1–4. http://hemisphericinstitute.org/hemi/en/e-misferica-72/72-editorial-remarks.

Lapointe, Ugo, and Colin Scott. Forthcoming. "A Balancing Act: Mining and Protected Areas in Wemindji." In *The Science and Politics of Protected Area Creation: Striking the Balance,* ed. Monica E. Mulrennan, Katherine Scott, and Colin Scott. Vancouver: UBC Press.

Lavabre, Marie-Claire. 1998. "Maurice Halbwachs et la sociologie de la mémoire." *Raison presente* (128): 47–56.

Lefranc, Sandrine. 2008. "La justice transitionnelle n'est pas un concept." *Mouvements* (Paris, France) 1 (53): 61–69. http://dx.doi.org/10.3917/mouv.053.0061.

Lemarchand, Rene. 1994. "Managing Transition Anarchies: Rwanda, Burundi, and South Africa in a Comparative Perspective." *Journal of Modern African Studies* 32 (4): 581–604. http://dx.doi.org/10.1017/S0022278X0001586X.

Llewellyn, Jennifer. 2002. "Dealing with the Legacy of Native Residential School Abuse in Canada: Litigation, ADR, and Restorative Justice." *University of Toronto Law Journal* 52 (3): 253–300. http://dx.doi.org/10.3138/utlj.52.3.253.

Mackey, Eva. 2013. "The Apologizer's Apology." In *Reconciling Canada: Critical Perspectives on the Culture of Redress,* ed. Jennifer Henderson and Pauline Wakeham, 47–62. Toronto: University of Toronto Press.

Mamdani, Mahmood. 2002. "Amnesty or Impunity? A Preliminary Critique of the Report of the Truth and Reconciliation Commission of South Africa." *Diacritics* 32 (3): 33–59. http://dx.doi.org/10.1353/dia.2005.0005.

McKiggan, John. 2007. "Indian Residential Schools: A Brief History of the Largest Abuse Claim Settlement Ever." *John McKiggan's Abuse Claims Blog,* May 4. https://abuseclaims.wordpress.com/2007/05/04/indian-residential-schools-a-brief-history-of-the-largest-abuse-claim-settlement-ever.

Mignolo, Walter. 2005. *The Idea of Latin America.* Malden, MA: Blackwell.

Miller, J.R. 1996. *Shingwauk's Vision: A History of Native Residential Schools.* Toronto: University of Toronto Press.

Million, Dian. 2011. "Intense Dreaming: Theories, Narratives and Our Search for Home." *American Indian Quarterly* 35 (3): 314–33.

–. 2013. *Therapeutic Nations: Healing in an Age of Indigenous Human Rights.* Tucson: University of Arizona Press.

Milloy, John Sheridan. 1999. *"A National Crime": The Canadian Government and the Residential School System, 1879–1986.* Winnipeg: University of Manitoba Press.

Morris, David B. 1997. "About Suffering: Voice, Genre, and Moral Community." In *Social Suffering,* ed. Arthur Kleinman, Veena Das, and Margaret Lock, 25–46. Berkeley: University of California Press.

Nagy, Rosemary L. 2013. "The Scope and Bounds of Transitional Justice and the Canadian Truth and Reconciliation Commission." *International Journal of Transitional Justice* 7 (1): 52–73. http://dx.doi.org/10.1093/ijtj/ijs034.

–. 2014. "The Truth and Reconciliation Commission of Canada: Genesis and Design." *Canadian Journal of Law and Society* 29 (2): 199–217.

Nagy, Rosemary L., and Robinder Kaur Sehdev. 2012. "Introduction: Residential Schools and Decolonization." *Canadian Journal of Law and Society* 27 (1): 67–73. http://dx.doi.org/10.3138/cjls.27.1.067.

Niezen, Ronald. 2004. *A World Beyond Difference: Cultural Identity in the Age of Globalization.* Malden, MA: Blackwell. http://dx.doi.org/10.1002/9780470776582.

–. 2013. *Truth and Indignation: Canada's Truth and Reconciliation Commission on Indian Residential Schools.* Toronto: University of Toronto Press.

Olick, Jeffrey K., and Joyce Robbins. 1998. "Social Memory Studies: From 'Collective Memory' to the Historical Sociology of Mnemonic Practices." *Annual Review of Sociology* 24: 105–40.

Olick, Jeffrey K., Vered Vinitzky-Seroussi, and Daniel Levy. 2011. *The Collective Memory Reader.* New York: Oxford University Press.

Preston, Jen. 2013. "Neoliberal Settler Colonialism, Canada and the Tar Sands." *Race and Class* 55 (2): 42–59. http://dx.doi.org/10.1177/0306396813497877.

Regan, Paulette. 2010. *Unsettling the Settler Within: Indian Residential Schools, Truth Telling, and Reconciliation*. Vancouver: UBC Press.

Royal Commission on Aboriginal Peoples (RCAP). 1996. *Report of the Royal Commission on Aboriginal Peoples*. Ottawa: Royal Commission on Aboriginal Peoples.

Smith, Linda Tuhiwai. 2012. *Decolonizing Methodologies: Research and Indigenous Peoples*. 2nd ed. London: Zed Books.

Snyder, Emily. 2010. "The Ethics of Reconciling: Learning from Canada's Truth and Reconciliation Commission." *Ethics Forum/Les ateliers de l'éthique* 5 (2): 36–48. https://papyrus.bib.umontreal.ca/xmlui/bitstream/handle/1866/4337/pdf_03_Snyder.pdf?sequence=4&isAllowed=y.

Stanton, Kim. 2011. "Canada's Truth and Reconciliation Commission: Settling the Past?" *International Indigenous Policy Journal* 2 (3): 1–18. http://ir.lib.uwo.ca/iipj/vol2/iss3/2.

–. 2012. "Looking Forward, Looking Back: The Canadian Truth and Reconciliation Commission and the Mackenzie Valley Pipeline Inquiry." *Canadian Journal of Law and Society* 27 (1): 81–99. http://dx.doi.org/10.3138/cjls.27.1.081.

Teitel, Ruti G. 2003. "Transitional Justice as Liberal Narrative." In *Out of and into Authoritarian Law*, ed. Andrà Sajò, 3–13. La Haye: Kluwer Law International.

Truth and Reconciliation Commission of Canada (TRC). 2012. *Interim Report*. Winnipeg, MB: Truth and Reconciliation Commission of Canada.

Tully, James. 2002. "Défi constitutionnel et art de la résistance: La question des peuples autochtones au Canada." In *Altérité et droit: Contributions à l'étude du rapport entre droit et culture*, ed. Isabelle Schulte-Tenckhoff, 263–300. Brussels: Bruylant.

Turner, Dale A. 2013. "On the Idea of Reconciliation in Contemporary Aboriginal Politics." In *Reconciling Canada: Critical Perspectives on the Culture of Redress*, ed. Jennifer Henderson and Pauline Wakeham, 100–14. Toronto: University of Toronto Press.

Walker, Connie. 2014. "New Documents May Shed Light on Residential School Deaths." *CBC News*, January 7. http://www.cbc.ca/news/aboriginal/new-documents-may-shed-light-on-residential-school-deaths-1.2487015.

Part 1
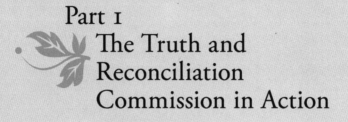 The Truth and
Reconciliation
Commission in Action

1

On the Making of a National Tragedy: The Transformation of the Meaning of the Indian Residential Schools

ERIC TAYLOR WOODS

INDIAN RESIDENTIAL SCHOOLS are widely represented in the Canadian public sphere as a terrible tragedy. Indeed, they have become the pre-eminent symbol of the deleterious consequences of Canada's colonial history for Indigenous peoples. This representation of the school system is in stark contrast to how it was represented by its founders, who likened the residential schools to a humanitarian – even sacred – enterprise designed to save Indigenous communities from extinction in the face of an ostensibly higher form of civilization. My aim here is to trace the process by which the transformation in the representation of residential schools occurred.

Research on residential schools has burgeoned in recent decades. The main thrust of the research has been on bringing to light empirical facts related to how the schools functioned and their impact on the students and their communities. There have been important findings on the school system as a whole (e.g., Miller 1996; Milloy 1999), as well as on individual schools (e.g., Coates 1984; Gresko 1992). Not only have historians and social researchers been involved in this research agenda, but health scientists have also played an important role, revealing the negative consequences of the schools for the health and well-being of the survivors (e.g., Claes and Clifton 1998; Kaspar 2014). Much continues to be unknown about residential schools and their impact, and it is clear that more of this important line of research needs to be undertaken. I focus here on the representation of residential schools – on their meaning rather than their reality. What follows, therefore, is not a story about the coming to light of the empirical reality of the tragedy of the residential school system but a story about how it came to be represented as a tragedy.

It should be made clear from the outset that the concern here is with how residential schools are represented in the (English) Canadian public sphere. Consequently, my focus on this representational process differs from, for example, sociologist Brieg Capitaine's focus on the meaning of the residential schools for former students and their communities, as well as from religious studies scholar Cheryl Gaver's focus on the perspective of the churches (Chapters 2 and 9 in this volume). The Canadian public sphere has notably undergone much change in recent decades. Until at least the 1960s, it reflected the Canadian ethnic hierarchy that John Porter ([1965] 2015) famously described as the vertical mosaic. In short, the public sphere was once nearly wholly dominated by male, heterosexual, white Protestants of British origin. However, since the 1960s, it has witnessed the entry of other identities that were once suppressed or ignored. The increased visibility of these identities reflects wider developments occurring across the West, which anthropologist Ronald Niezen attributes in this volume to the human rights revolution. The transformation of the public sphere in Canada is partly the result of a movement from below, in which once-excluded groups successfully made their concerns visible, and partly the result of a movement from above, in which the privileging of maleness, heterosexuality, and Protestant Britishness among the dominant group began to be replaced by an adherence to liberal principles associated with civic nationalism. The increasing visibility of Indigenous communities and their concerns, including public acknowledgment of the negative consequences of residential schools, are key components of this process.

The Strong Program

Nancy Fraser (1990) defines the public sphere as a theatre in which public opinion is enacted. This metaphor highlights the potential involvement of a wide variety of social actors in the attribution of meaning. On this score, the state is but one (albeit powerful) actor among many – a situation that is compounded in democracies. The notion that meaning is constructed and contested in a public sphere analogized as a social theatre sits well with the sociological approach referred to as the strong program in cultural sociology (Alexander and Smith 2003). Although sociologist Jeffrey Alexander is the principle architect of the strong program, many others have contributed to its development, with the Center for Cultural Sociology at Yale University providing an intellectual locus. A key area of research in the strong program is the process by which meaning is attributed to suffering. In this regard, the approach is particularly useful for bringing to light how the residential schools came to be represented as a symbol of suffering.

Where the strong program has arguably seen its greatest impact is in the study of the representational dynamics of suffering (for programmatic statements, see Alexander et al. 2004; Eyerman, Alexander, and Breese 2011). This research agenda seeks to explain why some instances of suffering are acknowledged and may even become important symbols of collective identity, whereas others are not. The starting point for answering this question is the possibility that what ultimately determines the representation of a particular tragedy is not its objective intensity but how it is represented by social actors. This premise paves the way for uncovering the often contested process by which shared meanings are attributed to suffering – a process that Alexander (2004), drawing on Victor Turner's dramaturgical framework, refers to as a trauma drama. The notion of a trauma drama also shares much with the concept of the signification spiral, which describes how a phenomenon can become ever more imbued with a particular meaning as more and more social actors engage with it (see Hall et al. 1978).

According to Alexander (2004, 11), the key players of a trauma drama are the carrier groups, a broad term comprising all social actors who consciously or unconsciously contribute to the public attribution of meaning, including politicians, activists, artists, researchers, journalists, and so on. Like theatrical performers, carrier groups creatively seek to convey intended meanings to their wider group, which, in modern societies, Alexander (2004, 12) analogizes as a potentially divided and critical audience. In their attempt to convey intended meanings, carrier groups seek to make an emotional and psychological connection with the wider group. To do so, carrier groups make use of available material resources, particularly various forms of mediation such as newspapers, radio, and film. Linked to this is also the carrier group's relative access to power. However, with respect to this last point, it should be added that although Alexander (2010) emphasizes the signal role of power in meaning making, he does not wholly reduce meaning to power, preferring to position meaning as a relative autonomous force with which power must interact.

By focusing on the case of the residential schools, this chapter provides an original application of the insights of the strong program. Researchers have heretofore seemed reticent to test the limits of their approach. In this regard, the tendency has been to focus on events that are already objectively so terrible that it is difficult to imagine them as anything other than a tragedy. This tendency is evident, for example, in Alexander's (2002) much-discussed essay on the transformation of the meaning of the Holocaust from a rather circumscribed symbol of Germany's wartime atrocities into a universal symbol of radical evil. By contrast, as described below, with the residential schools, we have a case that was initially described by its founders as an act of beneficence. Indeed, as I have suggested elsewhere (Woods 2013, 2016, 53–72), it is in part this particular representation of residential schools that enabled them to persist for so long. In this chapter, I submit that such a representation can also help us to understand why it has taken so long for the full tragedy of the residential schools to be acknowledged.

What follows is best understood as a history of the transformation of the public representation of residential schools. However, to provide structure, I focus on the representational dynamics associated with three key events in the meaning of the residential schools: their founding, their closure, and their return to the public sphere as a result of a child abuse scandal. In the language of historical sociology, these events can be seen as critical junctures in the meaning of the residential schools, which had bearing on how the school system was subsequently represented.

The Residential School System

By the nineteenth century, the Whig interpretation of history, which put Britain at the apex of human development, was ascendant. This representation of history enabled Britain's rapidly expanding empire to be defended on moral grounds, such that it would facilitate the so-called progress of colonized peoples (see Kumar 2004, 190–95). Indeed, this possibility was often framed as the very *mission* of empire – generally now known as its civilizing mission. In the service of the imperial civilizing mission, education was accorded special priority. In 1835, Thomas Macauley penned his now infamous "Minute on Indian Education," suggesting that the aim of education in British India should be "to form ... a class of persons, Indians in blood and colour, but English in taste, in morals, and in intellect" (quoted in ibid., 191).

The moral basis for the expansion and consolidation of British North America (now Canada) and the question of the status of the Indigenous communities within the emergent political order were similarly grounded in the ideology of the civilizing mission. By the mid-nineteenth century, there was a widespread view that Indigenous cultures – represented as primitive forms of human culture – would soon be rendered extinct in the face of mass settlement (Francis 2012, Chapter 2). For some observers, such as economist Stephen Leacock, this was the "natural" result of the collision between an ostensibly superior culture and a lesser culture, and there was therefore little that could be done (ibid., 54). However, many other observers took up the position that even if their cultures were dying, Indigenous peoples might nevertheless be saved. It was in this context that the idea of the residential school system arose.

Through the residential schools, Indigenous children would ostensibly acquire the culture and practice of "civilization" and thereby be saved. Assimilation was thus represented as a humanitarian policy. Nicolas Flood Davin's (1879, 11) oft-cited statement "kill the Indian to save the man," which was contained in the report that led to the creation of the residential school system, sums up this rather contorted idea well. Bringing civilization to Indigenous communities was also represented as a sacred obligation. In this view, it was divine providence that had bequeathed vast territories to the new nation, and there was, therefore, a sacred duty to be discharged in relation to its original inhabitants. Hence, Davin (ibid.) argued that the "Government of Canada had a sacred trust with which providence has invested in the country in the charge of and care for the aborigines committed to it."

It was in the service of such lofty ideals that the supporters of the residential schools justified the forcible separation of children from their parents. According to Davin (1879, 25), it simply was not possible for the adults to grasp the intricacies of civilization because they were already too deeply enmeshed in their own culture and practices. Moreover, as long as the adults were near their children, they were also seen as potentially having the malign influence of entreating their children back to "savagery." Thus, Davin (ibid.) suggested that "the more remote from the Institution and distant from each other are the points from which the pupils are collected, the better for their success."

The benign representation of the residential school system dominated for much of the period of its operation, despite the fact that there were frequent efforts to attribute to them a much less positive meaning. Problematically, such efforts were not taken up by carrier groups with sufficient access to power and resources to trigger a signification spiral capable of overturning the dominant representation of the residential schools. This is in large part because Indigenous peoples' efforts in this regard generally went unanswered, grappling as they were with much-depleted populations whose access to power and resources had been seriously curtailed during the consolidation of Canada – to say nothing of the fact that they also had to contend with their own public representation as childlike, primitive peoples who could hardly be trusted to assess their own situation. As a result, prior to the mid-twentieth century, the most significant efforts to represent the schools in a less-than-beneficent light tended to originate among non-Indigenous Canadians.

One of the more important episodes of criticism occurred in the first decade of the twentieth century, triggered by the publication in 1907 by Peter Bryce of a report for the Department of Indian Affairs on the health conditions of the residential schools. The Bryce Report presents a harrowing portrait, suggesting that overcrowding, poorly trained personnel, inadequate infrastructure, insufficient nutrition, and a lack of proper sanitation had led to an abnormally high rate of disease and death in the school system (Bryce 1907). Even though Indian Affairs buried the report, Bryce distributed it among members of Parliament, the churches, and the media (Milloy 1999, 90). The report subsequently triggered an internal struggle over the merits of the school system within the Anglican Church, and it led, as well, to calls from prominent government officials to withdraw from the school system (see Woods 2013).

Unfortunately, Bryce's efforts were not enough to trigger a full-blown trauma drama and destabilize the prevailing representation of the residential schools. Even as the conditions at many residential schools continued to worsen over the coming decades, they retained their benign representation. In seeming frustration, Bryce (1922) republished his report with a different title. Again, the impact was limited. Hence, seventeen years later, in 1939, the secretary of the Anglican Indian and Residential School Commission produced a pamphlet, aimed at inspiring donations, that continued to describe the residential schools as a blessing (Anglican Church of Canada 1939).

The End of the System

Notably, Bryce's criticisms of the residential schools did not extend as far as questioning the underlying logic of the civilizing mission. Instead, his critique hinged on whether the school system should be considered congruent with such a mission. By contrast, as the twentieth century progressed into the 1960s and Indigenous social actors became a major carrier group in the Canadian public sphere, it was the civilizing mission itself that became the object of criticism. In this context, the view that the residential schools should be seen as an attempted subjugation of Indigenous communities was forcefully put forward.

In the 1930s, in opposition to earlier predictions that the inevitable fate of Indigenous peoples in Canada was extinction, their populations had started to rapidly rebound, putting intense pressure on a school system whose infrastructure had continued to deteriorate as a result of years of underfunding (Miller 2000, 314). By the 1940s, the situation was so deplorable as to have become unavoidable. In other words, the gap between the benign representation of the residential schools and their malign reality had become so wide that it was no longer possible to ignore. For example, shortly after touring Mount Elgin Residential School, which he described as the most "dilapidated structure that [he had] ever inspected" and which was "literally alive with cockroaches and 'odours ... so offensive ... he could scarcely endure them,'" Indian Affairs superintendent R. Hoey recommended the closure of the residential schools, stating that it was "necessary and inevitable" (Milloy 1999, 193). Hoey's recommendation gained strength in 1948 when a joint committee of the House of Commons and the Senate proposed that the residential schools be replaced with an integrated system, in which Indigenous children would be educated alongside non-Indigenous Canadians. With this recommendation, the long process of ending the residential school system finally began.

Despite the inauguration of a new Indigenous education policy, assimilation remained its underlying aim. Although the language was softer and Indigenous cultures were attributed slightly more value (with "elevation to higher civilization" now referred to as "integration"), the ends of the new policy had changed little. Indeed, the new integrated system was even represented by its early defenders as an improved mechanism of assimilation. For example, a 1951 brief by the Department of Indian Affairs, which gave voice to the new policy, suggested that the integrated system would "quicken and give meaning to the acculturative process through which they [Indigenous children] are passing" (Milloy 1999, 196).

It seems likely that Indigenous educational policy would have continued to be informed by the paternal representation of Indigenous cultures if not for the winds of ideological change then blowing into Canada via the civil rights movement in the United States and decolonization movements farther afield. Minorities and colonized peoples who had long been ignored or suppressed were now forcing their way into the public sphere as subjects rather than objects. American Indians were prominent in this process, as most visibly seen in the Occupation of Alcatraz. Interestingly, at the same time as such voices from below were rising in prominence, the deepening norms of human rights among dominant groups throughout the West made them increasingly uneasy with their pasts and more amenable to the demands of the new social movements.

Indigenous representatives had long expressed their desire for cultural and political autonomy, and the assimilationist intent of Canadian Indigenous education policy was often the object of their critique. Unfortunately, their concerns tended to be ignored or downplayed. In the 1960s, this pattern exploded as Indigenous activists and intellectuals forced their concerns into an increasingly sympathetic Canadian public sphere. Going forward, "Aboriginal identity would gain momentum as an autonomous collective force in any discourse concerning the country's recognition of citizenship status and in the defining features of Canadian federalism" (Gagnon 2000, 18). Alongside such changes, prevailing representations of the Canada-Indigenous relationship began to be transformed.

Against the representation of the Canada-Indigenous relationship as one marked by peaceable and mutually beneficial relations, Indigenous carrier groups sought to instantiate a new historical narrative depicting the European settlement of North America as inaugurating a long period of suffering for Indigenous peoples. This new historical narrative was forcefully put forward in Montreal at Expo '67, where Indigenous leaders made use of their invitation to present a "critique of historical and contemporary relations between Aboriginals and non-Aboriginals [that] was by far the most comprehensive that had ever been presented in so public a forum" (Phillips 2004, 105).

A catalyst for the consolidation of the growing pan-Indigenous movement was the now-infamous *Statement of the Government of Canada on Indian Policy* (Canada 1969). The document, generally known as the "White Paper," suggested that the cause of the social problems afflicting Indigenous peoples in Canada was their differential treatment by the state. In an oft-cited statement, then prime minister of Canada Pierre Trudeau wrote, "we can't recognize Aboriginal rights because no society can be built on historical 'might-have-beens'" (Cairns 2011, 174). Thus, the dim view of Indigenous cultures that had been the hallmark of Canada's imperial era continued to find expression in the highest reaches of Canadian politics.

The White Paper galvanized the Indigenous leadership. Almost immediately following its release, activists mounted a highly visible campaign to have it rescinded. Leadership in this campaign was provided by Harold Cardinal, the talented young president of the Indian Association of Alberta. Cardinal was the lead author of a counter-report, which he mockingly referred to as the "Red Paper" (Indian Association of Alberta 1970). Cardinal (1969) also published his personal reflections in a book entitled *The Unjust Society: The Tragedy of Canada's Indians,* in which he takes aim at the broader historic maltreatment of Indigenous communities. In 1970 the book topped Canadian bestseller lists (Miller 2000, 337). Other regional Indigenous organizations across Canada soon joined the struggle against the White Paper.

In order to coordinate a pan-Indigenous response, the National Indian Brotherhood was formed. Although its membership was open only to status Indians, it was nevertheless the first truly effective pan-national Indigenous organization. In this way, the White Paper had the unintended effect of solidifying the unity of Indigenous communities. The National Indian Brotherhood reconstituted itself in 1984 as the Assembly of First Nations – which is presently the most powerful pan-Indigenous political organization in Canada. As a result of the coordinated effort by Indigenous leaders and the new support that they found in non-Indigenous Canada, which was expressed in numerous sympathetic editorials in broadsheets and magazines (see Miller 2000, 337), by the time Trudeau was presented with Cardinal's Red Paper in 1970, his government had already decided to retract the White Paper.

The residential schools were a central aspect of this period of heightened criticism of prevailing representations of the Canada-Indigenous relationship. For example, in *The Unjust Society,* Cardinal (1969) charges that the school system had been designed to subjugate Indigenous communities rather than to help them. But perhaps the most important incident in this period that focused attention on the residential schools involved the Presbyterian-run Cecilia Jeffrey Indian Residential School.

In 1965 Ian Adams, a journalist and author, wrote a highly negative article for the *Weekend Magazine* on the living conditions of Indigenous communities in Ontario, which included a bleak description of the Cecilia Jeffrey School: "[It has] an atmosphere of unutterable loneliness, desolate enough to stop time in a child's heart ... [Children who ran away] were locked in a room with just a mattress on the floor, left only their underclothes, and put on a bread-and-milk diet" (quoted in Milloy 1999, 288). The article was syndicated to dozens of English Canadian dailies (Hodgins and Milloy 2003, 222).

Then, approximately one year after Adams published his article on the Cecilia Jeffrey School, Charlie Wenjack, a twelve-year-old boy who had attempted to escape from the school, was found dead – having died while trying to return home. To make matters worse, until his body was discovered, Wenjack's parents had not been informed that he was missing. Adams returned to the topic of the Cecilia Jeffrey School, publishing a series of angry articles on the incident – one of which was featured in *Maclean's*, a widely read English-language magazine (Hodgins and Milloy 2003, 223). That same year, Canadian poet Joanne Bealy (1966) published a eulogy about the incident:

> Charlie Wenjack was 12 years old when he ran. 400 miles nothing but a number.
> Charlie Wenjack died alone and cold,
> > hungry,
> > probably scared,
> > just trying to get home.
> O Canada, glorious and free.
> O Canada, with breaking hearts we see thee.
> Oh.
> Canada.
> Oh.

Wenjack's death prompted a provincial inquest, which found clear problems at the Cecilia Jeffrey School. The inquest also highlighted more broadly the "tremendous emotional and adjustment problems" that students faced at residential schools and recommended that a study be "made of the present Indian education and philosophy" (quoted in Haycock 1971, 85). So much did the death of Wenjack penetrate the Canadian public sphere that the tragedy has become generalized as a symbol of the suffering of Indigenous peoples. At Trent University, a monument was built to memorialize the tragedy, and a building was named after the boy. Recently, a documentary about the incident was aired on national public radio (CBC 2012).

However, although Wenjack's death seemed to have all the ingredients necessary to trigger a broader trauma drama in which the scope of the tragedy might have been extended to represent the whole of the residential school system, this did not occur. The reason seems to have been the reticence in this period of many students to come forward with their negative experiences. Indeed, at this time, there continued to be many prominent former students, such as Edward Ahenakew (1965), who recounted their residential school experiences with fondness. As a result, the meaning of Wenjack's death remained relatively circumscribed.

To return to the surging pan-Canadian Indigenous political movement, given the attention to the residential schools and their representation by activists as a symbol of a historic effort by church and state to destroy Indigenous cultures, it is unsurprising that education was high on the agenda of the newly formed National Indian Brotherhood. Indeed, after its successful attack on Trudeau's White Paper, its first major order of business was education. In a 1972 report on the topic, the organization forcefully made the case that, where it was demanded, Indigenous communities should have administrative control over education and that curriculum should be modified to account for an Indigenous perspective (see National Indian Brotherhood 1972).

Remarkably, Trudeau's administration endorsed the report in full, dramatically changing the course of Canada's stance on Indigenous education after more than a hundred years of commitment to the civilizing mission. Going forward, Indigenous perspectives, cultures, and practices were ostensibly to be nurtured rather than eliminated. The former church partners in the residential schools also underwent a rapid volte-face; almost overnight, the civilizing mission was replaced with a new mission to defend Indigenous cultures (on the Anglican Church, see Woods 2016, Chapter 4; see also Gaver, this volume).

However, if church and state had suddenly distanced themselves from the civilizing mission, they nevertheless avoided prolonged reflection on the implications of their long commitment to such a mission. In part, this was possible because Indigenous activists used their newfound discursive power to press forward in their struggles, moving from education to unresolved land claims, among other issues. As a result, the residential school system fell away from the public sphere as a key concern, becoming more of a background symbol. There, its meaning remained unsettled and clouded in ambiguity. As discussed above, although there were now carriers of the meaning of residential schools as an instrument of colonization, there were others who continued to represent the school system as a benign enterprise.

The residential school system might have remained on the periphery of Canada-Indigenous relations, clouded in ambiguity and destined, if anything, to eventually be represented as but another exemplar of the paternalism and ethnocentrism of the Canadian state. However, as we shall see in the subsequent section, this was not to be the case.

Return of the Residential Schools

In the 1980s the resurgence of Indigenous activism and political organization that had begun in the 1970s continued apace. In the midst of this activism and organization, the meaning of the residential schools returned to the public sphere as an object of struggle. Notably, this phase of struggle marked a new phase in their representation, with the ambiguity of previous decades now being replaced with an ever-spiralling, sinister meaning.

Beginning in the mid-1980s, the long-held unwillingness of many former students to publicly discuss their sufferings at residential school began to dissipate. In the realm of published memoirs, with the exception of Jane Willis's (1974) harrowing account, the historic trend had been to represent the residential school experience in a fairly positive light (e.g., Ahenakew 1965; Moine 1975; Gladstone 1987). Toward the end of the 1980s, this situation would rapidly change: Basil Johnston's (1988) much-discussed memoir dwells at length on numerous instances of cruelty by residential school staff. Similarly, Celia Haig-Brown's (1988) book, *Resistance and Renewal*, the first academic study devoted to students' memories of their experiences, dwells at length on abuse and deprivation. Going forward, published recollections would become ever more sombre.

The new willingness to talk openly about abuses suffered at residential schools was also reflected in the legal realm, as former students began to bring their allegations into the courts, beginning in 1988 when eight former students of the Anglican-run St. George's Indian Residential School opened legal proceedings for sexual abuses. Initiating a pattern that would soon be followed by thousands of other former students, the allegations also marked the first time that sexual abuse was associated with the residential schools.

By the end of the 1980s, the growing presence of the residential schools in the public sphere meant that it was no longer only the former students and their communities who were involved in the struggle over their representation. In 1989 *Where the Spirit Lives,* a made-for-television film whose author and director are non-Indigenous, was broadcast across Canada (Pittman 1989). The film presents a highly negative portrayal of the staff members and the system as a whole. It remains the most watched film on the topic of the residential schools, doing much to bring them to the attention of the wider Canadian public (see Miller 2001).

If at the end of the 1980s the residential schools had returned to the public sphere, it was not yet clear that a spiralling national trauma drama had begun. Although the issue of sexual abuse meant that the residential schools now regularly appeared in mainstream media, the evil that they represented remained relatively circumscribed, and potential guilty parties therefore sought to distance themselves from responsibility. The worst abuses could be rationalized to have occurred only at select schools and could thereby be dealt with on a case-by-case basis. As a result, responsibility for abuse could be framed as residing with particular individuals, particular schools, or particular dioceses rather than institutions as a whole. Thus, in the case involving the St. George's School, the Anglican Church and the Canadian government initially contested the court's decision that they were liable for damages (Hayes 2004, 45). As for the general public, there was hardly mention at this point that they could also be held collectively responsible.

On October 30, 1990, the distancing strategies of the church and state were to suddenly become much more difficult when the charismatic leader of the Assembly of Manitoba Chiefs, Phil Fontaine, publicly alleged that he and his classmates had been sexually abused while attending residential school. Upon hearing that, as a result of two former parish priests being accused of sexual assault, a special committee had been set up by the Roman Catholic Archdiocese of St. Boniface to receive complaints of sexual abuse at the hands of the clergy, Fontaine alleged at the offices of the Archdiocese in Winnipeg that he and his former classmates had been sexually abused while students at Fort Alexander Residential School. Fontaine subsequently convened a press conference and repeated his allegations. It was these actions that provided the trigger for a trauma drama to unfold.

The initial attention to Fontaine's allegations in the mainstream press was intense. The following day, his allegations were reported in every major Canadian broadsheet and in the after-dinner news sections of the major national television networks. That evening, he repeated his allegations in an interview with tele-journalist Barbara Frum on national television (CBC 1990b). The subsequent evening, in the same prime time slot, Frum followed up with a hard-hitting interview with a representative of the Catholic Church in Manitoba (CBC 1990a).

Fontaine's willingness to come forward triggered a mass response among other former students. In the days, weeks, and years that followed, thousands came forward with similar allegations. Around this time, there was also a noticeable transition in the realm of cultural production. Previous silence on themes pertaining to sexual abuse in the residential schools gave way to an explosion of cultural works dealing with it directly (see Rymhs 2003).

The spiralling scandal prompted a political response by the Assembly of First Nations. Indigenous leaders overcame lingering doubts as to the wisdom of publicly confronting the issue of abuse and coalesced around an effort to obtain redress from church and state. Henceforth, the demand for redress would be a central component of the assembly's political aims. Notably, redress was sought for *all* former students rather than for only those who had suffered criminal abuse. Much as what occurred in the 1960s, the political movement sought to make the underlying assimilationist rationale of the residential schools central to the struggle over their meaning, rather than focusing only on the issue of criminal abuse. Indeed, right from the beginning, in Fontaine's (CBC 1990b) initial interview with Frum, he suggested that it was the effort to erase Indigenous cultures that truly made the residential schools so nefarious.

Focusing on the assimilationist intent of the residential schools is crucial to broadening their scope as a symbol of malignancy and thereby widening the circle of collective responsibility. It is their association with the civilizing mission that sets residential schools apart from other types of boarding schools. Consequently, this association is crucial to the claim that all former students have the right to redress, irrespective of whether or not they suffered abuse, for it implies that merely punishing specific criminals is not enough. Rather, responsibility also potentially lies with churches and the state, as well as with the wider Canadian citizenry as the inheritors of a state whose founding rationale is entwined with the founders' belief in their cultural superiority.

The force of the burgeoning trauma drama quickly impacted the former church partners. Faced with an increasing number of court cases and a state that was initially unwilling to share responsibility, as well as demonization in cultural productions and the press, church representatives were quick to acknowledge, and express regret for, their predecessors' role in the residential schools, as detailed in the introduction to this volume. Following this acknowledgment, the churches became key carrier groups in the movement demanding redress from the Canadian government.

As the symbol of residential schools became ever more imbued with a malign meaning, various other sectors began to engage with it, further contributing to the spiralling effect. The response from health scientists, social scientists, and historians, informed by their findings on the far-reaching negative consequences of the school system, was crucial in this regard. In the mid-1990s, former students began to be regularly described in the academic literature as survivors. A few years later, "Indian residential school syndrome" emerged in the health science community as a new diagnostic term to describe the long-term negative impact of the residential schools (see Brasfield 2001). Around this time, the residential schools also began to be defined by some social scientists as an attempted genocide akin to the Holocaust (e.g., Chrisjohn and Young 1997; Neu and Therrien 2003).

Also important in the transformation of the meaning of the residential schools was the work carried out by the Royal Commission on Aboriginal Peoples. Although it had been created in response to the 1990 armed standoff at Oka, Quebec, much of the work of the commission involved investigating the impact of the residential schools. The release of its report in 1996 provoked a response from the federal government, which in 1998 issued a "Statement of Reconciliation" and created a $350 million healing fund for former students (RCAP 1996; Canada 1998). By this point, it seems that the tragedy had become so saturated with a malign meaning that it was no longer possible for the government to approach it from the rather circumscribed legalistic position that it had initially adopted. Yet the progress of the trauma drama was such that from the perspective of many Indigenous and non-Indigenous carrier groups, the government's response was insufficient, and they pressed for a proper prime ministerial apology, as well as for more funds (see Nobles 2008, 115–18). Eventually, the government responded. In 2008 Prime Minister Stephen Harper apologized for the residential schools on behalf of the Canadian state. Harper's apology was accompanied by a $1.9 billion Common Experience Payment for all former students and a commitment to establish the Truth and Reconciliation Commission of Canada on the residential schools. The TRC is now complete, and its final report has been released. Although it is too soon to assess its impact, given that the final report of the TRC specifically refers to the school system as a cultural genocide, it seems reasonable to surmise that it will add fuel to the spiralling trauma drama (TRC 2015, 1).

❧

Drawing on the heuristic framework provided by sociologist Jeffrey Alexander and Philip Smith's (2003) strong program in cultural sociology, this chapter traces the process by which the Indian residential schools came to be represented as a symbol of terrible suffering. Alexander and Smith suggest attributing analytic autonomy to meaning, such that it is treated as an independent variable. In the case of the public meaning of the residential schools, rather than conveying the objective reality of the school system as such, this strategy helped to foreground the process whereby the underlying representational dynamics of the residential schools both constrained and enabled the acknowledgment of the schools' deleterious impact. This process was highly contingent and contested, and it was not at all obvious in the middle of the twentieth century that the residential schools would become the eminent symbol of the maltreatment of Indigenous peoples in Canada.

Public representation of residential schools had three broad phases, each of which had very real implications. In the first phase, the benign meaning that was initially associated with the residential schools seems to have constrained the acknowledgment of their failings, thereby contributing to their persistence. Unfortunately, at the outset of the twentieth century, the distribution of social power was such that attempts to convey an alternate meaning of the residential schools were ignored. It was not until Indigenous social actors acquired sufficient discursive power in the middle of the century that the prevailing representations of the residential schools began to be challenged, eventually leading to the government's withdrawal from the school system amid wider criticism of its historic commitment to the civilizing mission.

But if the residential schools lost their lustre in the 1960s, they were also not suddenly seen as a mechanism of imperial domination – despite several figures making such a charge. Instead, in the second phase in the public representation of the residential schools, the schools' meaning seems to have entered a period of ambiguity. This outcome was largely the result of their having receded in importance in Canada-Indigenous relations. Indigenous activists moved on with other pressing issues, and representatives of church and state sought to distance their organizations from the historic civilizing mission by stressing the possibility of a better future. Thus, the residential schools seemed destined to fade into the background of Canadian history.

Residential schools suddenly returned at the end of the 1980s, when numerous former students broke their long silence and began to publicly discuss some of the more horrific aspects of their residential school experiences. In this phase of the public representation of the residential schools, a trauma drama was finally triggered, with ever more sectors of Canadian society engaging with the residential schools, leading to their increasing association with a malign meaning. Eventually, the spiralling effect would reach the highest level of Canadian politics.

Looking ahead, with the meanings associated with the TRC not yet settled, it seems that the trauma drama has not reached its denouement. Will the public meaning of residential schools become further imbued with tragedy? This is far from clear. Although it is increasingly apparent that the shared traumatic experience of the residential schools is playing a key role in the emergence of a pan-Indigenous identity in Canada – as Capitaine details so well in this volume – it is as yet unclear what significance the residential school system will ultimately have for the non-Indigenous Canadian public. As demonstrated in this study, meaning making is highly contingent. A trauma drama requires continuous engagement from an ever-widening circle of social actors. Will this process continue to occur in the case of residential schools? Despite a series of highly mediatized events associated with the TRC, it seems that there are many people among the wider non-Indigenous Canadian public who remain resistant to the malign meaning of the residential school system and, indeed, to the fact that they are in some way collectively responsible for its deleterious consequences (see Gaver, this volume). Whether this resistance can be overcome is a key factor in the future representation of the residential schools.

There is also a further question raised by Ronald Niezen in the Foreword to this book. Niezen makes an important point that it has been the widespread incidence of physical and sexual abuse in the schools that have most captured the attention of the Canadian public. The risk is that the school system will come to be seen as an exemplar of the kinds of institutional child abuse perpetrated by churches that now seem to have been endemic throughout the West. Although this is certainly a critical aspect of the residential schools, by focusing solely on child abuse, one risks obscuring the association of the residential school system with Canada's colonial history. The reference to the residential schools as a cultural genocide in the TRC's (2015, 1) summary of its final report is aimed at ensuring that they retain this association. However, Harper's confident assertion in 2009 that Canada did not have a history of colonialism, despite his earlier apology for the residential schools, suggests that the effort to ensure the schools are symbolic, not just of child abuse but also of an emergent settler state intent on eliminating the cultures of its original inhabitants, will surely take a massive effort.

REFERENCES

Ahenakew, Edward. 1965. "Little Pine: An Indian Day School." *Saskatchewan History* 18 (2): 55–62.

Alexander, Jeffrey C. 2002. "On the Social Construction of Moral Universals." *European Journal of Social Theory* 5 (1): 5–86.

–. 2004. "Toward a Theory of Cultural Trauma." In *Cultural Trauma and Collective Identity*, ed. Jeffrey C. Alexander, Ron Eyerman, Bernhard Giesen, Neil Smelser, and Piotr Sztompka, 1–30. Los Angeles: University of California Press. http://dx.doi.org/10.1525/california/9780520235946.003.0001.

–. 2010. "Power, Politics, and the Civil Sphere." In *Handbook of Politics: State and Society in Global Perspective*, ed. K.T. Leicht and J.C. Jenkins, 111–26. New York: Springer.

Alexander, Jeffrey C., Ron Eyerman, Bernhard Giesen, Neil Smelser, and Piotr Sztompka. 2004. *Cultural Trauma and Collective Identity*. Los Angeles: University of California Press. http://dx.doi.org/10.1525/california/9780520235946.001.0001.

Alexander, Jeffrey C., and Philip Smith. 2003. "The Strong Program in Cultural Sociology: Elements of a Structural Hermeneutics." In *The Meanings of Social Life: A Cultural Sociology*, ed. Jeffrey C. Alexander, 11–26. Oxford: Oxford University Press. http://dx.doi.org/10.1093/acprof:oso/9780195160840.003.0011.

Anglican Church of Canada. 1939. *The Indian and Eskimo Residential Schools*, MSCC 9–5, Popular Information Series, GS 75–103, Box 130. Toronto: General Synod Archives, Anglican Church of Canada.

Barman, Jean, Yvonne Hebra, and Don McCaskill. 1986. *Indian Education in Canada: The Legacy*. Vancouver: UBC Press.

Bealy, Joanne. 1966. "Eulogy for a Truant." *Cahoots Magazine*. http://www.cahootsmagazine.com/?option=com_content&task=view&id=182.

Brasfield, Charles R. 2001. "Residential School Syndrome." *British Columbia Medical Journal* 43 (2): 78–81.

Bryce, Peter H. 1907. *Report on the Indian Schools of Manitoba and the North-West Territories.* Toronto: General Synod Archives, Anglican Church of Canada.

–. 1922. *The Story of a National Crime: Being an Appeal for Justice to the Indians of Canada, the Wards of the Nation, Our Allies in the Revolutionary War, Our Brothers-in-Arms in the Great War.* Ottawa: James Hope and Sons.

Cairns, Alan. 2011. "Review of *Aboriginal Title and Indigenous Peoples: Canada, Australia, and New Zealand,* edited by Louis A. Knalfa and Haijo Westra." *BC Studies* (170): 174–75.

Canada. 1969. *Statement of the Government of Canada on Indian Policy.* Ottawa: Indigenous and Northern Affairs.

–. 1998. "Statement of Reconciliation." In *Gathering Strength: Canada's Aboriginal Action Plan,* 2–3. Ottawa: Minister of Indian Affairs and Northern Development. http://www.ahf.ca/downloads/gathering-strength.pdf.

Canadian Broadcasting Corporation (CBC). 1990a. "The Catholic Church Responds to Fontaine's Abuse Charges." *The Journal,* October 31. http://www.cbc.ca/archives/entry/the-catholic-church-responds-to-fontaines-abuse-charges.

–. 1990b. "Phil Fontaine's Shocking Testimony of Sexual Abuse." *The Journal,* October 30. http://www.cbc.ca/archives/entry/phil-fontaines-shocking-testimony-of-sexual-abuse.

–. 2012. "Charlie Wenjack: The Runaway from Residential Schools." In *Dying for an Education: A CBC Thunderbay Special Report.* http://www.cbc.ca/thunderbay/interactives/dyingforaneducation/.

Cardinal, Harold. 1969. *The Unjust Society: The Tragedy of Canada's Indians.* Toronto: Hurtig.

Chrisjohn, Roland D., and Sherri Young. 1997. *The Circle Game: Shadows and Substance in the Indian Residential School Experience in Canada.* Penticton, BC: Theytus Books.

Claes, Rhonda, and Deborah Clifton. 1998. *Needs and Expectations for Redress of Victims of Abuse at Native Residential Schools.* Ottawa: Law Commission of Canada.

Coates, Ken. 1984. "'Betwixt and Between': The Anglican Church and the Children of the Carcross (Chooutla) Residential School, 1911–1954." *BC Studies: The British Columbian Quarterly* 64: 27–47.

Davin, Nicholas F. 1879. *Report on Industrial Schools for Indians and Halfbreeds.* Toronto: General Synod Archives, Anglican Church of Canada.

Eyerman, Ron, Jeffrey C. Alexander, and Elizabeth Breese, eds. 2011. *Narrating Trauma: On the Impact of Collective Suffering.* Boulder, CO: Paradigm.

Francis, Daniel. 2012. *The Imaginary Indian: The Image of the Indian in Canadian Culture.* Vancouver: Arsenal Pulp Press.

Fraser, Nancy. 1990. "Rethinking the Public Sphere: A Contribution to the Critique of Actually Existing Democracy." *Social Text* (25–26): 56–80. http://dx.doi.org/10.2307/466240.

Gagnon, Alain-G. 2000. "Canada: Unity and Diversity." *Parliamentary Affairs: A Journal of Comparative Politics* 53 (1): 12–26. http://dx.doi.org/10.1093/pa/53.1.12.

Gladstone, James. 1987. "Indian School Days." *Alberta Historical Review* 15 (1): 18–24.

Gresko, Jacqueline. 1992. "Everyday Life at Qu'Appelle Industrial School." *Western Oblate Studies* 2: 71–94.

Haig-Brown, Celia. 1988. *Resistance and Renewal: Surviving the Indian Residential School.* Vancouver, BC: Tillacum Library.

Hall, Stuart, Chas Critcher, Tony Jefferson, John N. Clarke, and Brian Roberts. 1978. *Policing the Crisis: Mugging, the State, and Law and Order*. London: Macmillan.

Haycock, Ronald. 1971. *The Image of the Indian: The Canadian Indian as a Subject and a Concept in a Sampling of the Popular National Magazines Read in Canada, 1900–1970*. Waterloo, ON: Wilfrid Laurier University Press.

Hayes, Alan. 2004. *Anglicans in Canada: Controversies and Identity in Historical Perspective*. Chicago: University of Illinois Press.

Hodgins, Bruce W., and John S. Milloy. 2003. "The Resistance of Little Charlie Wenjack and His Legacy at Trent University." In *Blockades and Resistance: Studies in Actions of Peace and the Temagami Blockades of 1988–1989*, ed. Bruce W. Hodgins, David McNab, and Ute Lischke, 221–28. Waterloo, ON: Wilfrid Laurier University Press.

Indian Association of Alberta. 1970. *Citizens Plus*. Edmonton: Indian Association of Alberta.

Johnston, Basil. 1988. *Indian School Days*. Toronto: Key Porter Books.

Kaspar, V. 2014. "The Lifetime Effect of Residential School Attendance on Indigenous Health Status." *American Journal of Public Health* 104 (11): 2184–90.

Kumar, Krishan. 2004. *The Making of English National Identity*. Cambridge, UK: Cambridge University Press.

Miller, Jim R. 1996. *Shingwauk's Vision: A History of Native Residential Schools*. Toronto: University of Toronto Press.

–. 2000. *Skyscrapers Hide the Heavens: A History of Indian-White Relations in Canada*. Toronto: University of Toronto Press.

Miller, Mary J. 2001. "*Where the Spirit Lives*: An Influential and Contentious Television Drama about Residential Schools." *American Review of Canadian Studies* 31 (1–2): 71–84. http://dx.doi.org/10.1080/02722010109481583.

Milloy, John. S. 1999. *"A National Crime": The Canadian Government and the Residential School System, 1879–1986*. Winnipeg: University of Manitoba Press.

Moine, Louise. 1975. *My Life in a Residential School*. Regina: Provincial Chapter 1.o.D.E., Saskatchewan, in cooperation with the Provincial Library of Saskatchewan.

National Indian Brotherhood. 1972. *Indian Control of Indian Education: Policy Paper Presented to the Minister of Indian Affairs and Northern Development*. Ottawa: National Indian Brotherhood.

Neu, Dean, and Richard Therrien. 2003. *Accounting for Genocide: Canada's Bureaucratic Assault on Aboriginal People*. Halifax: Fernwood.

Nobles, Melissa. 2008. *The Politics of Official Apologies*. Cambridge, UK: Cambridge University Press. http://dx.doi.org/10.1017/CBO9780511756252.

Phillips, Ruth. 2004. "Commemoration/(De)celebration: Super-Shows and the Decolonization of Canadian Museums, 1967–92." In *Postmodernism and the Ethical Subject*, ed. Barbara Gabriel and Suzan Ilcan, 99–124. Montreal and Kingston: McGill-Queen's University Press.

Pittman, Bruce, dir. 1989. *Where the Spirit Lives*. Written by Keith Ross Leckie. Ottawa: CBC Television.

Porter, John. (1965) 2015. *Vertical Mosaic: An Analysis of Social Class and Power in Canada*. Toronto: University of Toronto Press.

Royal Commission on Aboriginal Peoples (RCAP). 1996. *Report of the Royal Commission on Aboriginal Peoples*. Ottawa: Royal Commission on Aboriginal Peoples.

Rymhs, Deena. 2003. "A Residential School Memoir: Basil Johnston's *Indian School Days*." *Canadian Literature* (178): 58–70.

Truth and Reconciliation Commission of Canada (TRC). 2015. *Honouring the Truth, Reconciling for the Future: Summary of the Final Report of the Truth and Reconciliation Commission of Canada.* Ottawa: Truth and Reconciliation Commission of Canada. http://www.trc.ca/websites/trcinstitution/File/2015/Findings/Exec_Summary_2015 _05_31_web_o.pdf.

Willis, Jane. 1974. *Geniesh: An Indian Girlhood.* Toronto: New Press.

Woods, Eric T. 2013. "A Cultural Approach to a Canadian Tragedy: The Indian Residential Schools as a Sacred Enterprise." *International Journal of Politics, Culture and Society* 26 (2): 173–87. http://dx.doi.org/10.1007/s10767-013-9132-0.

–. 2016. *A Cultural Sociology of Anglican Mission and the Indian Residential Schools in Canada: The Long Road to Apology.* New York: Palgrave Macmillan.

2

Telling a Story and Performing the Truth: The Indian Residential School as Cultural Trauma

BRIEG CAPITAINE

"FEEL AT EASE TO tell your story. Wherever we have travelled, people are different, but the stories are basically the same." This statement was made by a member of the Survivors Committee at the opening of a sharing circle held at the Canadian Truth and Reconciliation Commission's national event in Edmonton. This statement provides a departure point for addressing the question, How is it that individuals of different backgrounds, ages, and sexes represent an event in the same way? More precisely, how is it that residential schools are understood as a trauma that has forever changed people's lives, not only the lives of residential school survivors but also the lives of their children and other family members who did not experience this event? To collect the life stories of Indigenous people – men, women, youth, or elders – is to be unavoidably confronted with the residential school event. Whether associated with destruction and violence (which is most often the case) or with emancipation (which is rarer), residential schools symbolize, paraphrasing the words of Wright Mills (1959), a rupture at the intersection of biography and history. Workplace discrimination, periods of unemployment, divorce, the arrival or loss of children, leaving or returning to the reserve – these are all events that entail social struggle and lend structure to individuals' life histories (Capitaine 2012). None of these events, however, has the power of residential schools to become a temporal and spatial marker between a "before" and an "after," as well as between an "us" and a "them." The residential school thus tends to become a key causal factor underlying a host of issues: psychological suffering and social vulnerability, cultural erosion and exclusion, unequal social and economic conditions, and the incapacity to act and react in the face of certain social challenges. In addition, as the TRC's (2015) final report shows, residential schools legitimize demands for social justice, reparation, and recognition that lie at the heart of much contemporary political activity among Indigenous peoples in Canada.

I seek to understand the social process by which an event such as residential school becomes a cultural trauma. In demonstrating the usefulness of bringing sociological analysis to bear upon what is primarily a psychological phenomenon, I first analyze the shared representations that structure the stories of former students. The public forums organized by the TRC have given rise to what sociologist Jeffrey Alexander terms a cultural classification. Alexander (2012, 17–19) identifies four elements that make up the cultural classification of trauma: the nature of the suffering, the nature of the victim, the relationship of the victim with the greater audience, and the attribution of responsibility. Second, drawing on the concepts of ritual and cultural performance, I show how the TRC showcased and participated in the production of this cultural classification.

The Social Theory of Cultural Trauma

The theory of cultural trauma holds that trauma has no inherent existence (Eyerman 2001, 2008; Alexander et al. 2004; Alexander 2012). Rather, actors socially construct trauma in the process of attributing meaning to an event. In distinguishing psychological from cultural trauma, sociologist Neil Smelser (2004, 37) writes, "cultural traumas are for the most part historically made, not born." From this perspective, an event is not intrinsically traumatic; it becomes so through the imaginative and subjective work of social actors. An event acquires the status of cultural trauma not because it is inherently damaging but because actors believe that the event has profoundly harmed the group's collective identity and meaning-system (ibid.). Adopting a similar theoretical approach, sociologist Eric Woods ably shows in this volume how the meaning given to Indian residential schools changed over time thanks to the efforts of carrier groups promoting an interpretation of the residential school as cultural trauma. This interpretation holds that the residential school system is not simply a pedagogical failure and is not only an expression of colonial domination but is also a key source of linguistic loss, cultural impoverishment, and shame and guilt of simply being oneself. Around this symbolic production coalesces a collective memory that provides the foundation for group identity (Eyerman 2001).

Since the mid-twentieth century, cultural trauma has become part of our everyday social interactions (Fassin and Rechtman 2009). In general, cultural trauma arises out of causal relationships established between events and behaviours. Public policy responses and civil reparations frequently accompany the identification of a trauma. Alexander (2012) notes that cultural trauma is so anchored in social life that it appears to be intuitively understood and shared by individual actors and groups that are extremely disparate. However, Alexander (ibid., 13) argues that "events are not inherently traumatic. Trauma is a socially mediated attribution." Drawing on the idea of religious imagination developed by sociologist Émile Durkheim in *The Elementary Forms of the Religious Life* (1912), Alexander (2012, 14) goes on to state, "it is only through the imaginative process of representation that actors have the sense of experience." What matters in this perspective are not the facts in and of themselves but the representations that actors produce and the beliefs shared by the group. The theory of cultural trauma is unshakably constructivist, positing that trauma emerges through a social process: "The gap between event and representation can be conceived as the trauma process" (ibid., 15). This process is the result of work performed by social actors engaged in a struggle to win recognition for the profound wounds they have suffered, as Woods shows in his contribution to this volume. The process of trauma construction requires that the group and its members become convinced of the traumatic nature of the event. The performative dimension of trauma occurs primarily through the narration of a new version of history that is composed of four primary elements: the nature of the suffering, the nature of the victim, the relationship between the victim of trauma and the audience, and the attribution of responsibility. These four elements constitute the framework for a new version of history. This history has to be compelling enough to generate self-identification not only by group members but also by Canadian society. Generating identification by Canadian society with this new version of history is the more complicated proposition, as we will see. As a cultural classification, it forms a new master narrative (ibid.) and is transmitted, with varying degrees of success, to different realms of society – media, governmental, legal, academic, and aesthetic. If the actors have social standing and an accompanying measure of power, this new history takes root and comes to form the basis for a new collective memory.

The socio-historical approach developed by Woods demonstrates how this process occurs. My own perspective in this text is different. Although the residential school historical counternarrative promoted by the TRC aims to raise the event of residential schooling to a suprasocial level and to create a collective identity crisis, this operation cannot function without individual actors. Trauma remains commonly understood as a singular and private experience. The goal of persuading others to identify with the new narrative is mainly accomplished by individuals sharing their personal stories. Thus an understanding of trauma as culture and as a system of meaning should not begin with an analysis of social systems or institutions but rather with the individual actors engaged in sharing their experiences. In other words, macro-sociology may not forego a micro-sociological approach. Identification with trauma becomes possible when the narrative is situated midway between biography and history – when a collective belief system is expressed through the singularity of an individual's experience. With the goal of illustrating this cultural classification, I begin by retranscribing the first testimony that I heard at the TRC national event in Montreal.

Telling the Residential School Story

"And We Went towards the Unknown"[1]

The sharing circle is ready to begin. The first witness is a man in his forties with long dark hair.[2] With his head lowered and his back hunched in his chair, he seems very nervous. One of the traditional support workers approaches. He crouches next to the man, places a hand on his shoulder, smiles at him in a friendly manner, and helps him to take off his coat. The support worker offers the man tobacco, which the man takes and rubs between his hands. The coordinator of the sharing circle, who is also a member of the Survivors Committee, opens the proceedings. He states, "thank you Creator, grandmother, grandfather. Be with us to help you in your path." The first witness then begins to speak:

> I am a survivor. It all started in 1962 when there were gatherings for the youth. The men came beforehand with candies. I never thought I would leave my home, my father, my mother. They took me, put me in the bus, I didn't know where I was going. I only spoke my own language. We were happy to be leaving with kids our own age. We were quite a big group.

They separated us by size: small and medium. "Put your things on the beds." There were numbers. Me, I will remember my number all my life. It was seventy-one. There were Cree, Anishnabe ... We tried to communicate, but it was difficult. It wasn't easy. At night, we cried. They asked us to pray, prayers that we didn't know. There were punishments that came down because we couldn't speak our language. And there was also ... [silence, sobs]. There was also something that ... Me, I was afraid. We were just kids. They came to get me. Me, I saw myself in there. Over all those years, from the smalls to the mediums, I went through what I had to go through: brainwashing. And I was scared to talk about it to my friends. I was ashamed of myself. I felt guilty. That's where my life got turned upside down. That's where my life started to be changed. When we did the sexual games with the boys, we locked ourselves up in the huts. In the rooms, we did the sexual games. That was what my life had to be. I had to hide for a very long time before I could talk about it. My grandmother said, "it's not true what you went through." For me, it's supposed to be normal what we go through. That's when my life as a grownup boy started. I left there in '71. I said to my father, "I never want to go back." My life was changed forever.

In this testimony, as occurs in most of the narratives that I heard in the context of the TRC's national events in Montreal, Edmonton, and Ottawa, the residential school event establishes a rupture between before the event and after. This temporal structure and the representations and symbols that constitute it become the framework for the collective memory of trauma. To analyze this structure, I identify the four elements that characterize the narrative framework of cultural trauma according to Alexander (2012): What is the suffering? Who is the victim? What is the relationship between the victim and the public? Who is responsible? These elements, as Alexander (ibid., 17) notes, do not follow in chronological order but are intertwined in the story, reflectively co-constructing each other. The following analysis is based on excerpts from testimonies given by former students or their families during the public TRC events that I attended.

The Pain

What happened? What did victims go through? In what ways do they still suffer? According to 37 percent of Canadians, the suffering of former students is primarily characterized by sexual abuse and physical violence

(Environics Research Group 2008).[3] Widely reported in the media and at the heart of legal proceedings,[4] this pain is also regularly expressed in survivors' testimonies. However, survivors' pain not only refers to concrete events talked about in the past tense but has also come to symbolize a loss and emptiness of meaning suffered by the collective as a whole in the present.

Residential schools represent a rift with parents, family, and community. They evoke the feeling of being alone, plunged into "darkness" and the "unknown."[5] In other words, pain represents a loss of meaning and a rupture in an individual's relationship with the collective. An Inuit put it this way: "I was surprised to find myself in residential school. I saw an airplane arrive. I approached the airplane and someone got out and gathered up the kids. It was the first time that I was in an airplane without my family. I was alone, it was scary."[6] Personal emotions, such as fear, arise out of solitude and intergenerational rupture. This interweaving of the individual psyche and community solidarity is rendered more acute because the victims are children. A woman declared, "in the morning, there were all these children. That was the moment. I would never see my parents again. I was alone."[7] Becoming separated is a recurring theme in survivors' testimonies. The deprivation of one's mother tongue, for example, is associated with the inability to communicate and to construct relationships.[8] One man said, "in Kenora, a dialect is spoken, so I was really lost."[9] The ways that survivors speak about past events show the collective and symbolic character of their pain. One witness said, sobbing, "I didn't know why." Another former student asked, "What was I doing there?"[10] Another stated, "My sisters were there. I couldn't see them. I don't know why."[11] This brutal loss of meaning, repeated in every testimony, symbolizes the crisis of the collective: "It made me crazy. Why? Why? Why?"[12] Since the victims were children, the loss of meaning regarding one's place in the world through being severed from the community seems heightened. One former student noted, "we were children, they gave us numbers, we had no names."[13] Another said, "They took us far away, we had no more family. We had to obey ... They hit hard on the hand."[14] Repeated references to separation and uprooting communicate to the audience that the community as a whole was brutally and enduringly plunged into darkness and the unknown.

Detailed explorations of specific cases of abuse or acts of violence were not the focus of survivors' testimonies, in contrast to testimonies delivered within the legal framework of the Independent Assessment Process (see Introduction, this volume). During the TRC public hearings that I attended, which were broadcast around the room on big-screen televisions, former students alluded to violence with a phrase, a gesture, or silence. The audience seemed to understand the meaning immediately, almost intuitively. "I was abused, I limp, but it is a physical wound – not serious. What's in my head ... It's what is in my head that is important. I was abused, but I can talk about it."[15] The individual is not the only victim here; also victims are the group's language, identity, and the community as a whole. This effect is heightened by survivors' frequent usage of the pronoun "us." "They told us that we were flea-ridden. I now have more respect for fleas (laughs) ... They destroyed us."[16] Former students frequently related their language and their identity to violence and trauma: "If I couldn't say the right word in English, I was hit. I would stand for four or five hours until I peed in my pants. That's one year that changed my life." Another man shared, "when I spoke Cree, I was whipped on the head and back. They kidnapped me to a hellhole with no humanity."[17] Former students described a form of violence that desubjecitvizes: it destroys the awareness of the actors and the collective (Wieviorka 2012, 6). The result of this deprivation of meaning, this isolation and solitude, and this brainwashing, as the first survivor mentioned, is individuals who have forgotten how to behave.

Frequent oscillation between "I" and "we/us" – as though these terms were equivalent – also shows the inability to separate individual experiences of violence and private emotions from the destruction of collective identity. Throughout the testimonies, the merging of the individual with the collective is reinforced by constant references to culture. Here, culture is perceived not as an aggregate of interdependent elements but as a universe of collectively shared meaning (Geertz 1973) that, according to former students' testimonies, has been destroyed by the violence of the residential school system. The pain experienced by the individual appears as everybody's pain: "I was abused. I had to face that. They hit us with a black strap when we didn't listen. I thought of my parents who didn't know what we were going through."[18] The narrative of violence returns to the separation of the individual from the group. The residential school pushes the former student, now grown up, into the void and strikes at the heart of the group's culture.

The Victim

Who has been most affected by this uprooting, this wrenching away, this emptiness that marks the pain contained in the testimonies of former students? Individuals? A distinct group? Society as a whole? The testimonies oscillate, as we have seen, between the "I" and the "we," while never explicitly referring to ethnic origin or to Indigenous peoples. The figure of the victim is constructed as a mirror image of the event itself and the pain associated with it. The victim thus fuses with the community as a whole. "I was born with my language,"[19] an elder declared, illustrating this holism in its purest form. In the testimonies, the child as victim emerges and exists only through its relationship with the collective. The assertion "I only spoke my language"[20] constructs the self as a simple product of culture. Themes that characterize the era prior to residential schools include community gatherings, family, neighbours, and the rejection of materialism. One man stated, "Before residential school, I lived with my family. We trapped, we hunted. I lived off of the love of my family."[21] Survivors do not generally speak of community in terms of its role in cultural organization and social reproduction. Rather, it is through the expression of emotions such as well-being and love that a positive, idealized image of the past, particularly of the community and the family, is constructed (see also Green, this volume). Along with the child, then, the family institution is a primary trauma victim:

> I remember that my mother went shopping and bought us things. It was bizarre. My mother held my hand. I didn't speak a word of English. I climbed the stairs, there were other children. I ate candies. My mother became smaller and smaller. I felt alone and rejected for the first time, and I had the feeling that my mother didn't love me and that's why she abandoned me. I didn't know what it was to be sad. I didn't understand.[22]

Although the identification of children with their family and their community of origin is primary, former students also refer to members of other Indigenous nations, such as the Cree and the Anishnabe, with whom they share the same lot. This allusion implicitly enlarges the "us." The expansion of the category of victim is also accomplished through the nostalgic representation of a more or less mythic past. One elder remembered, "I miss my food, I miss my past. Our life was good. There was no racism, cruelty. The smell of the pine helped us not to be sick."[23] Although the "us" is regularly associated with the victim (e.g., "they destroyed us"), it is not qualified in a precise way. In the testimonies, the status of victim is not assigned to a particular category, generation, or cultural group. The free-floating nature of the status of victim allows audience members to identify with it. This is especially the case among younger people, who attended the TRC events in large numbers.

The Relationship between the Audience and the Victims

The audiences at the TRC's national events were primarily composed of Indigenous people. At the events I attended, former students and elders circulated in the corridors, accompanied by their families. Also present were members of the various churches; in Edmonton, they formed a group at the back of the room during the hearings. Other than journalists, several researchers, and some unaccompanied individuals, few non-Indigenous people came to listen to the testimonies of former students. Although the testimonies were broadcast live on the Internet and recorded for the archives of the National Research Centre for Truth and Reconciliation at the University of Manitoba, the stories of former students seemed to resonate above all with an Indigenous audience.

As we have seen, on the one hand, this identification is facilitated by the constant reference to "us," which acts to diminish the gap between individual experiences and the collective memory of residential schools. On the other hand, the memory of trauma casts the figure of the survivor in a positive light. Through a return to the original community, resilience and holistic healing emerge from suffering, violence, and loss. One woman explained how she had come to identify as a residential school survivor:

> My husband and me, we watched *Schindler's List*. They took them into the gas chamber and suddenly, I couldn't breathe. I had to get out. I couldn't understand why I was like that. I asked a friend: "did that really happen [to us]?" Yes, she tells me. We were locked up there. It was hot and we couldn't breathe with all the steam. We banged on the little window and opened the door, but the nuns pushed us back. I erased that from my mind ... I wanted to share that with you because I had driven that from my mind.[24]

Continuing her testimony, this woman explained at length how she had "successfully survived" and "healed." By transitioning from an individual's incomprehensible experience to a collective narrative, the event becomes an agent in the creation of meaning and construction of a new culture. A man testified, "when I was young, I was abused like the other children. Growing up, I realized that I was a Survivor. It was hard, but I kept fighting because I was strong."[25] The relationships between former students are tenuous, but given the diversity of their experience, the relationships between the students and their children and grandchildren are even more so. Indigenous youth, not having gone to residential school, are even more estranged from the developing collective narrative. In theory, a generation constructs itself in opposition to the previous one. The previous generation seeks to maintain the singularity of its collective memory, which is made up of political struggle and trauma and is peopled with its own key personalities (Eyerman and Turner 1998, 97). However, even though the experience of Indigenous youth today is different from and much more heterogeneous than that of residential school survivors, numerous youth and other Indigenous people who did not go to residential schools testified at the TRC events and took on the cultural classification of survivors. Youth testified to a lack of love from their parents and, in some cases, to violence or sexual abuse perpetrated by family members or others. In Edmonton numerous adults testified that they had been "kidnapped"[26] by the Department of Social Services and talked about how this uprooting, combined with the shame of "being Indian,"[27] had pushed them into drug and alcohol abuse. The act of characterizing suffering as a crisis of meaning, along with a degree of vagueness in the qualification of the victim, permits individuals with no direct experience of residential school to represent certain events as traumatic. The identification of youth with the identity of survivor is so strong that they define themselves as intergenerational survivors or multigenerational survivors. Interestingly, this identification entails a shift in the attribution of responsibility for violence committed against youth. Parents, family members, or other members of the community who may remain objectively responsible for violent behaviour are in this case forgiven – because the bulk of responsibility is assigned to actors from outside of the collective, either to the "men who came" or to another representative of the "other."

As we will see, the media's portrayal of the TRC shows that the Canadian public does not fully identify with the narrative framework employed by former students and their families. The Canadian public appears to consider residential school trauma to be predominantly the concern of Indigenous people. For the Canadian public, the fact that survivors assign responsibility for this trauma mainly to the "other" constitutes a barrier to identification that trauma, even if raised to a cultural level, is unable to pierce.

The Perpetrators

Who is at fault? The churches? Residential school employees? The federal government? Canada? Does the fault lie with the Western ideologies that legitimized the residential school system? The question of who is responsible is equally unsettled for Indigenous youth and others who did not directly experience residential schools but who identify with the pain suffered by their close relatives and ancestors. Of course, when survivors refer to the perpetrators, the state or the church figures largely, but they are talked about as individuals, not legal entities. When former students make allusion to the church or the state, they denounce these perpetrators' professed ignorance of the abuse (e.g., "the church knew") but do not implicate them as actors in physical or sexual aggression. In their testimonies, survivors use both determinate and indeterminate pronouns to refer to the perpetrators of aggression: phrases such as "they did that," "they did that to me," and "the men came" are commonplace. The TRC's prohibition against naming perpetrators, unless the latter were already objects of lawsuits and/or legal decisions, contributed to this ambiguity. Although some may see this situation as evidence of the TRC's lack of power (James 2012), this ambiguity has allowed the audience to use its own imagination to fill in the blanks, and just about anybody can be imagined as responsible for the abuses that victims may have suffered. Imaginative work is certainly required in the case of identifying perpetrators of violence against intergenerational survivors, as behind their use of the pronouns "they" and "we" may be a foster family, a violent spouse, Social Services, or even kidnappers.[28] This ambiguity has also allowed those who testified at the TRC events to avoid speaking directly about community members. In listening to more than one of these testimonies, I lost track of the perpetrator's identity. Was the victim referring to a parent, a family member, or a residential school employee?

Whereas testimonies can often be somewhat fuzzy on the question of the perpetrator, the TRC was more clear-cut, as evidenced by the title of one of its publications, which explicitly identifies the perpetrator, the victims, and the event: *They Came for the Children: Canada, Aboriginal Peoples, and Residential Schools* (TRC 2012b). Although the cultural classification that lends structure to the testimonies is relatively indeterminate and accommodating with respect to pain, the victim, and the attribution of responsibility, the intermediary actors[29] – the TRC commissioners and honorary witnesses – commented on and interpreted witnesses' testimonies. This interpretive activity contributed to the forging of the truth about the residential school system and its legacy.

Performing the Truth

As anthropologist Ronald Niezen (2013, 103) notes, "the events of the TRC ... are not just sites of gathering knowledge; they are also active in producing it." Tanya Goodman (2009) makes the same observation about South Africa's Truth and Reconciliation Commission. Employing recently developed methodologies for studying the function of ritual in modernity, she defines that commission as "a public ritual which relied on narratives (and their interpretations) to connect the past and future trajectories of individual and collective lives – an endeavour which subsequently shifted the definition of who belongs" (ibid., 27). As Alexander (2006, 41) notes, "rites not only mark transitions but also create them, such that participants become something or somebody else as a result. Ritual performance not only symbolizes a social relationship or change; it also actualizes it" (quoted in Goodman 2009, 30). In Canada not only did the TRC provide a simple stage for the expression of collective representations conveyed through the testimonies of former students, but as a cultural performance, it also gave flesh and blood to this new memory of residential schools. Here, I can only outline certain aspects of this performance. What immediately becomes apparent, however, is that the TRC provided an analytic and conceptual framework for the individual stories through constant reference to psychiatric theories of trauma, thereby facilitating the emergence of a traumatic memory (Niezen 2013, 105). I also analyze how intermediary actors – honorary witnesses, commissioners, and the media – speak about the perpetrators, interpret pain, and participate in reproducing the identity of victims. These codifying and moderating activities, as we will see, do not operate without some contestation.

From the Event to the Trauma

The TRC operated with an intergenerational, even historical, understanding of trauma. The inclusion of youth and families as legitimate witnesses of the same order as former students was based on a number of concepts and theories drawn from the psychiatric literature. By the same token, the testimonies of these actors contribute to the recognition of these theories. The ability to transcend individual qualities such as age, history, and geographical context is accomplished, writes Niezen (2013, 103), "through concepts drawn from psychiatry, history, and human rights that are combined in ways to clarify the essence of the Survivor experience and make it possible for the category to be inhabited with certainty of conviction."

At the doors of the main ballroom in Montreal's Fairmont Hotel, where the commissioners' sharing panels were taking place in 2013, each spectator was offered a small plastic bag containing paper tissues and a card containing the phone numbers of free, twenty-four-hour emergency and support hotlines. The TRC's mandate included mention of protecting the health and safety of participants (IRSSA 2006). Support staff members, easily identifiable by their coloured vests, were constant companions of survivors and present in the audience during public hearings. They monitored the proceedings, on the alert for vulnerable people present both to testify and to listen. They handed out tissues in Montreal and water in Edmonton. That these measures to protect mental health were omnipresent is an indication of the traumatic nature of the testimonies. The free distribution of tissues and the continuous attention of health service workers to survivors and audience members created an atmosphere wherein everyone was vulnerable. There was a sense of risk that the hearings may lead to the sudden resurfacing of a traumatic event buried in the unconscious. Niezen (2013, 107), who observed all of the TRC events, writes that "if triggering is the specific form by which psychological pain is expressed among Survivors, the general background in which it takes place is often referred to as 'trauma.'" Taken together, these physical and human resources materialize the trauma. The presence of health service personnel at TRC events was not due to an extraordinary event, as may be the case during a humanitarian crisis or a catastrophe, but instead appeared to the outside observer as natural and normalized. This understanding of trauma was contained in the mandate of the TRC and materialized as a set of technical measures. This understanding of trauma is found in psychoanalytic theory, particularly in the psychiatric literature on Indigenous peoples (Brave Heart 1999; Brave Heart et al. 2011). These studies attempt to explain the high rates of disorders, including mental health and drug use, through the concept of historical trauma. Historical trauma is defined as a "collective complex trauma inflicted on a group of people who share a specific group identity or affiliation ... It is the legacy of numerous traumatic events a community experiences over generations and encompasses the psychological and social responses to such events" (Evans-Campbell 2008, 320, quoted in Gone 2013, 687). This concept is not recent, but its formalization is.[30] Its popularity has increased in recent years. Although not all psychiatrists accept this concept, notably because of its anachronistic character (Gone 2013), the intergenerational trauma that is the legacy of Indian residential schools legitimizes the concept of historical trauma and gives it a concrete visibility (Bombay, Matheson, and Anisman 2014).

The second aspect of this theory is its commitment to healing trauma through "the re-cathexis or re-attachment to traditional ... values" (Brave Heart 1999, 109). After a TRC sharing circle, an Innu friend invited me to accompany him to a lounge in order to undergo a purification ritual. "After emotions like that, you need to be purified," he told me. The ubiquitous smell of sage wafting from various rooms near the sharing spaces served as a constant reminder to those present of both the pathological nature of the event and of the healing methods associated with a renewed commitment to, and recognition of, Indigenous healing knowledge.

By placing its activities within the concept of historical trauma, the TRC went beyond classical psychoanalytic theories that treat trauma as coming from the event itself. Here, trauma is rooted directly in the ethnic origins and cultural identities of Indigenous peoples, which are structured by colonization. The traumatic event becomes mythologized and tends to place on an equal footing survivors, youth, women, and men from different communities all over the country, including those excluded from the Indian Residential Schools Settlement Agreement (see Gadoua 2010; and Molema, this volume).

Cultural Genocide or Real Genocide?

Intermediary actors also participated in the characterization of pain. Testimonies that I heard contained tears, nightmares, separation from siblings, shame of being Indigenous, sadness, sexual abuse, and physical brutalities. The TRC also opened the floor to parents and children of survivors, who spoke of a lack of love (see Green, this volume), incomprehension, alcohol, depression, and having to leave their communities in order to "escape." The assessment of these disparate experiences is contested terrain, both among scholars (Woolford 2009; MacDonald and Hudson 2012; Mako 2012) and among political leaders. For example, former Canadian prime minister Paul Martin, who appeared at a Montreal TRC national event, summed up these experiences using the term "cultural genocide."[31] The next day, the highly politically active Mohawk Ellen Gabriel refuted this classification, declaring that what had occurred was a "real genocide." Politicians, intellectuals, and Indigenous leaders all partake in this process of assessment and codification, which is not as straightforward as it may seem. Along these lines, the TRC created a Working Group on Missing Children and Unmarked Burials, mainly in response to media interest in the topic. The disappearance of Indigenous children and scientific experiments performed on Indigenous children are sensitive topics that illustrate and reinforce the idea of genocide (Mosby 2013). The counting of children who have disappeared, died, or were buried in mass graves is an issue that commissioners and survivors either did or did not mobilize in qualifying the pain they had experienced or witnessed. At the official release of the TRC's findings on the residential school system, Commissioner Marie Wilson highlighted with emotion the results of the investigation by the Working Group on Missing Children and Unmarked Burials:

> We learned the stories of those who could not speak and these 3,200 students sent to residential schools never returned home. In almost one third of those cases, the student's name wasn't even recorded ... A quarter of the time the student's gender was not reported ... For almost half of the children who died, the cause of death was not reported ... The indignity of this ... the utter sadness of this ... the currental devastation of this ... Can you imagine?[32]

During its events and in its reporting, the TRC proliferated analogies with the Holocaust without making explicit reference to it. These analogies were not lost on some non-Indigenous observers, judging by certain oppositional reactions in the editorial sections of newspapers. The history detailed in the TRC's (2012a) interim report perfectly illustrates this analogy. Repeated recourse to the terms "the people," "the parents," and "the children" allows for all ethnic connotations to be removed from history. It tells of the bus ride, sorting, taking of personal items, disrobing, hair cutting, delousing, assigning of numbers, uniforms, walking in single file, and inhumane treatment (TRC 2012b). The technical dimension and the consistent character of the description cannot help but remind readers of the precision with which the Nazis assembled, deported, and exterminated

European Jews. The video portrayals, where we see close-ups of tearful witnesses who are blowing their noses and losing control of their emotions, also contribute to this process of universalization of trauma. When I inquired at one point whether the transcriptions of testimonies were available, a person from the TRC explained to me that at the time, only the videos should be used as material. The speeches or comments of the honorary witnesses and commissioners during the sessions titled "Call to Gather," "Expressions of Reconciliation," and "Honorary Witness Reflections" also became occasions for them to expand the frontiers of the identity of victim by referring to or identifying with other survivors whose fundamental rights were also violated.

From the Indian Child to the Victim of Evil

One of the aspects of the TRC's work consisted of enlarging the scope of the traumatic event so that it went beyond being an Indigenous problem. Through a process of universalization, the TRC worked to make people perceive the event as having damaged the sacred values on which Canadian democracy was founded. In other words, the TRC wanted the retelling of this trauma to initiate a process of identification that would elicit empathy and solidarity from Canadian civil society where none had previously existed. This process of universalization relied in large part on relationships that the TRC was building with other survivors whose trauma was also anchored in collective memory and featured a struggle with evil. I am thinking here especially of the Shoah and the Rwandan genocide.

Workshops bringing these disparate survivors together were organized by the TRC. In Vancouver one of these was entitled "Be the Change: Young People Healing the Past and Building the Future." This workshop brought together four youth "who are facing the intergenerational impacts of human rights violations such as residential schools, Holocaust, Japanese internment and Chinese head tax" (TRC 2013). One of the TRC's honorary witnesses, a Tutsi survivor of the Rwandan genocide, spoke at the Montreal and Edmonton events. After situating his personal experience as a consequence of colonization, which had "destroyed the unity of our country" by dividing Hutu from Tutsi on the basis of simple physical observations, Eloge Butera stated, "I want to tell you that you are not alone and that we can assure you that your word is taken seriously to change us and change this country." His speech gave rise to numerous personal reactions that the mediator systematically translated as racism and colonialism and that he related to his own experience. Oscillating incessantly between singularity and universality, Indigenous people present at the conference were still able to identify with the speaker. "You have the same story as us," one woman commented. "I understand what happened to you [black people], to the slaves. On my path, compassion is important because that's what makes me a woman." Another audience member declared, "When we learn from books, we wonder if what we read is true. When we listen ... [we believe it]." Particularly performative, the speech of this honorary witness generated an extension of "us" through the recognition of shared pain. That is one of the strengths of trauma when the performance meets its goal.

Performative Success and Failure

In *Performance and Power,* Jeffrey Alexander (2011, 53) writes,

> The goal of secular performances, whether on stage or in society, remains the same as the ambition of sacred ritual. They stand or fall on their ability to produce psychological identification and cultural extension. The aim is to create, via skilful and affecting performance, the emotional connection of audience with actor and text and thereby to create the conditions for projecting cultural meaning from performance to audience.

The TRC produced a representation of the truth as a counternarrative of residential schools. This counternarrative is the foundation for a collective memory around which the identity of a people is constructed (Eyerman 2001, 2008). As Bernhard Giesen (2004, 113) states, "like birth and death, which set the frame for the continuity and unity of the individual existence, referring to a past as a collective triumph or a collective trauma transcends the contingent relationships between individual persons and forges them into a collective identity." By situating themselves spatially and temporally within the traumatic story that characterizes their suffering and by qualifying their aggressor, individuals accomplish two things: they give form to the collective, and they include themselves within the collective through the identity of survivor. The individual testimonies both broadcast and carry out the work of collective memory. By narrating their personal experiences, survivors come across to the audience as authentic victims bearing a traumatic memory. But does the audience identify with the survivors? This unification of survivors and audience is potentially quite powerful, as it does not depend on a rupture. Nor does it divide the generations, such as around a new interpretation of history. To the contrary, testimonies speak more of healing the intergenerational relationship than they do of healing the individual. They explicitly seek unification of the different Indigenous social and cultural groups under one identity and one truth. Anthropologist Simone Poliandri (this volume) shows how, in Mi'kmaw communities, new intergenerational solidarities are being reconstructed around the identity of survivor. An Innu confided to me in the hallway outside a TRC event, "You know, we come from all over Quebec. We have never seen each other, and yet we are all telling the same story. That means it's the truth." The memory of Indian residential schools as traumatic is becoming progressively entrenched among the Indigenous public, as evidenced by the numerous youth who define themselves as intergenerational or multigenerational survivors and by local-level investigations. However, the contributions in this volume by anthropologists Karine Vanthuyne and Arie Molema allow us to nuance this fact. Certain actors refuse to identify with this collective memory, which tends inevitably to reduce the uniqueness of individual and local experiences to the extent that the collective memory becomes institutionalized. As some survivors alluded to, this collective memory and the work of the TRC can appear to be artificial. Two factors that contributed to a sense of superficiality were the periodic reminder to survivors of the time limits allotted for speaking during the commissioners' audiences and the explicit mention of the narrative structure encouraged by the TRC during the "How to Share Your Truth" workshop. This superficiality does not attach to the testimonies themselves but rather to the TRC, in spite of the freedom to think and act that it accorded to former students in the context of its hearings.

In its interim report, the TRC (2012a, 9) describes the challenges it encountered in "raising awareness, among non-Indigenous Canadians, of the residential school history and legacy. This presents an enormous limitation to the possibility of long-term understanding and meaningful reconciliation." This observation (also made in the chapters by Hughes and Gaver, this volume), shows that reconciliation was not something that could be enacted through political will. Rather, reconciliation depended on the ability of the TRC to produce a narrative framework compelling enough to overturn the uncivil discursive codes that legitimize the exclusion of Indigenous people in Canada. However, the work of the TRC was quite underreported compared with other investigative commissions in Canada. When the TRC's national events occurred, provincial newspapers often ran several articles dealing with witness testimony or with the speeches of honorary witnesses or commissioners. A partial analysis of these articles shows that residential schools are considered to be an Indigenous issue and that Canadian society does not seem to identify with the associated trauma. The issue of the receptivity of Canadian society to this new history of residential schools deserves further research; only one poll on the topic has been conducted, and that was done before the TRC began (Environics Research Group 2008). No exhaustive analysis of the media treatment of the TRC has yet been undertaken. It can be asserted that the identity of the perpetrator responsible for genocide, which has a large role in this new history of residential schools, poses an obstacle to Canadian society. The gap between the event and most people's own prior representations of the event is too wide for the TRC's narrative to generate identification on behalf of Canadian society.

❧

Telling the truth about one's experience of residential school does not consist only of sharing one's personal history. Through this telling, a set of shared representations is broadcast into the public sphere, representations that qualify, regulate, and codify the event. A discourse analysis of witness testimonies shows the traumatic and collective dimension of the residential school. The event is considered to have damaged the collective and to have forever transformed Indigenous identity. It acquires, for the collective as a whole, the status of cultural trauma. This traumatic memory is not limited to physical violence or sexual abuse suffered by individuals but speaks to a loss of culture understood here as a web of significance (Geertz 1973, 5). The elevation of the narrative of trauma to the cultural level and its transcendence of the individual manifest as a process of reconstruction of meaning and rebuilding of alliances that were destroyed by the event itself. "They destroyed us" sums up this process of expansion – of indeterminacy, some might say – that allows the suffering of the victim of trauma and the actions of the perpetrators to transcend the level of strict personal experience. Thus, even those who did not directly experience residential school come to identify with the community of survivors. These survivors are united by a shared desubjectification arising out of the event of residential schooling.

The TRC did not give a voice to victims only so that they could heal from their trauma. By codifying, organizing, and giving form to testimonies, the TRC contributed to the creation of this traumatic memory. Through incessant analogies and associations with other traumas that depict absolute evil such as the Holocaust or the Rwandan genocide, residential schools were represented as having damaged and undermined the sacred values of the collective. Thus, the truth is no longer situated ethnically, geographically, or temporally, allowing people who did not directly experience residential school (e.g., Indigenous youth) and Canadian society in general to identify with this narrative. Indigenous identity is manifested and expressed through constant reference to the collective identity of survivor, which transcends classic categories of social belonging (i.e., sex, place, class, age, etc.) and which the work of the TRC has differentiated into the categories of multigenerational survivor, intergenerational survivor, and so on. The power of the TRC may be only symbolic power, but that is not necessarily a weakness. The TRC's work may not lead to the reparation of colonial injustice, but by making the residential school into a cultural trauma and by broadcasting this collective memory, it participated in giving, around the identity of survivor, flesh and blood to the abstract category of Indigenous peoples.

ACKNOWLEDGMENTS

A preliminary version of this chapter was presented at the annual seminar of Yale University's Centre for Cultural Sociology. The author thanks especially Jeffrey Alexander for his invitation and all the graduate students and scholars at the event for their comments and constructive input. The author also thanks the three anonymous reviewers for their close reading and their comments, which contributed to improving the text, as well as Wren Nasr for the translation of the text. This research was made possible by a postdoctoral grant from the Social Sciences and Humanities Research Council of Canada.

NOTES

1 Élisabeth, TRC Sharing Circle, Montreal National Event, April 27, 2013.

2 Unknown, TRC Sharing Circle, Montreal National Event, April 26, 2013..

3 For 20 percent of the Canadian population, it is the separation of children from their families that is mentioned. For 14 percent, the residential schools are associated with racial discrimination and mistreatment perpetrated against Indigenous peoples. For 10 percent, the residential schools are associated with the refusal to allow children to speak their language. A table contained in the study shows in detail the levels of awareness of the Indian residential schools among the general population, the off-reserve population, and new Canadians.

4 Carole Blackburn (2012) shows how, in the case of *Blackpint v. the Crown,* the loss of language and culture was not recognized by the courts.

5 Élisabeth, TRC Sharing Circle, Montreal National Event, April 27, 2013.

6 Mathias Suganaqueb, TRC Commissioners Sharing Panel, Edmonton National Event, March 29, 2014.

7 Unknown, TRC Sharing Circle, Montreal National Event, April 27, 2013.

8 This link between language and the capacity to rebuild social relationships is especially apparent among certain former students for whom learning English or French was the key to finding a job, going to school, or integrating into mainstream society. It is notable that most of the testimonies were delivered in English or French (in Montreal), even though the majority of former students had been able to conserve or relearn their Indigenous languages. Communicating in English or French, then, seems to be a means by which relationships can be shared and reconstructed – through the act of telling one's private story to others.

9 Mathias Suganaqueb, TRC Commissioners Sharing Panel, Edmonton National Event, March 29, 2014.

10 Élisabeth Minnie, TRC Commissioners Sharing Panel, Montreal National Event, April 27, 2013.

11 Unknown woman, TRC Commissioners Sharing Panel, Montreal National Event, April 27, 2013.

12 James Whiteduck, TRC Commissioners Sharing Panel, Edmonton National Event, March 28, 2014.

13 Norman, TRC Commissioners Sharing Panel, Edmonton National Event, March 29, 2014.

14 Élisabeth, TRC Sharing Circle, Montreal National Event, April 27, 2013.

15 Peter Stonechild, TRC Commissioners Sharing Panel, Edmonton National Event, March 29, 2014.

16 Marie Moreau, TRC Commissioners Sharing Panel, Montreal National Event, April 28, 2013.

17 Ibid., Edmonton National Event, March 27, 2014.

18 Élisabeth Minnie, TRC Commissioners Sharing Panel, Montreal National Event, April 27, 2013.

19 Unknown, TRC Sharing Circle, Montreal National Event, April 27, 2013.

20 Ibid.

21 Mathias Suganaqueb, TRC Commissioners Sharing Panel, Edmonton National Event, March 29, 2014.

22 Ibid.

23 Marie Moreau, TRC Commissioners Sharing Panel, Montreal National Event, April 28, 2013.

24 Marguerite Simpson, TRC Commissioners Sharing Panel, Edmonton National Event, March 27, 2014.

25 Peter Stonechild, TRC Commissioners Sharing Panel, Edmonton National Event, March 29, 2014.
26 Unknown woman, TRC Sharing Circle, Edmonton National Event, March 29, 2014.
27 Linda Minoose, TRC Commissioners Sharing Panel, Edmonton National Event, March 29, 2014.
28 The narrative of Donald Morin, in his forties, at the Edmonton National Event was particularly eloquent. He recounted that at the age of twelve, he was sent by his foster family to buy cigarettes. On the way, he was kidnapped and raped by two men who confined him overnight.
29 I use the term "intermediary" here to account for the position these actors occupy. They are situated midway between the survivors and the greater audience in the communication process. For example, the term "cultural genocide," used by former Canadian prime minister Paul Martin, appeared widely in media reports.
30 Maria Yellow Horse Brave Heart and colleagues (2011, 284) write, "There has been a groundswell of positive reactions to the concept of historical trauma ... as evidenced by significant requests for workshops and training on this topic across tribes throughout the United States and Canada, the number of 'hits' on the website www.historicaltrauma.com, an increase in literature on this topic, and local as well as national and international conferences about historical trauma and related topic areas."
31 The term "cultural genocide" was used in the TRC's (2015) final report in reference to the Indian residential schools. Debate around the use of this qualification of the event is ongoing.
32 Commissionner Mary Wilson, TRC Closing Event, Ottawa, June 2, 2015.

REFERENCES

Alexander, Jeffrey C. 2006. *The Civil Sphere*. Oxford: Oxford University Press.

—. 2011. *Performance and Power*. Cambridge, UK: Polity.

—. 2012. *Trauma: A Social Theory*. Cambridge, UK: Polity.

Alexander, Jeffrey C., Ron Eyerman, Bernhard Giesen, Neil J. Smelser, and Piotr Sztompka. 2004. *Cultural Trauma and Collective Identity*. Berkeley: University of California Press. http://dx.doi.org/10.1525/california/9780520235946.001.0001.

Blackburn, Carole. 2012. "Culture Loss and Crumbling Skulls: The Problematic of Injury in Residential School Litigation." *Political and Legal Anthropology Review* 35 (2): 289–307. http://dx.doi.org/10.1111/j.1555-2934.2012.01204.x.

Bombay, Amy, Kim Matheson, and Hymie Anisman. 2014. "The Intergenerational Effects of Indian Residential Schools: Implications for the Concept of Historical Trauma." *Transcultural Psychiatry* 51 (3): 320–38.

Brave Heart, Maria Yellow Horse. 1999. "Oyate Ptayela: Rebuilding the Lakota Nation through Addressing Historical Trauma among Lakota Parents." *Journal of Human Behavior in the Social Environment* 2 (1–2): 109–26. http://dx.doi.org/10.1300/J137v02n01_08.

Brave Heart, Maria Yellow Horse, Josephine Chase, Jennifer Elkins, and Deborah B. Altschul. 2011. "Historical Trauma among Indigenous Peoples of the Americas: Concepts, Research, and Clinical Considerations." *Journal of Psychoactive Drugs* 43 (4): 282–90. http://dx.doi.org/10.1080/02791072.2011.628913.

Capitaine, Brieg. 2012. "Autochtonie et Modernité: L'expérience des Innus au Canada." PhD diss., School for Advanced Studies in the Social Sciences, Paris.

Durkheim, Émile. 1912. *The Elementary Forms of the Religious Life*. London: Allen and Unwin., 1976.

Environics Research Group. 2008. *IRSRC – 2008 National Benchmark Survey*. Prepared for Indian Residential Schools Resolution Canada and the Truth and Reconciliation Commission of Canada. Ottawa: Environics Research Group.

Evans-Campbell, T. 2008. "Historical Trauma in American Indian/Native Alaska Communities: A Multilevel Framework for Exploring Impacts on Individuals, Families, and Communities." *Journal of Interpersonal Violence* 23 (3): 316–38. http://dx.doi.org/10.1177/0886260507312290.

Eyerman, Ron. 2001. *Cultural Trauma: Slavery and the Formation of African American Identity*. Cambridge, UK: Cambridge University Press. http://dx.doi.org/10.1017/CBO9780511488788.

–. 2008. *The Assassination of Theo Van Gogh: From Social Drama to Cultural Trauma*. Durham, NC: Duke University Press. http://dx.doi.org/10.1215/9780822391449.

Eyerman, Ron, and Bryan S. Turner. 1998. "Outline of a Theory of Generations." *European Journal of Social Theory* 1 (1): 91–106. http://dx.doi.org/10.1177/136843198001001007.

Fassin, Didier, and Richard Rechtman. 2009. *The Empire of Trauma: An Inquiry into the Condition of Victimhood*. Princeton, NJ: Princeton University Press.

Gadoua, Marie-Pierre. 2010. "The Inuit Presence at the First Canadian Truth and Reconciliation Commission National Event." *Études/Inuit/Studies* 34 (2): 167–84. http://dx.doi.org/10.7202/1004096ar.

Geertz, Clifford. 1973. *The Interpretation of Cultures*. Basic Books: New York.

Giesen, Bernhard. 2004. "The Trauma of Perpetrators: The Holocaust as the Traumatic Reference of German National Identity." In *Cultural Trauma and Collective Identity*, by Jeffrey C. Alexander, Ron Eyerman, Bernhard Giesen, Neil J. Smelser, and Piotr Sztompka, 112–54. Berkeley: University of California Press. http://dx.doi.org/10.1525/california/9780520235946.003.0004.

Gone, Joseph P. 2013. "Redressing First Nations Historical Trauma: Theorizing Mechanisms for Indigenous Culture as Mental Health Treatment." *Transcultural Psychiatry* 50 (5): 683–706. http://dx.doi.org/10.1177/1363461513487669.

Goodman, Tanya. 2009. *Staging Solidarity: Truth and Reconciliation in a New South Africa*. Boulder, CO: Paradigm.

Indian Residential Schools Settlement Agreement (IRSSA). 2006. "Schedule N." In *Indian Residential Schools Settlement Agreement*. Ottawa: Government of Canada. http://www.trc.ca/websites/trcinstitution/File/pdfs/SCHEDULE_N_EN.pdf.

James, Matt. 2012. "A Carnival of Truth? Knowledge, Ignorance and the Canadian Truth and Reconciliation Commission." *International Journal of Transitional Justice* 6 (2): 182–204. http://dx.doi.org/10.1093/ijtj/ijs010.

MacDonald, David, and Graham Hudson. 2012. "The Genocide Question and Indian Residential Schools in Canada." *Canadian Journal of Political Science* 45 (2): 427–49. http://dx.doi.org/10.1017/S000842391200039X.

Mako, Shamiran. 2012. "Cultural Genocide and Key International Instruments: Framing the Indigenous Experience." *International Journal on Minority and Group Rights* 19 (2): 175–94. http://dx.doi.org/10.1163/157181112X639078.

Mills, C. Wright. 1959. *The Sociological Imagination*. New York: Oxford University Press.

Mosby, Ian. 2013. "Administering Colonial Science: Nutrition Research and Human Biomedical Experimentation in Aboriginal Communities and Residential Schools, 1942–1952." *Social History* 46 (91): 145–72.

Niezen, Ronald. 2013. *Truth and Indignation: Canada's Truth and Reconciliation Commission on Indian Residential Schools.* Toronto: University of Toronto Press.

Smelser, Neil J. 2004. "Psychological Trauma and Cultural Trauma." In *Cultural Trauma and Collective Identity,* by Jeffrey C. Alexander, Ron Eyerman, Bernhard Giesen, Neil J. Smelser, and Piotr Sztompka, 31–59. Berkeley: University of California Press. http://dx.doi.org/10.1525/california/9780520235946.003.0002.

Truth and Reconciliation Commission of Canada (TRC). 2012a. *Interim Report.* Winnipeg, MB: Truth and Reconciliation Commission of Canada.

–. 2012b. *They Came for the Children: Canada, Aboriginal Peoples, and Residential Schools.* Winnipeg, MB: Truth and Reconciliation Commission of Canada.

–. 2013. *Reconciliation Dialogue – Be the Change: Young People Healing the Past and Building the Future.* Video. https://vimeo.com/78638476

–. 2015. *Honouring the Truth, Reconciling for the Future: Summary of the Final Report of the Truth and Reconciliation Commission of Canada.* Ottawa: Truth and Reconciliation Commission of Canada.

Wieviorka, Michel. 2012. *Evil.* Cambridge, UK: Polity.

Woolford, Andrew. 2009. "Ontological Destruction: Genocide and Canadian Aboriginal Peoples." *Genocide Studies and Prevention* 4 (1): 81–97.

3

Loving to Reconcile: Love as a Political Emotion at the Truth and Reconciliation Commission

ROBYN GREEN

> Without justice there can be no love.
>
> – bell hooks, *All about Love*

AT THE OPENING CEREMONIES of the Truth and Reconciliation Commission of Canada's Atlantic National Event,[1] Chief Commissioner Murray Sinclair stated,

> Reconciliation is about love. And in this way, I need you to think about how we can use that term. If you love your children, if you love your grandchildren, if you love your family, then we need to do something about this. We need to think about what the solutions can be. We need to start to get beyond all of those things that are burdening us. (TRC 2011c, 93–94)

Prior to my departure to attend the Halifax event, I considered the theme "It's about Love" awkward for a setting that emphasized the narration and witnessing of residential school stories that frequently depicted experiences of violence and abuse. Yet, in his address, Commissioner Sinclair linked familial love to the intergenerational effects of historic trauma in order to convey an urgent need to alleviate the circulation of bad feelings (Ahmed 2005, 72–73) in Indigenous families and communities. Drawing on public speeches and testimony from the Atlantic National Event, I document in a creative tension between the Truth and Reconciliation Commission of Canada as a formal quasi-judicial institution and as a public space that was routinely transformed by participant testimonies to address the following question: what was the relationship between the conceptualization of love and the conceptualization of reconciliation at the TRC's Atlantic National Event?

I argue that references to love at this particular national event can be read in two ways: as a desire for sameness and unity among the nation's citizenry (Hardt and Negri 2009) or as a powerful emotion to express self-determination (see Collins 1991; hooks 2000; Baker 2005). Against the backdrop of these two readings of love, I draw a correlation between Emerance Baker's (2005) concept of loving Indianness, which situates love alongside survivance,[2] and Paulette Regan's (2010) concept of restorying, which refers to a "decolonizing space for Indigenous history – counter-narratives of diplomacy, law, and peacemaking practices – as told by Indigenous Peoples themselves" (Corntassel, Chaw-win-is, and T'lakwadzi 2009, 138). I argue that although the extent to which the Truth and Reconciliation Commission of Canada fostered a space for decolonial politics remains contested (Nagy 2012; James 2012; Niezen 2013), the possibility of restorying Indigenous histories at national events still existed.

First and foremost, it is important to note that many scholars are reluctant to endorse reconciliation as a viable political process or a meaningful concept for recuperating Indigenous-settler relations (Alfred 2009b; Simpson 2011). As noted in the introduction to this volume, reconciliation functions as a constitutional mechanism; it is a concept that describes either the potential for reconstructing Indigenous-settler relations or a process of acknowledging historical injustice. According to Dale Turner (2013, 100), reconciliation is a process that "attempts to heal Aboriginal Peoples and communities," yet some scholars insist that in the Canadian context, this concept may emphasize a foreclosure of the past (Simpson 2011) since material redistribution (Alfred 2009b) and the reconciliation of sovereignties (Ladner and Dick 2008, 89) were underemphasized in the Truth and Reconciliation Commission's official mandate. Jennifer Henderson and Pauline Wakeham (2009, 15) suggest that reconciliation's "more abstract resonances of overcoming differences lend the term to cooptation by governments seeking to cleanse the national image through more symbolic measures." This understanding of reconciliation remains in contradistinction to their definition of redress, which represents "aggrieved constituencies' movements from below to achieve state recognition and material forms of compensation for injustices" (Henderson and Wakeham 2009, 15). Although this reconciliation-redress binary may be helpful in conceptualizing the consequences of institutionalizing justice seeking in Canada, it may be less beneficial in analyzing the Truth and Reconciliation Commission in action since national events organized spaces that could be mobilized to disquiet settler-colonial logics in much the same way that the settler state "produces the materials and possibilities of its own unsettlement" (LeFevre 2013, 138–39). What follows, however, should not be read as an endorsement of the TRC but as a way to demonstrate its limitations in shaping a coherent or ideological public message concerning what it means to *reconcile*.

I explore the intersection of reconciliation and a decolonizing politics of love based primarily on my experience participating in the Truth and Reconciliation Commission's national events. In concert with my attendance, I reviewed transcripts of survivor testimonies and media responses to the Atlantic National Event (both official and personal) in order to examine expressions of love, which carried with them numerous assumptions that I believed required critical intervention. Because of the Atlantic event's theme, I assert that a specific relationship and tension existed between the affect of love and the concept of reconciliation that may not have existed at other national events. For this reason, I focus on this national event only to avoid projecting specific interpretations of the tensions between love and reconciliation onto the testimonies of other events.

I assumed that love would be deployed as a nationalist strategy to shore up narratives of belonging or would function as an affective mechanism to engender therapeutic outcomes for participants. Yet, upon reviewing the Atlantic event's transcripts and recordings, I realized that love was often deployed in ways that circumvented paternalistic or sentimental inferences to romance or conciliation. Each of the TRC's event themes coincided with one of the Seven Sacred Teachings. *Zaagi'idiwin,* an Anishnaabe word for "love," is the teaching that represented the Atlantic National Event.[3] Zaagi'idiwin is described as *unconditional* emotion, which represents a holistic teaching expressed as a love of others, of the Creator, and of oneself (Bouchard and Martin 2009). I observed that the expression of love in the context of the Atlantic event's theme demonstrated a radical response to colonialism and its legacy. I argue that love was deployed for cross-purposes at the Atlantic National Event to express national sentiment and to assert Indigenous self-determination.

Conceptualizations of Love

This chapter contributes to "culture of redress" scholarship (Henderson and Wakeham 2009; Martin 2009; Youngblood Henderson 2013) but also to a burgeoning field of affect studies that explores emotion either as a central component of anticolonial resistance (Carpenter 2008; Million 2013) or as a technology used to maintain settler histories and authority (Rifkin 2011). Love as an emotion is endowed with great importance for individuals, families, and communities, but it often functions as a contradiction, representing a source of joy and pain, or salvation and struggle. Michael Hardt and Antonio Negri (2009, 182) state,

> Love is deeply ambivalent and susceptible to corruption. In fact, what passes for love today in ordinary discourse and popular culture is predominantly its corrupt forms. The primary locus of this corruption is the shift in love from the common to the same, that is, from the production of the common to a repetition of the same or a process of unification.

These corrupted forms of love may reinforce the status quo as a means to marginalize difference and universalize the experience of citizenship. Indeed, narratives of nationhood are often deployed as allegories, highlighting familial or romantic forms of love. Building on Gramscian thought, Doris Sommer (1994, 178) describes romantic love as a potentially "hegemonic political project" that subdues "the antagonist through 'love' rather than coercion." This assertion coincides with Roland Chrisjohn and Tanya Wasacase's (2009, 221) critique of matrimonial metaphors that are used to represent reconciliation. These authors observe that

> The path of true love rarely runs smoothly, and the union may be dissolved for one reason or another. There is and has been for centuries any number of interventions ... aimed at healing the rift, whatever its basis. *Reconciliation,* then, is the success of these enterprises, a restoration to the earlier condition of a single, shared and combined effort. (Emphasis in original)

This quote demonstrates how the emotion of love is a popular trope used to represent the renewal of harmony, teamwork, or partnership even where it was absent in the first place.

Despite its being taken up by queer and anticolonial literatures, some scholars suggest that love often remains outside of most scholarly analyses "because love continues to be a feminized topic, associated with 'private' space and feelings" (Morrison, Johnston, and Longhurst 2013, 506). Consequently, and in response to this elision, the study of love in the works of feminist scholars situates this emotion as a mechanism to contest white supremacy and capitalist authority upon its public expression (hooks 2000; Akiwenzie-Damm 2003; Baker 2005). For instance, Lisa Amanda Palmer (2012, 16) states that "love within black feminist thought also becomes a weapon against racism and all other systems of domination, thus creating a social climate of revolutionary democracy where political acts of love cannot exist in the same spaces of domination." Following bell hooks, Baker's (2005, 115) paper "Loving Indianness" suggests that "a loving perception is necessary in the face of so much ongoing racism and oppression." Affective strategies such as the deployment of love or healing, combined with the practice of restorying, can be used to contest the so-called innocence of the settler state (Regan 2010; see also Episkenew 2009) and to challenge narratives of Indigenous dysfunction or pathology (Baker 2005; Million 2013).

The importance of taking up such affective strategies as part of a politics of decolonization is highlighted by Eve Tuck (2009, 416), who argues "that a desire-based framework is an antidote to damage-centred research." An analytic framework based on a politics of love works as such an antidote because it "stops and counteracts the effects of a poison, and the poison I am referring to here is not the supposed damage of Native communities, urban communities, or other disenfranchised communities but frameworks that position these communities as damaged" (ibid.). Indigenous perspectives on love and erotica have been the subjects of two recent literary anthologies and a collection of short stories (Akiwenzie-Damm 2003; Taylor 2008; Simpson 2013),[4] yet narratives of trauma and suffering are still overemphasized in mainstream representations of Indigenous peoples, especially in the context of residential schooling.

The emotionalization of society has been critiqued by scholars as displacing structural violence and material disparity (Furedi 2004; Moon 2008), what is brought to the fore in the works of Indigenous feminists is an affirmation of the relationship between feeling, cultural recovery, and sovereignty, since the emotion of love functions as a central force in the process of healing. The importance of acknowledging the depth of trauma and social suffering inflicted through colonial relationships is crucial (Irlbacher-Fox 2009; Alfred 2009a), and love remains central to the context of reconciliation even if it seems misplaced alongside survivor commentary.

Residential Schools and the Denial of Love

In speaking on the theme of love at the opening ceremonies of the Truth and Reconciliation Commission's Atlantic National Event on October 27, 2011, Commissioner Murray Sinclair addressed the contradiction between the event's theme and the history experienced by survivors:

> This particular theme is about love, and in our community hearings it has been raised with us about the inappropriateness of that term because, as we have been told, many of the Survivors found no love within the schools. They did not experience love within their home because they went back to people who had themselves been damaged by residential schools. They did not feel love as they were growing up either within the schools or within their communities or within their families, and they continue to live a life in which they wonder whether love exists. (TRC 2011c, 93)

In keeping with the feminist interventions about love noted above, I maintain that the history of Indigenous-settler relations in Canada should not be regarded simply as one without "love" but also as one based on a logic of elimination (Wolfe 2006). The logic of elimination was legitimized and maintained through Indian Act legislation, which was used to enforce residential school policy.[5] John Borrows (2008, 14) notes that the Indian Act

> is anti-family, and thus stands in the way of love. Love forges and wields family ties in the present and through the generations. The Indian Act does not. Love would promote legislation and community approaches that recognized and affirmed family relationships, like husband and wife, parent and child, grandparent and grandchild, aunts and nephew, uncles and nieces, cousins, siblings, and other kinship bonds. We are spiritually and sociologically a people of extended kinship and clan relations. The Indian Act severs these traditions.

Consequently, the emotion of love, or more accurately its absence, in residential school narratives is characteristically situated alongside the concept of *loss* in reference to the *loss of family* and the *loss of self.*

In his testimony at the Atlantic event, Rev. Fred Hiltz of the Anglican Church of Canada recognized the relationship between love and the *loss of family:*

> The theme of this Atlantic National Event, "It's About Love," it moves me to think of a mother's love, a father's love, the love of brothers and sisters, the love of grandparents, and the love of an extended family. I am sorry. I am sorry that our church was part of a system, a policy of assimilation, in which we took you from your homes. (TRC 2011c, 158–59)

Hiltz's apology recognizes that students were removed from their families, yet survivor testimonies describe the residential schools as punitive or carceral spaces that resembled nothing like a "new" home. Building on this, the Assembly of First Nations' (1994, 88) report, titled *Breaking the Silence: An Interpretive Study of Residential School Impact and Healing as Illustrated by the Stories of First Nations Individuals,* helps to situate the intergenerational impacts of dismantled familial relationships:

> Fundamental to adulthood is raising a family. Among other things, raising a family requires a high level of intimacy with at least one other person. Fundamental to intimacy is the willingness to communicate openly, to reveal oneself to another person. It is impossible to be intimate and maintain silence. For those living in the world after residential school, the challenge of an intimate relationship was often an exercise in frustration, and frequently led to failure.

The report suggests that familial ties were eroded through the imposition of residential school due to the policies of removal. Kim Anderson notes that "undertaking a loving perception, while necessary, is complex in that it is about establishing intimacy and responsibility while simultaneously acknowledging the problems in Native communities" (Baker 2005, 116). Some of these problems illustrate the effects of spiritual, familial, and epistemological dispossession, which was central to the logic of the residential school system. The lack of love coincides with cultural shaming, where assimilationist logic manifests as a form of cultural *hatred* directed against

Indigenous peoples, often fuelling forms of self-hate in former students (see Gaudet and Martin, this volume). Isolation and shame only increased as communication between generations became increasingly fraught due to widening language barriers and prolonged removal from community, which undermined cultural knowledge production and transmission (Grant 1996; Monture-Angus 1999; James 2012).

Testimonies given by survivors at TRC national and community events detail a lack of caring and compassion from caretakers that resulted in an absence of love. The narrative of absent love can also be told in a more nuanced way through a process of *restorying*. For example, Cree leader Madeleine Dion Stout (2012, 49) affirms the absence of affection in residential schools but, at the same time, reveals how her experience of second-hand love afforded her some semblance of healing:

> I also remember looking up to a window and catching an unmistakable aura of affection between a Cree woman who worked at the school and her Dene suitor. She was radiant as she beamed down on us from the window, large and paned, while he, strikingly handsome, beamed at her. While I was deprived of love in residential school, I lived it second-hand to the fullest. Love literally filled my empty heart and soul, even though it was not rightfully mine.

Through its juxtaposition of romantic love with a space where love is not only absent but also actively oppressed, Stout's memory indicates how powerful witnessing love can be. Her story cannot be reduced to an allegory of romance or matrimony but serves as a reminder of the possibility of hope and healing in the wake of love's absence. The Truth and Reconciliation Commission of Canada presented an opportunity for sharing a vast array of narratives where Indigenous survivors represented themselves as individuals and community members opposed to the products of cruel and discriminatory practices.

The TRC's Atlantic National Event

As detailed in the Introduction to this volume, the Truth and Reconciliation Commission of Canada was created as one of the main prongs in the 2006 Indian Residential Schools Settlement Agreement. The history of this legal action has direct links to the survivors of the Shubenacadie Residential

School, the only officially recognized school in Atlantic Canada.[6] In 1996 survivor Nora Bernard organized nearly a thousand former students in a bid to launch a class action claim against the administrators of the school; this successful undertaking resulted in claimants eventually joining the Baxter class action lawsuit in 2005, which would later form the template for the Settlement Agreement.

The Truth and Reconciliation Commission's national events constituted a variety of programming, such as educational workshops, film screenings, literary readings, plays, talent shows, educational days for elementary school students, memorials, the induction of honorary witnesses, and numerous dialogues with parties to the Settlement Agreement and with settler participants. However, the collection and preservation of public and private testimonies was the mainstay of the TRC. Testimony in the wake of historical injustice is a deeply political act, which can "begin to draw the focus back to community and family processes of restorying justice and history, as a means to challenge the colonial relationship with Canada" (Corntassel, Chaw-win-is, and T'lakwadzi 2009, 144). In conceptualizing the process of restorying, Regan (2010) believes that the narration and witnessing of residential school testimony at these events demonstrated great pedagogical promise as a decolonial strategy. Other scholars withheld an endorsement of the Truth and Reconciliation Commission as a space where restorying could take place (Corntassel, Chaw-win-is, and T'lakwadzi 2009, 141–46).

The "Atlantic National Event Concept Paper" (TRC 2011a, 3) states that "National Events will honour all these former little ones [survivors of residential school] by involving an appropriate number of intergenerational Survivors, including young children" because this will "help other Canadians 'feel' and relate to the enormity of the impact on family and community of having so many children removed from them." Therefore, feeling served as an act of pedagogy deployed to impact settler participants. Nonetheless, the expression of emotional testimony – be it sadness, happiness, or anger – to an Indigenous and non-Indigenous audience was central to the TRC's truth-telling events. However, this form of pedagogy must be voluntarily sought since few mainstream Canadians outside of members of church congregations ended up participating in these events. This situation may indicate the TRC's limited reach (see the chapters by Gaver, Hughes, and Niezen, this volume). In the following section, I explore the complex ways that love was deployed at the Atlantic National Event by focusing on two major themes: *love as teamwork* and *love as home*.

All Is Fair in Love and Sport

At the welcoming ceremony on October 27, 2011, to frame the national event's theme of love, Commissioner Marie Wilson used a comment she had heard from a survivor at a regional meeting that preceded the event. In recounting this survivor's assertion that it had taken "50 years to realize I come from a loving community," Commissioner Wilson stated that the comment "left [her] with this question: how long will it take us to realize we come from a loving country?" (TRC 2011c, 110). As the survivor's statement is rearticulated as a question concerning the broader context of Indigenous-settler reconciliation, "loving community" becomes an unintended placeholder for "nation-state." Given the genocidal outcomes experienced by Indigenous peoples due to the imposition of Canadian policy in both the past and present (Ladner and Dick 2008; Woolford 2009), reflections of Canada as a loving country may seem premature at this stage of reconciliation. Commissioner Wilson's statement may also exemplify what Regan (2010, 83–111) calls the peacemaker myth, which routinely positions Canada as a protective nation and a benevolent power through processes of historical revision. The survivor's reference to loving in the original statement depicts the recognition of community solidarity, whereas Commissioner Wilson's question presents this affect in allegorical terms. This shift may undermine the potential for self-determination acknowledged in the original assertion.

Following the reference to Canada as a loving country, Commissioner Wilson built on her question by noting,

> The work of the Truth and Reconciliation Commission is not a spectator sport. It is a full contact sport. Full contact at the level of spirit and at the level of heart and at the level of love. *Love for what is right, love for what is fair, love for how things should have been and love for how things should be and can still become.* That cannot happen in our country of Canada if the work of the Truth and Reconciliation Commission is limited to Indigenous peoples and residential school Survivors talking to themselves. It cannot happen without the defining and the living out of new

relationships. And it cannot happen if we do not find meaningful ways not only to reconcile each other, but as a first step to even come to know each other. (TRC 2011c, 110, emphasis added)

Commissioner Wilson's "athletics of the heart" metaphor valorizes the difficult task of fostering Indigenous-settler dialogue if certain forms of participation are ghettoized. However, the underlying message that ignorance breeds contempt appeals to a particular type of liberal humanism that reinforces the belief that "if people simply understood Native peoples better, Natives would then become fully human – they would be free and self-determining" (Smith 2010, 42). However, as Andrea Smith (ibid.) notes, "the project of aspiring to 'humanity' is always already a racial project; it is a project that aspires to a universality and self-determination that can exist only over and against the particularity and affectability of 'the other.'" Smith's view of universal narratives forms a caveat similar to that of Hardt and Negri's (2009) conceptualization of a corrupted love that privileges *sameness*, or what legal scholar Jula Hughes (this volume) recognizes as a form of *colonial mimicry*. Indigenous difference is reduced to forms of cultural and linguistic expression that can be universally accommodated, whereas the distinctiveness of Indigenous knowledge systems and historical experience is frequently jettisoned in the public sphere.

I counter Wilson's sports metaphor with Smith's critique of the "Oppression Olympics" as a means to anticipate potential problems of *shared* narratives. Smith (2006, 66–67) argues that organizing by women of colour becomes constrained when diverse communities organize themselves around the concept of shared subjugation. Under these conditions, the demarcation and ranking of various oppressions may occur, leaving the kaleidoscope of white authority hidden from view. This kaleidoscopic trick is evident in the way the TRC represents the act of sharing. As outlined in "Schedule N" of the Settlement Agreement (IRSSA 2006), the act generally refers to truth sharing and therefore implies an exchange of knowledge. However, sharing in this context, as well as in Wilson's metaphor, is reinforced by the assumption of fairness, which perceives individual players – although representative of collective identities – as engaging with a similar but *equal* opponent. The opportunity to share one's testimony publicly does not disrupt larger structural barriers within Indigenous-settler relationships. A more robust version of sharing can be found in the *Final Report* of the Royal Commission on Aboriginal Peoples (1996, n.p.), where "the principle of sharing calls for the giving and receiving of benefits in fair measure. It is the basis on which Canada was founded, for if Indigenous Peoples had been unwilling to share what they had and what they knew about the land, many of the newcomers would not have lived to prosper." Here, sharing is depicted as a historical practice between nations and ultimately a source of settler survival. Nonetheless, the impetus for the settler state to share resources, jurisdiction, or power with Indigenous peoples was underdeveloped in the TRC's pedagogical mandate.

As a result of the mandate's focus on dialogue, Commissioner Wilson's sports metaphor was later rearticulated by other TRC participants as a violent assault against the *settler*. For instance, during the Circle of Reconciliation,[7] Wilson's statement was reiterated by Anglican Bishop Sue Moxley:

> I really appreciated Commissioner Wilson's comment about this is not a spectator sport, it's a contact sport. And I felt like I'd been hit by a seven foot fullback as I listened to one after another of those stories. And I had to recognize the truth of the situation, was, that was *the church that I loved had this great big black blotch on its history. And I had to come to terms with that.* (TRC 2011c, 200, emphasis added)

As noted by religious studies scholar Cheryl Gaver (this volume), Moxley's statement literally demonstrates an example of colliding world-views that serves to obscure the entire story of residential schooling by registering how jarring the act of listening is for settlers. The violence experienced by the settler in Moxley's statement functions as an emotion of shame. Yet, according to Sara Ahmed (2005, 76), "the intimacy of love and shame is indeed powerful" because individuals are redeemed by recognizing and demonstrating shame in their "failure to live up to a social ideal." Here, the relationship between shame and love registers hurt on behalf of the settler, but the ability to face and withstand this shame nonetheless manifests as a noble act. So, although there is potential to achieve reconciliation through the frame of shared trauma narratives, which is a strategy reinforced by discourses of love, this approach may engender further opportunity for settler colonial logics to go unchallenged through an emphasis on understanding and pedagogy.

Jennifer Henry, executive director of the ecumenical organization KAIROS, cited Wilson's "contact sport" metaphor in her reflections after the first day of the TRC's national event in Saskatoon. Henry (2012, n.p.)

refashioned Wilson's sports metaphor into a new form of intimacy by claiming that reconciliation "is more like a dance. It is listening with our whole hearts. It is finding our place in the circle. It is acting out the justice of our heart's truth. It is joining our hands with others until the circle includes us all." The emphasis here is on the prospects of *social inclusion* (Rifkin 2011, 350), a goal that legitimizes settler authority by emphasizing equality, fairness, and togetherness while the forced assimilation of Indigenous peoples into the nation-state goes relatively unchallenged.

Home Is Where the Heart Is

The context of home was especially important to the TRC's Atlantic National Event. As also discussed by sociologist Brieg Capitaine (this volume), the removal of survivors from their familial homes recurs in both survivor and settler testimonies but is often referred to as the first act of trauma experienced by former students and as an egregious practice that provides legal purchase for accusations of genocide (Woolford 2009; Gordon 2010). The emotion of love becomes infused with the reclamation of home and is fundamentally important to survivors, to which Commissioner Wilson's original reference attests. Lottie Mae Johnson, a member of the TRC's Survivors Committee, referred to a personal experience of returning to her community:

> And during that time, I heard four eagle cries, and as I looked around, it dawned on me that this here was where love was, this here was family and where there's family, there's love. Only we didn't realize it, and I was always looking for home after I had left there, and I could never find a sense of home. So for me, I believe the eagle brought this home, and it was through traditional teachings, and this is one of the teachings, ours here is love. Our national event here is based on love. (TRC 2011c, 105)

Johnson's statement can be linked to Borrows (2008, 15) claim that "love grows in an atmosphere where people are welcomed and given messages that they belong." This coincides with the assertion that "'bodies that feel love' do so in particular *spaces* and *places*" and thereby make it necessary to "think about love as a spatial process because bodies cannot be divorced from the spaces and places in which they are constituted" (Morrison,

Johnston, and Longhurst 2013, 512, emphasis added). The body and the space it inhabits serve as an important referent in residential school testimonies precisely because bodies are "always being constructed through and mediated by sociocultural processes" (Lupton 1998, 32). The residential school system functioned as the direct embodiment of land dispossession, and it was the direct removal of bodies from the land, coupled with assimilative curricula, that disrupted the experience of *home*.

The Mi'kmaq, Maliseet, and Passamaquoddy territories are governed by Peace and Friendship Treaties that were established between 1725 and 1760. These treaties are unique in relation to modern treaties in Canada because Peace and Friendship Treaties "did not involve First Nations surrendering rights to the lands and resources they had traditionally used and occupied" (AANDC 2010, n.p.).[8] The Peace and Friendship Treaties originated as a means to mitigate growing conflicts between Indigenous peoples and settlers, or, stated more plainly, these treaties sought (and seek) to establish amiable relationships between these parties. At the Atlantic National Event, Grand Keptin Andrew Denny affirmed that "even today when we look at the laws, they are not our laws. We have never given up any of our laws in any of our treaties" (TRC 2011c, 74–75). Denny noted the ongoing existence of these treaties but also acknowledged that settler adherence to these treaties had been gradually eroded at the expense of Indigenous jurisdiction (ibid., 65–66).

The erosion of jurisdiction coincided with the loss of land. Mi'kmaw elder and author Isabelle Knockwood reminded the audience of the importance of the land in her testimony:

> Everything is based on our land. Our heritage, (I'm sorry), our culture, our traditions and our heritage is all land based. And when they put us on reserves and Indian Residential Schools, the purpose was for land ... And when they established the Indian Residential Schools, they entered into a joint venture with the church. Any joint venture, each of the parties expects to benefit. And the government expected to benefit from our land, and the church expected to benefit from our souls. Those were the two things they wanted from us. (TRC 2011c, 142)

By identifying the connection between residential schooling and land dispossession, Knockwood moves outside narratives of individual experience to assert the role of residential schools in the larger project of dispossession.

Knockwood's testimony refuses settler narratives of inclusion or sharing and instead calls attention to the benefits reaped by the settler state in appropriating Indigenous lands. Too often, "the issue of land is treated as a separate issue from that of the residential school, ignoring the fact that the issues with which Survivors from the residential school era contend are rooted in the forced removal of entire families and communities from their homelands" (Corntassel, Chaw-win-is, and T'lakwadzi 2009, 146). Acknowledging that love can be experienced spatially is important because, as I noted above, the expression of emotion for family and culture cannot be separated from the desire to reclaim Indigenous territories (see also Million 2013).

The disrespect for First Nations treaty rights in the Atlantic region has resulted in massive protests, such as the one witnessed in Elsipogtog, New Brunswick, in October 2013 over corporate fracking. Not only did protesters experience aggressive attacks from police, but treaty rights were also questioned when officers of the Royal Canadian Mounted Police (RCMP) were recorded making racist slurs toward Indigenous protesters and denying their rights to the land (CBC 2013). Two years prior to these protests at the Atlantic National Event, the RCMP had provided the Truth and Reconciliation Commission with a report detailing its lack of culpability in the crimes committed against students in the residential school system. This documented denial, in concert with the marked lack of love and regard for both treaties and human rights in this region by RCMP personnel, calls into question the purchase of shared narratives of reconciliation in this region.

However, although love may be absent from Indigenous-settler relationships, this emotion is emphasized in Indigenous forms of resistance such as those witnessed in Elsipogtog. In her reflections on the 1990 standoff at Kahnesatake, Quebec, Wanda Nanibush (2010, 172) insists,

> It is an image of vulnerability that connects love to resistance. I think of how there were families behind the blockade who continued to laugh and learn and the image of love includes responsibility linked to resistance. If we know how to love well then we know how to see another's needs, claims, desires and demands as necessary expressions of self-determination rather than threats to our own autonomy. Rather than a struggle for power, love expresses a shared space of equality that allows us to maintain our differences from one another.

Nanibush's claims are similar to those of Bonita Lawrence and Kim Anderson (2005, 6), who suggest that "if we love ourselves back into being as Indigenous women, surely we can reclaim much of the territory that has been lost." The reclamation of culture and home is directly linked to the emotion of love, despite its loss or disruption as a result of colonial policies, because love helps to formulate an assertion of difference instead of loyalty to the Canadian nation-state.

☙

During the TRC's national event in Montreal in April 2013, a town hall was held to elicit settler responses to the history of residential schooling. In describing the difficult task of creating a dialogue between the various Settlement Agreement parties, Commissioner Murray Sinclair jokingly remarked that although discussion was necessary and productive, the TRC was "not asking you [former students] to *marry* the government." Commissioner Sinclair was confronting the assumption that reconciliation requires a formal solicitous relationship between Indigenous peoples and the settler state. Yet, after this statement, he went on to remind the audience that survivors must "let go of their anger," lest they pass it on to future generations. By contrast, Indigenous scholar Glen Coulthard (2014, 126) notes that "Indigenous Peoples' individual and collective resentment – expressed as angry and vigilant unwillingness to forgive – ought to be seen as an affective indication that we care deeply about ourselves, about our land and cultural communities, and about the rights and obligations we hold as First Peoples." Coulthard's assertion of Indigenous difference through his reference to caring combines love and anger to demonstrate the complexity and importance of emotion as part of a decolonizing politics. I argue that love should be read as an ambivalent emotion, one that can either reinforce colonial relations or gesture toward the realization of Indigenous sovereignty, both political and territorial. Although attempts to bring Indigenous peoples and settler Canadians together through allegorical love was evoked at TRC events, the emotion of love also refuses the constraints of therapeutic logics. The love expressed by survivors at the TRC events focused on love of family, home, territory, and self, despite the efforts of colonial projects to dismantle these things. "Love," in this context, is not a sentimental term that necessitates a search for settler empathy (Carpenter 2008); rather, the expression of love acknowledges survivance (Baker 2005, 114) and works to interrogate acts of wrongdoing enacted by the settler state. Lastly, as Nanibush (2010) suggests, the emotion of love can help to imagine the possibility for different but equitable futures that oppose the constraints of a shared status quo.

NOTES

1 This event was held in Halifax, Nova Scotia, October 27–29, 2011.
2 Baker (2005, 111) describes Gerald Vizenor's concept of survivance as "a state in which we are moving beyond our basic survival in the face of overwhelming cultural genocide to create spaces of synthesis and renewal."
3 These teachings are also referred to as the Seven Grandfather Teachings. The other teachings are *nibwaakaawin* (wisdom), *minaadendamowin* (respect), *aakode'ewin* (bravery), *gwayak-waadiziwin* (honesty), *dabaadendiziwin* (humility), and *bebwewin* (truth).
4 Richard Van Camp uses the failure of romantic love to situate reconciliation in his novella *The Lesser Blessed* (1996) (see Green 2014). Tomson Highway's *Kiss of the Fur Queen* (1998) and Robert Arthur Alexie's *Porcupines and China Dolls* (2009) also feature the importance of romantic love in the process of healing for survivors in the aftermath of residential school trauma. Moreover, Leanne Simpson's careful use of love in her collection of poetry and short stories *Islands of Decolonial Love* (2013) is juxtaposed with the threat of violence that haunts her characters as they confront calamity. Yet a closer reading of the text reveals that relationships formed between friends (old and new), between family members, and with the land serve as an important link to safety, renewal, and reprieve.
5 The Indian Act of 1876 is a legislative framework that "specifies who is an Indian for entitlement purposes, where they may live, and what they may do" (Maaka and Fleras 2005, 18). Indian Act legislation soon began to govern Indigenous-settler relations after its conception, therefore denying the authority of the treaty process. The Indian residential school system became enshrined in this legislation, making residential school mandatory for students by 1920. Parents unwilling to comply with mandatory schooling were subject to arrest and imprisonment.
6 The release of Ian Mosby's (2013) article "Administering Colonial Science: Nutrition Research and Human Biomedical Experimentation in Aboriginal Communities and Residential Schools, 1942–1952" sent shockwaves through this community in July 2013, as the Shubenacadie Residential School was cited as one of five schools that had carried out nutritional experiments on its students.
7 The Circle of Reconciliation is described as follows: "Survivors and Representatives of the Settlement Agreement will come together to discuss the importance of Reconciliation. Each speaker has been asked to answer the questions: What does Reconciliation mean to you? How will this be addressed by the organization, government or entity that you represent?" (TRC 2011b, n.p.).
8 More recently, the Mi'kmaq–Nova Scotia–Canada Framework Agreement of 2007 was negotiated to "create stable and respectful relationships and to reconcile respective interests of the Parties through a Mik'maq of Nova Scotia Accord" (Mi'kmaq Rights Initiative 2016, n.p.). During the Circle of Reconciliation, the regional director of Indian Affairs and Northern Development Canada, Ian Gray, stated, "Our treaties are Peace and Friendship, they're treaties about establishing that relationship and maintaining it. And recently in

October, and every October, we gather and we celebrate Treaty Day and we reaffirm that concept of peace and friendship" (TRC 2011c, 220). Although his promising acknowledgment of the treaties was well received, he went on to state that Treaty Day serves as "an opportunity for me to rise above that day to day grind of programs and the terms and conditions and the rules and the problems, and the difficulties that we have to surmount" (ibid.).

REFERENCES

Aboriginal Affairs and Northern Development Canada (AANDC). 2010. "Peace and Friendship Treaties." http://www.aadnc-aandc.gc.ca/eng/1100100028589/1100100028591.

Assembly of First Nations. 1994. *Breaking the Silence: An Interpretive Study of Residential School Impact and Healing as Illustrated by the Stories of First Nations Individuals.* Ottawa: Assembly of First Nations.

Ahmed, Sara. 2005. "The Politics of Bad Feeling." *Australian Critical Race and Whiteness Studies Association Journal* 1 (1): 72–84.

Akiwenzie-Damm, Kateri. 2003. *Without Reservation: Indigenous Erotica.* Cape Croker Reserve, ON/Wellington, New Zealand: Kegedonce/Hula.

Alexie, Robert Arthur. 2009. *Porcupines and China Dolls.* Penticton, BC: Theytus Books.

Alfred, Taiaiake. 2009a. "Colonialism and State Dependency." *Journal of Aboriginal Health* 5 (2): 42–60.

–. 2009b. "Restitution Is the Real Pathway to Justice for Indigenous Peoples." In *Response, Responsibility and Renewal: Canada's Truth and Reconciliation Journey,* ed. Gregory Younging, Jonathan Dewar, and Mike DeGagné, 179–87. Ottawa: Aboriginal Healing Foundation.

Baker, Emerance. 2005. "'Loving Indianess': Native Women's Storytelling as Survivance." *Atlantis: Critical Studies in Gender, Culture and Social Justice* 29 (2): 111–21.

Borrows, John. 2008. *Seven Generations, Seven Teachings: Ending the Indian Act.* Ottawa: National Centre for First Nations Governance. http://fngovernance.org/ncfng_research/john_borrows.pdf.

Bouchard, David, and Joseph Martin. 2009. *Seven Sacred Teachings: Niizhwaaswi gagiikwewin.* Vancouver: More Than Words.

Canadian Broadcasting Corporation (CBC). 2013. "First Nations Say Reclaiming Crown Land a 'Desperate' Move." *CBC News,* November 1. http://www.cbc.ca/news/canada/new-brunswick/first-nations-say-reclaiming-crown-land-a-desperate-move-1.2325052.

Carpenter, Cari. 2008. *Seeing Red: Anger, Sentimentality and American Indians.* Columbus: Ohio State University Press.

Chrisjohn, Roland, and Tanya Wasacase. 2009. "Half-Truths and Whole Lies: Rhetoric in the 'Apology' and the Truth and Reconciliation Commission." In *Response, Responsibility, and Renewal: Canada's Truth and Reconciliation Journey,* ed. Gregory Younging, Jonathan Dewar, and Mike DeGagné, 217–29. Ottawa: Aboriginal Healing Foundation.

Collins, Patricia Hill. 1991. *Black Feminist Thought: Knowledge, Consciousness and the Politics of Empowerment.* New York: Routledge.

Corntassel, Jeff, Chaw-win-is, and T'lakwadzi. 2009. "Indigenous Storytelling, Truth-Telling and Community Approaches to Reconciliation." *English Studies in Canada* 35 (1): 137–59. http://dx.doi.org/10.1353/esc.0.0163.

Coulthard, Glen. 2014. *Red Skins, White Masks: Rejecting the Colonial Politics of Recognition.* Minneapolis: University of Minnesota Press.

Episkenew, Jo-Ann. 2009. *Taking Back Our Spirits: Indigenous Literature, Public Policy, and Healing.* Winnipeg: University of Manitoba Press.

Furedi, Frank. 2004. *Therapy Culture: Cultivating Vulnerability in an Uncertain Age.* London: Routledge.

Grant, Agnes. 1996. *No End of Grief: Indian Residential Schools in Canada.* Winnipeg, MB: Pemmican.

Gordon, Todd. 2010. *Imperialist Canada.* Winnipeg, MB: Arbeiter Ring Publishing.

Green, Robyn. 2014. "Recovering Pedagogical Space: Trauma, Education and *The Lesser Blessed.*" In *Canadian Literature and Cultural Memory,* ed. Cynthia Sugars and Eleanor Ty, 354–72. Don Mills: Oxford University Press.

Hardt, Michael, and Antonio Negri. 2009. *Commonwealth.* Cambridge, MA: Harvard University Press.

Henderson, Jennifer, and Pauline Wakeham. 2009. "Colonial Reckoning, National Reconciliation? Aboriginal Peoples and the Culture of Redress in Canada." *English Studies in Canada* 35 (1): 1–26. http://dx.doi.org/10.1353/esc.0.0168.

Henry, Jennifer. 2012. "Spirited Reflection: Back to the Circle." *KAIROS Canada.* June 22. http://www.kairoscanada.org/back-to-the-circle.

Highway, Tomson. 1998. *Kiss of the Fur Queen.* Toronto: Doubleday Canada.

hooks, bell. 2000. *All about Love: New Visions.* New York: William Morrow.

Indian Residential Schools Settlement Agreement (IRSSA). 2006. "Schedule N." In *Indian Residential Schools Settlement Agreement.* Ottawa: Government of Canada. http://www.trc.ca/websites/trcinstitution/File/pdfs/SCHEDULE_N_EN.pdf.

Irlbacher-Fox, Stephanie. 2009. *Finding Dashaa: Self-Government, Social Suffering and Aboriginal Policy in Canada.* Vancouver: UBC Press.

James, Matt. 2012. "A Carnival of Truth? Knowledge, Ignorance and the Canadian Truth and Reconciliation Commission." *International Journal of Transitional Justice* 6 (2): 182–204. http://dx.doi.org/10.1093/ijtj/ijs010.

Ladner, Kiera, and Caroline Dick. 2008. "Out of the Fires of Hell: Globalization as a Solution to Globalization – An Indigenist Perspective." *Journal of Law and Society* 23 (1–2): 63–91. http://dx.doi.org/10.1017/S0829320100009583.

Lawrence, Bonita, and Kim Anderson. 2005. "Introduction to 'Indigenous Women: The State of Our Nations.'" *Atlantis: Critical Studies in Gender, Culture and Social Justice* 29 (2): 1–8.

LeFevre, Tate A. 2013. "Representation, Resistance and the Logics of Difference: Indigenous Culture as Political Resource in the Settler-State." *Settler Colonial Studies* 3 (2): 136–40. http://dx.doi.org/10.1080/2201473X.2013.781926.

Lupton, Deborah. 1998. *The Emotional Self: A Sociocultural Exploration.* London: Sage Publications.

Maaka, Roger, and Augie Fleras. 2005. *The Politics of Indigeneity: Challenging the State in Canada and Aotearoa New Zealand.* Dunedin, New Zealand: University of Otago Press.

Martin, Keavy. 2009. "Truth, Reconciliation, and Amnesia: *Porcupines and China Dolls* and the Canadian Conscience." *English Studies in Canada* 35 (1): 47–65. http://dx.doi.org/10.1353/esc.0.0169.

Mi'kmaq Rights Initiative. 2016. "Made in Nova Scotia Process." http://mikmaqrights.com/negotiations/made-in-nova-scotia-process.

Million, Dian. 2013. "Trauma, Power, and the Therapeutic: Speaking Psychotherapeutic Narratives in an Era of Indigenous Human Rights." In *Reconciling Canada: Critical Perspectives on the Culture of Redress*, ed. Jennifer Henderson and Pauline Wakeham, 159–80. Toronto: University of Toronto Press.

Monture-Angus, Patricia. 1999. *Journeying Forward: Dreaming First Nations' Independence.* Halifax: Fernwood.

Moon, Claire. 2008. *Narrating Political Reconciliation: South Africa's Truth and Reconciliation Commission.* Lanham: Lexington Books.

Morrison, Carey-Ann, Lynda Johnston, and Robyn Longhurst. 2013. "Critical Geographies of Love as Spatial, Relational and Political." *Progress in Human Geography* 37 (4): 505–21. http://dx.doi.org/10.1177/0309132512462513.

Mosby, Ian. 2013. "Administering Colonial Science: Nutrition Research and Human Biomedical Experimentation in Aboriginal Communities and Residential Schools, 1942–1952." *Social History* 46 (91): 145–72.

Nagy, Rosemary. 2012. "The Scope and Bounds of Transitional Justice and the Canadian Truth and Reconciliation Commission." *International Journal of Transitional Justice* 7 (1): 52–73. http://dx.doi.org/10.1093/ijtj/ijs034.

Nanibush, Wanda. 2010. "Love and Other Resistances: Responding to Kahnasata:ke through Artistic Practice." In *This Is an Honour Song: Twenty Years since the Blockades,* ed. Leanne Simpson and Kiera Ladner, 165–94. Winnipeg, MB: Arbeiter Ring.

Niezen, Ronald. 2013. *Truth or Indignation? The Truth and Reconciliation Commission of Canada.* Toronto: University of Toronto Press.

Palmer, Lisa Amanda. 2012. "The Politics of Loving Blackness in the UK." PhD diss. University of Birmingham.

Regan, Paulette. 2010. *Unsettling the Settler Within: Indian Residential Schools, Truth Telling and Reconciliation in Canada.* Vancouver: UBC Press.

Rifkin, Mark. 2011. "Settler States of Feeling: National Belonging and the Erasure of Native American Presence." In *A Companion to American Literary Studies,* ed. Caroline Levander and Robert Levine, 342–55. Malden, MA: Blackwell.

Royal Commission on Aboriginal Peoples. 1996. *Report of the Royal Commission on Aboriginal Peoples.* Ottawa: Royal Commission on Aboriginal Peoples.

Simpson, Leanne. 2011. *Dancing on Our Turtle's Back: Stories of Nishnaabeg Re-creation, Resurgence, and a New Emergence.* Winnipeg, MB: Arbeiter Ring.

–. 2013. *Islands of Decolonial Love.* Winnipeg, MB: Arbeiter Ring.

Smith, Andrea. 2006. "Heteropatriarchy and the Three Pillars of White Supremacy: Rethinking Women of Colour Organizing." In *Color of Violence: The Incite! Anthology,* ed. Incite! Women of Color against Violence, 66–73. Cambridge, MA: South End.

–. 2010. "Queer Theory and Native Studies: The Heteronormativity of Settler Colonialism." *GLQ: A Journal of Gay and Lesbian Studies* 16 (1–2): 41–68.

Sommer, Doris. 1994. "Love and Country: Allegorical Romance in Latin America." In *Reading World Literature: Theory, History, Practice,* ed. Sarah Lawall, 177–202. Austin: University of Texas Press.

Stout, Madeleine Dion. 2012. "A Survivor Reflects on Resilience." In *Speaking My Truth: Reflections on Reconciliation and Residential School,* ed. Shelagh Rogers, Mike DeGagné, and Jonathan Dewar, 47–51. Ottawa: Aboriginal Healing Foundation.

Taylor, Drew Hayden, ed. 2008. *Me Sexy: An Exploration of Native Sex and Sexuality.* Toronto: Douglas and Mcintyre.

Truth and Reconciliation Commission (TRC). 2011a. "Atlantic National Event Concept Paper." Winnipeg, MB: Truth and Reconciliation Commission of Canada. http://www.myrobust.com/websites/atlantic/File/Concept%20Paper%20atlantic%20august%2010%20km_cp%20_3_.pdf
–. 2011b. "Circle of Reconciliation." Winnipeg, MB: Truth and Reconciliation Commission of Canada. http://www.myrobust.com/websites/atlantic/index.php?p=423
–. 2011c. *Transcripts: Atlantic National Event.* Winnipeg, MB: Truth and Reconciliation Commission of Canada.
Tuck, Eve. 2009. "Suspending Damage: A Letter to Communities." *Harvard Educational Review* 79 (3): 409–28. http://dx.doi.org/10.17763/haer.79.3.n0016675661t3n15.
Turner, Dale. 2013. "On the Idea of Reconciliation in Contemporary Aboriginal Politics." In *Reconciling Canada: Critical Perspectives on the Culture of Redress,* ed. Jennifer Henderson and Pauline Wakeham, 100–14. Toronto: University of Toronto Press.
Van Camp, Richard. 1996. *The Lesser Blessed.* Vancouver: Douglas and McIntyre.
Wolfe, Patrick. 2006. "Settler Colonialism and the Elimination of the Native." *Journal of Genocide Research* 8 (4): 387–409.
Woolford, Andrew. 2009. "Ontological Destruction: Genocide and Canadian Aboriginal Peoples." *Genocide Studies and Prevention* 4 (1): 81–97.
Youngblood Henderson, James (Sa'ke'j). 2013. "Incomprehensible Canada." In *Reconciling Canada: Critical Perspectives on the Culture of Redress,* ed. Jennifer Henderson and Pauline Wakeham, 115–29. Toronto: University of Toronto Press.

4

Learning through Conversation: An Inquiry into Shame

JANICE CINDY GAUDET AND LAWRENCE MARTIN/
WAPISTAN

THE TRUTH AND RECONCILIATION Commission of Canada was mandated to contribute to the process of truth, healing, and reconciliation specific to the history of Indian residential schools in Canada (IRSSA 2006). The TRC created formal and culturally centred testimonial spaces where survivors of the schools could share their experiences, publicly or privately. As its mandate stated, "the truth telling and reconciliation process as part of an overall holistic and comprehensive response to the Indian Residential School legacy is a sincere indication and acknowledgement of the injustices and harms experienced by Aboriginal people and the need for continued healing" (ibid., 1). The testimonies, also recognized as truth-telling spaces, were central to the TRC's mandate. Truth-telling spaces were created across Canada over a five-year period on both the national and community levels. Some of their purposes were to acknowledge the lived experiences of the survivors, to establish a holistic framework for healing, and to educate Canadians on the history of the Indian residential schools and their effects on Indigenous peoples. The TRC released its final report on December 15, 2015. The overarching vision of the TRC was to carve new pathways of mutual understanding and reconciliation between Indigenous peoples of Canada and settler Canadians.

Subsequently, on the heels of formalized testimonial spaces, the TRC broadened the definition of truth-telling spaces. These were not necessarily formalized but subsequently occurred. These were spaces of conversation. They occurred in the kitchen, at boardroom tables, on walks, around the fire, in the corridors, in classrooms, and in homes. Although these informal conversations occurred at the margins of the TRC process, they too served to reimagine ways of relating to ourselves and to one another. In this chapter, we suggest that informal conversations act as interventions into shame-based experiences. They disrupt the effects of discriminating practices, such as residential schools, that were imposed through the so-called civilizing agenda (Eigenbrod 2012, 288). We explore the power of conversations on the outer edges of formalized truth telling. Grounding our discussion in the context of inquiries into shame through conversation, we transcribe our own conversation in order to critically examine shame from within our distinctive lives. And Wisakedjak, a Métis and Cree trickster, teaches us how to apply 360-degree peripheral vision when examining truth telling, conversations, and shame.

Toward an Understanding of Shame

The feeling of shame is commonly expressed in conversations pertaining to systems that undermine (Simpson 2011, 2013; Stout and Kipling 2003; Wesley-Esquimaux and Smolewski 2004). At a lecture series in 2012 at Carleton University, Ottawa, Harry Snowboy – a well-respected Cree ceremonialist from the James Bay region – referred to the undermining of politically driven assimilationist agendas as shame-based systems. This terminology speaks to ways that government impositions like residential schools and displacement from ancestral lands shattered kinship systems and undermined individual and community well-being. Nishnaabeg educator Leanne Simpson (2011, 14), addressing the displacement of shame in the context of loss of land and lives, refers to colonial shame as a form of trickery: "I placed that shame as an insidious and infectious part of the cognitive imperialism that was aimed at convincing us that we were a weak and defeated people, and that there was no point in resisting or resurging." Simpson attests, like many Indigenous people, that when we are disconnected from our respective stories and ways of the land, shame can take hold of our lives.

Western science has also studied shame. David Hawkins (1995, 77) explains how "shame is used as a tool of cruelty, and its victims often become cruel to themselves ... Shame results in vulnerability to the other negative emotions, and therefore, often produces false pride, anger and guilt." Hawkins's study demonstrates that the individual level of consciousness correlates to shame as well as to many other emotions, perceptions, or attitudes.[1] His study focuses on individual consciousness rather than systematic methods that disfigure collective identities. Although it can be useful to focus on individuality, the aim of this chapter is to deploy conversation as an Indigenous method for gaining insights into the systemic structures of shame.

Shame comes from action and actors. Dominance is valorized; peoples' ways of life are denigrated. Shaming sets out to control human dynamism, uniqueness, and creativity. Human identity is disfigured. Shame gives the message of inadequacy and imperfection – a message that seeps through the dark crevices of generations, deep into our bone marrow and into our blood. Much research on the legacy of the Indian residential schools makes known the systemic structures of shaming (Wesley-Esquimaux and Smolewski 2004; Simpson 2013). Systems of shame are based on ideologies motivated by a narrow vision of what is socially acceptable, or "civilized." Ideologies dictate social and cultural norms that control human identity and relationships.

In the Canadian context of residential schools, Eurocentric systems of shaming were detrimental to Indigenous community formations and cultural continuity (Wesley-Esquimaux and Smolewski 2004; Simpson 2011; Kusugak 2012; Rogers, DeGagné, and Dewar 2012). Ojibwe author Richard Wagamese (2012, 158) exemplifies this experience in describing the impacts of the residential school system on his family life and on his journey back to harmony:

> All the members of my family attended residential school ... Each of them had experienced an institution that tried to scrape the Indian off of their insides, and they came back to the bush and river raw, sore, and aching. The pain they bore was invisible and unspoken. It seeped into their spirit, oozing its poison and blinding them from the incredible healing properties within their Indian ways.

The adverse effects of shame are wide-ranging, complex, and enduring. Its legacy has been documented, felt, and examined in scholarship. Research studies identify the connection between residential schools and drug and alcohol addiction, family violence, dysfunctional leadership, and youth suicides (Bopp, Bopp, and Lane 2003; Chansonneuve 2007; Kirmayer et al. 2007). It is tragic that many more examples overshadow the well-being of our communities, both urban and rural. Many stories remain untold, yet shame-based systems remain part of the harsh realities of Indigenous peoples. Sites of resistance are not limited to conversation but also give substance to positive action, healing, and transformation (Rogers, DeGagné, and Dewar 2012).

Conversations as Sites of Resistance

Margaret Kovach (2010, 40), an Indigenous educator from Saskatchewan of Plains Cree and Saulteaux ancestry, explains the conversational method in Indigenous research: "It involves a dialogic participation that holds a deep purpose of sharing story as a means to assist others. It is relational at its core." Solidarity is affirmed in speaking our truth. From this ontological perspective, conversation helps to differentiate between the shame-based system and the individual reality. It invites a deeper process of thinking critically rather than undermining self, relatives, and settler society.

Kovach (2010) describes conversation as a research method stemming from an Indigenous worldview. This approach to research, in which conversations become our teachers, offers a form of learning, teaching, and seeking multiple truths. It permits us to move beyond duality, to grow in our knowledge and experiences, and to elucidate understanding. Conversations can move us away from shame-based systems and toward renewal of Indigenous thought and stories in today's time. Wagamese (2012, 165) reminds us of the importance of returning to harmony: "You create harmony with truth and you build truth out of humility. That is spiritual. That is truth. That is Indian."

Conversations play a critical role in this process of returning to harmony. They can confront the shameful decisions, beliefs, and actions that we knowingly or unknowingly carried as our own (Eigenbrod 2012; Simpson 2011). Kovach (2010, 42) explains that "the conversational method aligns with an Indigenous worldview that honours orality as means of transmitting knowledge and upholds the relational which is necessary to maintain a collectivist tradition." African American author bell hooks (2010, 46) offers a compelling argument: "Conversation – true conversation – is the way we cleanse poisons, such as false assumption, prejudices, ignorance, misinformation, lack of perspective, lack of imagination, and stubbornness[,] from the system." Shawn Wilson (2008), an Opaskwayak Cree, elaborates on conversation as inclusive of both sharing and listening. This type of conversation is a way to build strong relationships. Upholding a responsibility to the well-being of our kinship relations is an expectation that we, as academics and authors, carry with us in our diverse roles and responsibilities within our community work, lives, and research. In this research, we have both, in our own way, come to understand how shame permeates the intricacies of concentric relationships through time and space.

Examining Shame through Conversation

Curious and perplexed about the energetics of shame, we sought to examine shame more deeply. This was done through conversation. We began to consider more deeply the shame-based systems that permeated our lives and our ways of relating to ourselves and to one another. We were unknowingly seeking to become intimate with this five-letter word. Listening to and reading personal testimonies about residential schools, we saw that shame was most often associated with a deep-rooted sense of failure or deficiency. "We were humiliated out of culture and spirituality. We were told that these ways were of the devil. We were punished for speaking the only language we ever knew" (Kelly 2012, 64). It will take generations and radical changes in societal consciousness and colonial structures to alleviate the pain and undo the damage of shame-based systems. Yet, Madeleine Dion Stout (2012, 179), a Cree leader from Kehewin First Nation in Alberta, is hopeful of change:

> Colonization, healing, and resilience reveal themselves to me. As Survivors, we ride waves of vulnerability for a lifetime and for generations. We were subjected to real risk factors including hunger, loneliness, ridicule, physical and sexual abuse, untimely and unseemly death. As we struggle to throw off the shackles of colonialism we lean heavily toward healing, and resilience becomes our best friend.

The survivors and the future generation of elders strengthen our commitment to co-creating old yet new schools of thought, ways of being, and ways of relating. The next section – our conversation – moves to our own ways of thinking about shame. Its personal accounts tell of where we live and how we live. They tell a story not only of the past but also of today with an aim to change tomorrow.

Our Conversation

CINDY: One of my first memories of feeling shame was being called a "petite sauvagesse" (little squaw) as a young girl in school. The tone of what felt like derogatory name calling stuck inside of me. It became a part of my web of life. I had witnessed how women who came from the nearby reserve were demeaned because they were Cree. I later learned that my grandmother had endured the same derogatory treatment. This was part and parcel of the squaw life, an accepted norm. Yet from what I experienced and understood, my grandmother's values, faith, and self-dignity remained intact. This was because she knew herself as a woman of the land.

Métis people represented, according to Adele Perry (2001), the failed attempt of colonization. My Métis ancestors were considered a humiliation to the British Empire. It was my mother, my sister, and other Métis women who taught me about Canada's history and the treatment of Métis people after the 1885 Resistance in Batoche, Saskatchewan.[2] Thanks to their courage, I began in my mid-thirties to recognize the lies I had been telling others and myself. I painted my skin white and fantasized about being someone other than me.[3]

LAWRENCE: We cannot see shame, but we see its impacts for the actions of or the lack thereof. I remember, too, as a kid, feeling shame. Growing up in a small village in Moose River, we didn't have a reserve, and none of my family went to IRS [Indian residential school], so I can't contribute to anything along those lines. But my shame came from who I am, my father being white and my mother being Cree, and not being able to fit in in either world, so one side of me would feel ashamed of the other side quite equally. So trying to walk a certain way became shameful.

C.: We rarely put it on the table, speak of shame, or talk back to shame. It remains unspoken and therefore unforgiven, like a shadow that lurks in the background or deep within the belly.

L.: Not being able to fit in, the white kids would say stuff about my Native side and vice versa, so I felt the shame of being part of the other side. They were all derogatory. I think I carried that shame for a long time, and I did not celebrate that duality I had until I was much older, probably in my late twenties. I started working in business and being involved in government. That way I could mix in, I could get in as an Irish man or I could go in as a Cree, so I started using my identity to get me to places. So I turned shame around and made it into a positive thing, I like to think anyways. But I carried it for a long time. I did not know what the impact would have been when I left my community at age fourteen. It would pop up every once in a while when I would meet white kids who resented Natives. Then I'd meet up with Native kids and would hang out with Native kids, but then as soon as something "white" came up, they'd look at me and question whether they could trust me. There was always that game at play. But it wasn't until I took ahold of myself and said, "hey that's who I am." You know, I learned about my culture through my grandmother and my parents. It has to be your own search for yourself and how you want to handle it, who you are, what you are, and celebrate that. Even my songs, I sing in Cree. I do the chanting. I talk about Cree things and Native things, and that makes me feel good. The Irish side of my music is in the melodies, not so much in the words, so I utilize the influence of that.

c.: I wonder if shame begins with identity, and then we go through our lives and play it out.

l.: Where else can it start?

c.: I would imagine that it starts with who I perceive myself to be or not to be? And the desire to belong and to be a part of something other than a part of the colonial curse.

l.: I see different levels of shame in the community. For example, the ones who drink and the ones who don't. There are different forms of that in every community. This has always been my question: If a whole generation of people went through residential school, how does it impact on families that did not have any families that went?

c.: I just found out that my gramma attended a provincially run boarding school in Duck Lake, Saskatchewan. I asked my mom if she knew anything about her experience. She said that all Gramma told her was that there was a devil hanging outside of the building, and they would use it to make them afraid. Fear was associated with shame.

l.: Yeah, sometimes we mix shame, fear, and anger. When I see and hear about Indian residential school, in all honesty, I don't feel ashamed. I can't derive shame from what happened, but I can sure feel the anger.

You mention fear. Why would parents allow their kids to go to residential school? They feared the repercussions: the police, the "white

people," and the threats. The fear was a big part of it. I remember –
again trying to draw from my own life – I didn't go to school until
I was eleven because my grandparents thought it was important to be
in the bush with them, learning the language and the culture. So they
said, "no you can't go." But then the white people in the community,
which was only one family, said that if you don't bring him to school,
we will report you to the authorities, and they will come and take him
away. So out of fear, they sent me to school at age eleven in the community where I was raised. The conflict in this is that the white family
was my grandfather on my father's side.

c.: It is complex for sure. Oftentimes, I hear non-Native people say,
"well if you say that your culture is so strong and spiritually centred,
how could they have let that happen?" When I hear this, it brings up
frustration. I am afraid of saying the wrong thing or, more honestly,
not knowing the answer to such a question. My great-grandfather
was hired as *l'agent des sauvages* [Indian Agent] of the One Arrow
Cree Reservation, just nearby our farm where I grew up.

l.: Is being fearful a right to be shameful? Just because you are scared, it
doesn't mean that you have to be ashamed. There are two different reactions that you have. You can stand your ground just as much as you can,
but sometimes there comes a point of compromise to live another day.
I think even the first sightings of white people in our area evoked fear.

c.: I wonder if the white people experienced the same kind of fear.

l.: I think that Europeans were people looking for conquest. This is a different level of fear, while survival is another. One thing I have learned
through this is to see both sides of a situation. It helps me to know
myself as whole. Otherwise, it evokes a sense of feeling powerless because I didn't act or do something I could have. I would feel ashamed.

c.: It would appear that feeling powerless comes from shame-based
systems. So do we need to critique shame, or is it enough to expose it,
understand, and resist identifying ourselves within the shame-based
systems? Even in just articulating this question, I feel as though the
accumulated layers of assumption and biases begin to crack the inter-
nalized colonial system.

l.: You have to define those words exactly right. And what tools do we have,
what laws do we have to do this, and what already exists in our culture
to help us reverse shame-based systems? What does this look like?

c.: Good question. On a personal level, I have to ask myself, "what does it look like to be in my own humanity?" My everyday experiences of relating to different kinds of people teach and help me to understand what the elders teach. I hope to challenge in a good way the thinking that feeds the harmful stereotypes and distorted representations of Indigenous people. I feel like this conversation itself is shedding another skin, like snake medicine.

To be honest, I believed that shame was part of my identity. It was my burden to carry. With the help of others, I am unlearning this. I can now see more clearly the damage of shaming. Is there fault in the desire to tell and to live another story about identity?

We had a previous conversation about a healing ceremony with ayahuasca. I was sharing with you how the plant Spirit invited me to critically self-examine at what point I needed to be something other than what I was – whether it was a wife, an educator, a doctor, a lover, a student, and the list goes on. Then you asked me, "When actually did you start thinking you couldn't be those things?"

l.: So you were ashamed? That is a belief and you believed in it. Someone said that to you, and you took it to heart.

c.: Yes, I believed it like the truth. This is again part of the internalizing of the colonial mindset.

l.: Then spit it out. Then spit it out.

What I had to deal with, growing up with two heritages, was being called a bastard. I carried that for a long time, and it created shame. Who am I? I am a bastard. And of course, it made me angry as well. One day, I am playing my banjo in the parking lot of the train station in North Bay. I was about fifteen years old, and I'm going home at the end of the school year. The guidance counsellor came out to the train to see us off. There was a whole bunch of Native kids going back to Moose Factory. And so he is standing there listening as I am picking away at my banjo. And he starts asking me who my parents are. I didn't want to use the word "bastard." But it's the first thing that came to my mind: "I don't have a father. I am an illegitimate." He said, "that's a terrible word to use." I said, "yeah but 'bastard' is even worse." He said, "no, no." And we talked it through and came to a mutual understanding. I even forgot about my banjo playing.

c.: Did you forget you were a bastard?

L.: No, but I was able to look at it more humorously after that point. But that was a big part of my burden I had to carry at that stage of my life. These words can have a lot of strength in causing shame.

C.: Yes, I am learning to celebrate and honour the squaw in me, and make her visible rather than keeping her hidden in the dark, like it is something to be ashamed of.

L.: We know it as a derogatory word, but "squaw" is so close to the word *iskwew* in Cree, which means "woman." The English could not pronounce many of the words.

C.: Speaking of words, "decolonizing" and "empowering" people are common language in academia. It can be quite frustrating because I do not always know what the words really represent in the context of truth telling. They can be so many different things in different contexts.

L.: When you think you are decolonizing people and empowering people, they are actually two different things, which is why it is so important to define our words. Wording is very important. I have noticed that the government often believes it is empowering First Nations peoples. For example, First Nations people may have developed their own election process, but what they did in fact was follow the Canadian legislation. So now they are applying it, thinking it is now theirs and applying it to their own people. Is there shame in that? But their own people are not familiar with that system, so they behave differently. They don't follow the rules in terms of certain timing and documentation. When working in these systems, it evokes the bad feelings because we have to learn to navigate the rules and try to do something good for our people. It usually comes back on us again, recreating the feeling of failure.

C.: Interesting what we are confronted with when working within certain frameworks. This conversation has helped me to reflect critically on how shame permeates so many of our social institutions, from birth to death – both inclusive of one another as the cycle of life. It is what the elder Isabelle Meawasige refers to as the life teachings that reorient my thinking. Back to decolonization and empowerment, I never thought of these as two separate experiences.

L.: Well, yes, consider that you have to build a house, and you must follow all the regulations, practices, and procedures of the state. Does this empower you? There could be some trickster medicine in that. Be aware of deceit, how it plays in our life.

c.: Ah yes, the trickster, Wisakedjak. When I hear Wisakedjak stories, my seriousness relaxes. Being educated in the Catholic school system, I am not aware of our stories and legends. But as a little girl, I vaguely remember hearing about the *loup garou,* a character in Métis and Acadian stories.

l.: So many people don't know their culture or don't know the stories of certain characters of stories like this. So how to handle the feelings of shame if you don't know something like that? It's like building a house. You are not going to find shelter and warmth until you build a house. So we need to build a house first and to focus on building the culture so when you get rid of the shame you can have a place to go to and celebrate it.

Culture is our business. The Wisakedjak character is one of our cultural teachers that help us to understand ourselves. To reflect on what happened, we refer to the knowledge held in the legends. In growing up, this is how we learned telling of legends from the grandfathers, grandmothers, the aunties. Pretty much everyone in the family shared a piece of it. It was their way of telling me a lesson that I should be learning in that moment. It was a gentle way rather than being scolded and punished.

Being with Wisakedjak

Our conversation led us to *kiskendemowin,* the Cree word for "knowledge." The knowledge of our people is shared through the legends. It may have something important to teach all of us about reducing the effects of shame in our lives. Even in a place of shame, there is a learning moment. There exist various characters in Cree and Métis legends (Ellis 1995; Fleury et al. 2008) who invite a perspective to help us to meet our humanity.

One of these characters is Wisakedjak – a well-respected trickster. This character shows up in our own actions and in the mishaps that take place in our lives. Knowing this character gives us the ability to laugh at ourselves, to remain playful, and to examine situations beyond right or wrong. The character of Wisakedjak is also called Wiisakaychak, Nanabush, and Chi-Jean in both Cree and Métis cultures (Fleury et al. 2008). This character plays a specific role in bringing balance, humour, and understanding (ibid.). Although the Cree and Métis stories are expressed and told differently, they are similar in portraying their tricksters as "the Creator's intermediaries to humans, and their adventures, through stories, [explain] the workings of the natural environment" (ibid., ii).

The teachings of the Wisakedjak help us to travel the bumpy roads. For instance, this character speaks of matters that were to remain unspoken within the shame-based systems. Wisakedjak wants to teach us that shame can be a part of disempowering structures; therefore, when confronted by shame, exercise discretion, caution, dignity, and humour. Other legends that we have in our cultures are about different feelings and experiences in regard to sexuality, vanity, happiness, and the whole relationship with other people and the animal world. Rules of conduct, laws, and respectful relationships are all present in the cultural teachings. The teachings contain cultural philosophies designed to support us through life's rites of passage from birth to death.

Wisakedjak keeps us innocent and humble so that we may grow compassionate and wise. For instance, if we think we are on a particular path, Wisakedjak will teach us to consider what the possibilities of falling off are. Wisakedjak plays with the notion that the anus is all-encompassing. In many of the Cree legends, the anus is very self-centred because it knows it is important. It is the boss, so it always plays that part. If the boss is not working, the body falls apart; this is another important teaching in the legends of Wisakedjak. The trickster wants to teach us that there are two sides to everything. Our principles can be strong, yet if something intrigues us, we may stray from our path, allowing chaos to emerge. Yet Wisakedjak reminds us that everything is part of the path itself, if you choose it to be.

To further situate the role of Wisakedjak in the context of where we began this article – with truth telling, reconciliation, and conversation – can we consider Wisakedjak to have played a part in historical events, particularly the Harper Government Apology on Indian Residential Schools in 2008? Again, in our ways of being taught, we reflect on the knowledge of Wisakedjak – an effective method to recognize the tricksters among us today.

Wisakedjak has a way of orchestrating events as a means to help us find the unique lesson that is necessary for a person to learn. As we are told in one of the old legends, Wisakedjak invited the ducks to come into the dance. The ducks were blindfolded. Wisakedjak sang songs and got them to dance. As they danced, Wisakedjak yanked them, one at a time, outside into the bush to kill them for food. During the dance, one of the ducks got suspicious, so he lifted his blindfold. He noticed many of his duck friends missing. He yelled out, "its Wisakedjak, he's tricking us again." The rest scrambled out and away, but Wisakedjak had taken many of them. Later, Wisakedjak made a fire and ate as many as he could. After his meal, he felt tired and wanted to sleep, but he was worried that someone would steal his remaining ducks. He buried the ducks in the sand, with just their feet sticking out. He asked his anus to watch over them and the fire while he slept. Wisakedjak said to his anus, when you hear or see anything or anyone trying to steal my ducks, you make sure you wake me up by farting loudly. While Wisakedjak slept, a wolf came along to steal one of the birds. His anus was not sure whether he saw the wolf, so he remained quiet. Again, the wolf came along and took another duck. His anus did nothing. Soon all the ducks were gone. Wisakedjak finally woke up, stretched, and said that he would like to snack on another duck. He looked, but there were no ducks in the sand. Wisakedjak was upset. He began to yell at his anus. He got really upset with his anus. Wisakedjak got so angry at his anus that he chapped it with the ambers of the burning wood. His anus cried out. Wisakedjak jumped all over the place, leaving marks on the rocks and ground. His decision to deceive the ducks left a lasting mark on himself and on the earth, where his actions will forever be remembered.

❧

In our research, we opened a relational space to examine shame in conversation. The process gently disrupted the emotional and physical charge shame held. It cleansed us of the pollutants of colonial shame – even for a short time. Conversation as a self-reflexive and relational approach to healing helped us to break shame into smaller manageable pieces, thereby giving it less control over our bodies, hearts, and minds.

Two simultaneous processes occurred in our conversation, one of decolonization and the other of renewal. We created a little more space for truth telling from within our personal and collective narratives, thus unbinding ourselves from the undermining social attitudes of oppression. According to Māori scholar Linda Smith, "'The talk' about the colonial past is embedded in our political discourses, our humour, poetry, music, storytelling, and other common sense ways of passing on both a narrative of history and an attitude about history" (Corntassel, Chaw-win-is, and T'lakwadzi 2009, 137). Whether or not these many forms of conversation have words, they express something clearly and completely about the meaning of the good life for Indigenous peoples.

NOTES

1 For further understanding of the energetics of shame and its interplay with consciousness and healing, see Hawkins (1995).
2 For more information on the history of 1885, see McLeod (2007) and Peterson and Brown (1985).
3 For further reading on this subject, see Gaudet (2014).

REFERENCES

Bopp, Michael, Judie Bopp, and Phil Lane, Jr. 2003. *Aboriginal Domestic Violence in Canada.* Ottawa: Aboriginal Healing Foundation.

Chansonneuve, Deborah. 2007. *Addictive Behaviour among Aboriginal Peoples in Canada.* Ottawa: Aboriginal Healing Foundation.

Corntassel, Jeff, Chaw-win-is, and T'lakwadzi. 2009. "Indigenous Storytelling, Truth-Telling, and Community Approaches to Reconciliation." *English Studies in Canada* 35 (1): 137–59. http://dx.doi.org/10.1353/esc.0.0163.

Eigenbrod, Renate. 2012. "For the Child Taken, for the Parent Left Behind: Residential School Narratives as Acts of 'Survivance.'" *English Studies in Canada* 38 (3–4): 277–97.

Ellis, Douglas, ed. 1995. *Cree Legends and Narratives.* Manitoba: University of Manitoba Press.

Fleury, Norman, Gilbert Pelletier, Jeanne Pelletier, Joe Welsh, Norma Welsh, Janice DePeel, and Carrie Saganace. 2008. *Stories of Our Peoples: A Métis Graphic Novel Anthology.* Saskatoon: Gabriel Dumont Institute.

Gaudet, Janice Cindy. 2014. "Dismantling the Patriarchal Altar from Within." *AlterNative: An International Journal of Indigenous Peoples* 10 (1): 58–66.

Hawkins, David R. 1995. *Power vs Force: The Hidden Determinants of Human Behaviour.* Carlsbad, CA: Hay House.

hooks, bell. 2010. *Teaching Critical Thinking and Practical Wisdom.* New York: Routledge.

Indian Residential Schools Settlement Agreement (IRSSA). 2006. "Schedule N." In *Indian Residential Schools Settlement Agreement.* Ottawa: Government of Canada. http://www.trc.ca/websites/trcinstitution/File/pdfs/SCHEDULE_N_EN.pdf.

Kelly, Fred. 2012. "Confession of a Born-Again Pagan." In *Speaking My Truth: Reflections on Reconciliation and Residential Schools,* ed. Shelagh Rogers, Mike DeGagné, and Jonathan Dewar, 11–43. Ottawa: Aboriginal Healing Foundation.

Kirmayer, Laurence J., Gregory M. Brass, Tara Holton, Ken Paul, Cori Simpson, and Caroline Tait. 2007. *Suicide among Aboriginal People in Canada.* Ottawa: Aboriginal Healing Foundation.

Kovach, Margaret. 2010. "Conversational Method in Indigenous Research." *First Peoples Child and Family Review* 5 (1): 40–48.

Kusugak, Jose A. 2012. "On the Side of Angels." In *Speaking My Truth: Reflections on Reconciliation and Residential School,* ed. Shelagh Rogers, Mike DeGagné, and Jonathan Dewar, 109–27. Ottawa: Aboriginal Healing Foundation.

McLeod, Neal. 2007. *Cree Narrative Memory: From Treaties to Contemporary Times.* Saskatoon: Purich.

Perry, Adele. 2001. "The State of Empire: Reproducing Colonialism in British Columbia, 1849–1871." *Journal of Colonialism and Colonial History* 2 (2). http://dx.doi.org/10.1353/cch.2001.0028.

Peterson, Jacqueline, and Jennifer S.H. Brown, eds. 1985. *The New Peoples: Being and Becoming Métis in North America*. Winnipeg/St. Paul: University of Manitoba Press/ Minnesota Historical Society Press.

Rogers, Shelagh, Mike DeGagné, and Jonathan Dewar, eds. 2012. *Speaking My Truth: Reflections on Reconciliation and Residential School*. Ottawa: Aboriginal Healing Foundation.

Simpson, Leane. 2011. *Dancing on Our Turtle's Back: Stories of Nishnaabeg Re-creation, Resurgence, and a New Emergence*. Winnipeg, MB: Arbeiter Ring.

–. 2013. *Islands of Decolonial Love*. Winnipeg, MB: Arbeiter Ring.

Stout, Madeleine Dion. 2012. "A Survivor Reflects on Resilience." In *Speaking My Truth: Reflections on Reconciliation and Residential Schools*, ed. Shelagh Rogers, Mike DeGagné, and Jonathan Dewar 179–83. Ottawa: Aboriginal Healing Foundation.

Stout, Madeleine Dion, and Gregory Kipling. 2003. *Aboriginal People, Resilience and the Residential School Legacy*. Ottawa: Aboriginal Healing Foundation.

Wagamese, Richard. 2012. "Returning to Harmony." In *Speaking My Truth: Reflections on Reconciliation and Residential School*, ed. Shelagh Rogers, Mike DeGagné, and Jonathan Dewar, 157–67. Ottawa: Aboriginal Healing Foundation.

Wesley-Esquimaux, Cynthia C., and Magdalena Smolewski. 2004. *Historic Trauma and Aboriginal Healing*. Ottawa: Aboriginal Healing Foundation.

Wilson, Shawn. 2008. *Research Is Ceremony: Indigenous Research Methods*. Halifax: Fernwood.

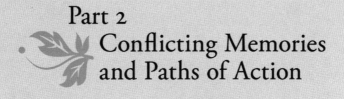

Part 2
Conflicting Memories
and Paths of Action

5

Surviving as Mi'kmaq and First Nations People: The Legacies of the Shubenacadie Indian Residential School in Nova Scotia

SIMONE POLIANDRI

I NEVER MET a Mi'kmaw individual – whether a former residential school student, a family member of a former student, or a member of any Mi'kmaw community – who did not speak of the Shubenacadie Indian Residential School as one of the instruments of the Canadian government's assimilation policy that has had the greatest emotional, physical, and psychological impact on the lives of this First Nations people. Mi'kmaw elder and former student Isabelle Knockwood (2015, 161) – author of *Out of the Depths,* the most comprehensive collection of testimonies of the Mi'kmaw people's experiences in the Shubenacadie School – states, "Those who ran the school tried to rob us of our collective identity by punishing us for speaking our language, calling us 'savages' and 'heathens.' They also tried to take away our individual identities." Historian John Milloy (1999, xiv, xvii) mirrors this sentiment when discussing Indigenous education at the national level: "It is clear that the schools have been, arguably, the most damaging of the many elements of Canada's colonization of this land's original peoples and, as their consequences still affect the lives of the Aboriginal People today, they remain so ... The schools produced thousands of individuals incapable of leading healthy lives or contributing positively to their communities."

In this chapter, I discuss some of the legacies, often intergenerational, of the Mi'kmaw people's experiences in the Shubenacadie School, which operated from 1930 to 1967 in the town of Shubenacadie, Nova Scotia.[1] I illustrate how the residential school experience resulted in the emergence of an additional layer in many Mi'kmaw people's individual and collective identities, namely, the "residential school survivor." I argue that the survivor's experience represents the twofold way that a pan-Indian identity has been forged among the Mi'kmaq and, by extension, all Indigenous groups in Canada. On the one hand, the shared experiences of many survivors and their family members are often the sad markers of one widespread Indigenous lifestyle characterized by elements including psychological imbalance, substance abuse, violence, suicidal tendencies, and crippled social skills. Such a lifestyle somewhat mirrors the community of destiny that Otto Bauer (1907, 51), in his classic Marxist discussion of the character of the modern nation, defined as not "just subjection to a common fate, but rather *common experience* of the same fate in constant communication and ongoing interaction with one another" (emphasis added). On the other hand, those past experiences have recently empowered the Mi'kmaw survivors and their families to claim distinct status as First Nations people who underwent a specific assimilationist policy and, as a result, to acquire political leverage for the purpose of demanding and obtaining acknowledgment and compensation.

The analysis of identity discussed here shares common ground with the perspectives offered by other contributors to this volume. In particular, the Shubenacadie School case highlights the creation of a collective experience that aligns with sociologist Brieg Capitaine's notion (this volume) of cultural trauma, intended as the source of both collective memory of the residential school and the solidarity extending between and beyond generations as a result of exposure to residential school life. At the same time, the fluid and relational nature of the Mi'kmaw identities that have developed as a result of residential school experiences, which I discuss here, mirrors anthropologist Arie Molema's discussion (this volume) of the dialectic and relational creation of the Canadian national memory of the Labrador Inuit and, more broadly, Indigenous residential school experiences in this era of reconciliation.

A couple of disclaimers are in order. First, I use the term "survivor" as both an objective and a subjective category. In the former sense, the term refers to those who attended the residential schools, and it acknowledges that they self-define and are defined as survivors. Indeed, during my residence in Mi'kmaw territory, I had numerous conversations with many people – both survivors and nonsurvivors – who used the term "survivor" to indicate individuals who had attended the Shubenacadie School. In the latter sense, the term identifies a constructed identity that has resulted from people's experiences in the residential school and from the subsequent efforts (or lack of) to heal and deal with the scars. In this sense, many – if not most – former students of the Shubenacadie School have added the survivor layer of identity to their other layers of identity, including gender, age, tribe, indigeneity, and nation. For many of these people, being a survivor has become their primary form of identity. Furthermore, as a subjective category, "survivor" includes intergenerational survivors, family members of survivors who have suffered indirectly from the damage done to their loved ones in the schools. In this perspective, identifying oneself as a survivor creates a sense of solidarity and common destiny.[2]

Second, I intentionally make ample use of direct statements by Mi'kmaw survivors and nonsurvivors as a way to give them voice, which I deem one of the best purposes and greatest achievements (alongside the many short-falls) of the Canadian Truth and Reconciliation Commission, as well as of scholarly studies like this one. In doing so, I aim to understand how the social actors involved in this case make (often involuntarily) the social problems and dark legacy of the school into sources of identification and, at the same time, how they transform (often voluntarily) these problems and this legacy into sources of empowerment.

The Shubenacadie Indian Residential School

The Canadian government had planned to build a residential school in Nova Scotia for the Maliseet and Mi'kmaq peoples as far back as 1892. Yet, as Mi'kmaw historian Daniel Paul (2006, 283) comments, "Probably because education was not much of a priority in the [Indian Affairs] Department's estimation, the decision to actually build such a school was not made until 1927."

The school was finally established in 1929 on a hill near the centre of Shubenacadie, eight kilometres from the Indian Brook First Nation community (then known as the Shubenacadie Band Reserve). It officially opened in 1930 at a time when, as Knockwood (2015, 19) says, "despite the threat to our survival as a people, we still had a language and a culture of our own."

James Miller (2004, 225) defines assimilation as "a wide-ranging ideology and policy that seeks to eradicate a people's identity and cultural practices in favor of another group's ways of doing things." The Shubenacadie School made this definition its primary goal. Run by Catholic personnel embodied by the well-remembered figures of Father Jeremiah P. Mackey and Father J.W. Brown of the Roman Catholic Diocese of Halifax and a group of Sisters of Charity nuns, the school was instrumental in eradicating the culture, values, language, and identities of many Mi'kmaq in the span of just a few generations – a process that Molema (this volume) calls "the loss of Indigenous cultural memory" and the disruption of "intergenerationally transmitted knowledge." In many cases, the school succeeded in full. In other cases, Mi'kmaw children managed to retain full or partial fluency in the Mi'kmaw language and to hold on to their identities, although they were scarred and changed forever (Knockwood 2015; Poliandri 2011, 223ff).

The goals and procedures implemented in the Shubenacadie School were comparable to those regulating the functioning of similar institutions in both Canada and the United States.[3] They often involved the use of physical and psychological violence as well as an all-but-straightforward system of rewards and punishments to make the pupils conform to a new set of religious and mainstream values.

Regina, a Mi'kmaw elder who attended the Shubenacadie School in the 1940s, described the nuns' teaching philosophy in these terms: "At the residential school you were sent to be taught love, honor, and obey. Honor and obey were beaten into us. Love, we did not know anything about. Catholicism was beaten into us in the residential school."[4]

Regina's words exemplify the extension of the logic of elimination underpinning the Canadian settler state's colonial strategy (epitomized by the nineteenth-century Indian Act) into the goals and methods that characterized Indian residential schooling in the twentieth century (see also Green, this volume).

Lisa, a middle-aged Mi'kmaw survivor who had attended the Shubenacadie School in the 1960s, spoke extensively about her experiences at the school, or the "resi," as she and other Mi'kmaw people have nicknamed it:

> I went to the "resi" when I was five years old. My parents told me that they'd come back, but they never did. I mean, they did! But that was on Easter, Christmas ... special occasions.
>
> That was no place to be for a little kid. You didn't get your education. You learned how to clean and pray. That's about it.
>
> We learned to read, but it was hard because a lot of us spoke our language and we didn't know how to speak English. It was hard for me. I spoke Mi'kmaq. I could only speak some English. Everybody used to speak [Mi'kmaq].

My parents sent me to the residential school because they thought it was a bigger school [than the day school on the reserve], and "you'll learn and get educated." They didn't know what happened in there. And there was no way of you telling them because you didn't want to cause any trouble. A lot of the kids hid it from their families. They hid their feelings for years because they did not want to cause trouble to the parents. You were considered a troublemaker if you'd said what happened.

They [the school personnel] were strict back then. We prayed three, four times a day, and we got strappings and ears pulled and cheeks pulled ... everything. It was awful, especially for a four, five year old going into the building, and they put you into the tub and cut your hair right above your ears. And they put you in uniforms. Everybody was dressed alike. Everybody looked alike after a while ... People cried at night that they wanted to go home.

The school was awful. It was good in a way ... like you had your meals ... but it wasn't in other ways. And if you were sick and you could not eat your food, the nun would come and force it into your mouth. It was awful to see as a little kid. I saw a lot.[5]

Lisa linked her experiences at the residential school with the later emergence of social problems. She revealed that, after she left the school, she had difficulties adjusting to everyday life. She eventually became an alcoholic, something that she blamed in part on the need to overcome painful memories and the confusion instilled by her experience in the school. After years of struggling, Lisa quit drinking and acquired greater control over her life.

It is worth noting that the residential school program in Nova Scotia was coupled with the centralization policy implemented by the federal government between 1942 and 1950. Centralization, which targeted the Mi'kmaq and Maliseet of the Maritimes, aimed at optimizing the government's administration of the dispersed Indigenous population by moving it, mostly by force or intimidation, onto four designated reserves, two in Nova Scotia and two in New Brunswick. The selected locations in Nova Scotia were Eskasoni and Shubenacadie (Poliandri 2011, 39–40; see also Paul 2006, 281–319). In addition, centralization responded to requests from the general population to remove Indigenous people from their vicinity: "As with other colonial policies, [it] constituted what we now understand to be institutionalized racism" (Hanrahan 2008, 30). The Mi'kmaw and Maliseet peoples resisted centralization vigorously, thus making it difficult for the government to implement it effectively.

The late Nora Bernard, a Mi'kmaw survivor and former director of the Shubenacadie Indian Residential School Association, which has operated on behalf of more than nine hundred Mi'kmaw survivors since 1995, stated that the ill effects of the Catholic educators' teaching practices and methods extended to the descendants of the former students – the intergenerational survivors, whom anthropologist Ronald Niezen (2013, 98) defines as "those whose lives were in some way adversely affected by the actions of a close relative with a background of traumatic experience in residential school." The results of this can be seen in social and cultural disruptions, including alcohol and drug abuse, lack of parenting and marital skills, psychological and physical violence as common practices in childrearing, and the persistence of language and cultural loss.[6] Most Mi'kmaw survivors I talked with framed their illustration of the Shubenacadie School in terms of these social problems and the related cultural disruption. Fittingly, and more broadly, it is significant that in August 1992, when formally requesting that the government share responsibility for the abuses and consequences of Indigenous residential schools, the Aboriginal Rights Coalition referred to "the loss of language through forced English speaking, the loss of traditional ways of being on the land, the loss of parenting skills through the absence of four or five genera-tions of children from Native communities, and the learned behavior of despising Native identity."[7] I address these elements of disruption later.

The Shubenacadie School closed in 1967 following an investigation that exposed the inhumane conditions in which the children were boarded and educated, as well as the ineffectiveness of its methods. Nevertheless, the damage had already been done to generations of Mi'kmaq – as unanimously revealed by the work of the Shubenacadie Indian Residential School As-sociation, innumerable testimonies of survivors and their family members (Knockwood 2015),[8] and several scholarly works (see Prins 1996; Paul 2006; and Poliandri 2011). After the school was closed, the large brick building marked the Shubenacadie landscape until 1986, when it was burned to the ground by unknown hands.

Today, the school's name is synonymous with a dark period in the recent history of the Mi'kmaw First Nation. It still evokes memories and sentiments of pain, discomfort, humiliation, violation, dispossession, rage, impotence, inadequacy, disillusionment, retaliation, injustice, and, rarely, forgiveness and normalcy among Mi'kmaq of all generations, whether survivors, inter-generational survivors, or unrelated people.

"Survivor" as a Reconceived Identity

I began to reflect on the idea of the residential school survivor after several years of developing relationships with many Mi'kmaw former students and their family members. By definition, being a survivor means having outlived a life-threatening experience; it also entails that there may be people who did not survive, whether culturally or physically. Indeed, in this case, residential school survivors and family members of former students have recently mounted protests in and around Catholic, United, and Anglican churches in several Canadian cities, including Vancouver and Toronto, explicitly demanding information regarding the whereabouts of the Indigenous children who died while in the schools but whose remains were never found. In more common terms, residential school survivors are those who emerged from such institutions both culturally wounded and emotionally scarred. For many of them, healing is still an unfinished journey.

Over the past decade, I was invited to attend several healing workshops for Mi'kmaw survivors. The focus of such gatherings included anger management, acknowledgment, forgiveness, and a regaining of self-confidence and a sense of belonging in the Mi'kmaw communities. It was in these workshops that I learned to distinguish between those survivors who had tackled their emotional issues, overcome them, and moved on and those who still had not come to terms with their problems or who simply struggled to face them. The former usually spoke of loss of language, self-esteem, childhood, innocence, culture, spirituality, and identity. They told stories of the hardships, punishments, humiliations, and, in some cases, sporadic moments of normalcy and even joy that characterized day-to-day life in the school.

In contrast, the latter hardly ever mentioned any of those things. They made no references to language, culture, beatings, identity loss, family, hair, punishments, church, or uniforms. All that they spoke of, when they chose to do so, was pain – "right here, deep inside my guts," to cite the most frequent clarification given at any time – a pain inside that would not go away and would resurface regularly in many ways. Anger, mostly directed at their children and other family members, was one manifestation. Others included nightmares, depression, profound insecurity, suicidal thoughts, and alcoholism.[9]

Although healing programs have recently become available to survivors, many of these former students still struggle to confront their pain. Nora Bernard illustrated this point clearly:

> Only recently there has been help with healing. And some of the survivors don't want healing. Some survivors don't want to hear or talk about the residential school. They pushed it back in the backburner. They tell me that I am very strong. That's only because I started my healing in 1955. Fifteen years ago I would not talk to you about my pain like I am doing now. I used to have nightmares when I started writing about my experiences in the school. Every night or every second night, I used to wake up sobbing my heart out.[10]

This account, I argue, reveals a reconceived sense of individual and Indigenous self that survivors have acquired through their experiences in the residential schools. It is undeniable that the survivors' life histories and identities are often marked by elements of a common path that many Indigenous people's lives, unfortunately, converge upon – a path that is characterized by social and familial disconnect, emotional and psychological imbalance, and substance abuse. Similarly, Niezen (2013, 7) states that the survivor is a category of people that stems "from recognition of a common experience by which tradition was interrupted." He goes on to add that informal gatherings of survivors and their participation in the TRC proceedings both provided "a sense of solidarity behind the interruption of silence and stigma" and, more relevant to my discussion, offered survivors another way to "to form a common identity based on shared experience" (ibid., 30).

Solidarity and a sense of shared identity have also characterized formal healing workshops and events organized by intertribal associations and programs, many of which I attended in the Canadian Maritimes. However, Indigenous identities that were transformed by the residential schools, and partially by the indirect experience of interacting with family members who attended the schools, also have a unique nature, as they are not available to those Indigenous people who did not attend the schools or did not suffer from the consequences of interacting with a family survivor. Thus, they highlight a cleavage between the life experiences available to survivors – and, to a lesser degree, intergenerational survivors – and those available to non-survivors. The discussion of language, of alcoholism and anger, and of family disruption and a lack of parenting skills clarifies this point.

Language

Fluency in the Mi'kmaw language is an important component of Mi'kmaw identity that was disrupted in the residential school. Many children entered the Shubenacadie School unable to speak English and left it unable to speak Mi'kmaq. Discussing his wife's experience in the school, Philip, an elder from Indian Brook, said, "She could not talk English when she went in there. She came out that she could not speak Mi'kmaq."[11] Leonard, a survivor from Indian Brook, told me that after he left the institution, common Mi'kmaw words were abruptly unavailable to him. Losing his language forced him to adapt to an English-speaking worldview.[12]

This process also negatively affected many Mi'kmaw children's sense of Indigenous pride and individual self-confidence. Clyde, a middle-aged Mi'kmaq, said, "The priest and nuns used to beat us for speaking our language. If you are beaten up for that, you start believing that there is something wrong with you."[13] Knockwood (2015, 60) recalls the confusion Mi'kmaw children experienced when being reprimanded for saying what they considered inoffensive words like *pipnaqn* (bread) in the presence of the nuns.

Furthermore, and maybe less intuitively, I argue that the destructive process carried out in the school contributed to disrupting the social relationships between those Nova Scotia Mi'kmaq who are fluent in their language and those who are not (Poliandri 2011, 73–80). Consider that the Mi'kmaw people who reside on the reserves of Cape Breton Island, the northern and more isolated part of Nova Scotia, have mostly retained their language and still use it as their principal form of communication. In contrast, the Mi'kmaq from the rest of Nova Scotia are mostly illiterate in Mi'kmaq. Territorial and historical factors, dating back to the French and British colonial presence beginning in the seventeenth century and predating the impact of the Shubenacadie School, account for this phenomenon. Unlike the mainland Mi'kmaq, the Cape Breton Mi'kmaw people's greater geographic isolation and stronger ties with the less invasive French colonists allowed them to retain their language.[14] However, the Shubenacadie School shared responsibility for shaping this phenomenon. While discussing the legacy of the school, Susan, a middle-aged daughter of former students, told me, "In Cape Breton they kept the language. Residential school was only here [on the mainland]."[15]

When conversing with Mi'kmaw individuals from Cape Breton, I was often presented with the perspective that they feel "more Mi'kmaq" than the mainland Mi'kmaq, because the majority of the latter are not fluent in the Mi'kmaw language and, therefore, have lost a significant part of their Mi'kmaqness.

Interestingly, the question "what do you think about the idea that Mi'kmaw speakers are more Mi'kmaq?" usually generated a different response when posed to a residential school survivor or to one of their descendants. For instance, Susan told me, "My parents went to the residential school. That's why they would not speak Mi'kmaq to us kids. They were afraid we would get hurt by the nuns and the priest." She added, "It's not my fault that I don't speak it but the residential school's."[16] Her statements mirror those of many survivors and their descendants who link their crippled cultural identity to their fate as residential school survivors. Being either a survivor or an intergenerational survivor provides a sense of Mi'kmaw and, more broadly, Indigenous shared destiny that somewhat replaces the missing "Mi'kmaqness," perceived as having been lost along with the language.

Alcohol and Anger

Many Mi'kmaq ascribe their alcoholism directly or indirectly to their experiences in the residential school. Bill, who attended the Shubenacadie School for a few years starting at age five, said that the pain he suffered in the school led him to the bottle in adulthood as a way to find relief and numbness: "Alcohol helped me not to get hurt, and for that I blame the residential school. After the abuse I suffered in the school, alcohol gave me a safe environment."[17] Bill eventually healed, sobered up, and moved on.

Clara spent three years in the Shubenacadie School, and her mother had been there before her. She told me that such an experience deprived her of language, cultural identity, and self-esteem and that it also built rage within her. That rage, Clara said, used to be directed at family members in sudden outbursts. That rage, she added, led her to alcoholism. Clara finally recovered and has been sober for years.[18]

Of course, alcoholism has not been a problem exclusive to residential school survivors. Abundant literature and countless testimonies speak of a long-term history of Indigenous substance abuse extending well beyond the realm of residential schooling.[19] In this sense, in fact, it is appalling that the survivors' reconnection with some form of Indigenous lifestyle and identity, perceived as lost or damaged in the residential schools, often entails the descent into a challenged lifestyle unfortunately common to many Indigenous people. Yet, without intending to oversimplify the very complex issue of substance abuse, I argue that survivors' alcoholism is different from that of Indigenous non-survivors. Whereas nonsurvivors may often employ alcohol as a way of evading, numbing, or blurring an uncomfortable reality, survivors often perceive it also as a vehicle by which they can return to or reacquire a sense of normalcy and stable self, which were disrupted in the schools. In this perspective, healing entails shifting the perception of stability away from alcohol and learning to accept the consequences of having survived residential school abuse.

Hate and anger, which many Indigenous students developed as a form of reaction to the abuses they suffered, are also by-products of residential school education. In her research on the experiences of the Shuswap people of British Columbia, Celia Haig-Brown (1988, 86) illustrates that such hostility was primarily directed toward the parents who sent the children to the school, or were perceived as having done so, as well as toward the priests and nuns for their treatment of the pupils. This was also common among the Mi'kmaq in the Shubenacadie School.

In addition, anger was also directed toward other children, who served as either substitute targets for the unreachable educators or sacrificial victims of self-preserving oppressors. Knockwood (2015, 95–96) reports several cases in which violence and punishments received in the Shubenacadie School instilled rage that many students directed toward other students: "'Ratting' on other students [thus triggering punishment] became a way of working off old scores ... Older boys would also intimidate younger ones." Haig-Brown (1988, 55) reports that the "oppressive atmosphere at the school produced aggressive behavior in the [Shuswap] children, which [was] vented onto other children." As a result, hate and anger were felt both by those survivors who had been oppressors and had developed aggressive behaviour as a result of the violence received in the school as well as by those survivors who had been victims of other children and had developed hate and resentment toward the former. Arguably, such an outcome has contributed to deteriorating the social fabric of the Mi'kmaw communities.

Hate and anger have played a significant role in many survivors' process of identity formation. Maureen Smith (2001, 76) writes, "Because the students were so segregated from other groups and because of the extremely oppressive nature of the schools, students formed a them versus us mentality." Such a confrontational pattern of social interaction has been experienced first and foremost by family members and close friends in the households. Many survivors still struggle to come to terms with their hate and anger. If and when they decide to address these issues, doing so often entails participating in counselling and anger management programs.

Family Disruption and a Lack of Parenting Skills

There is another way that residential schooling contributed to disrupting the relationship between parents and children, as well as between children and other family members. Regina said that one of the most important elements of Mi'kmaw social life that the residential school sought to eradicate was the extended family: "gram, granddad, aunt and uncles."[20] Several survivors, intergenerational survivors, and other Mi'kmaq with whom I discussed residential schooling between 2003 and 2009 provided similar statements.

Nora Bernard, for instance, described the undermining of family ties in these terms:

> The residential school effects on people in extended families had their toll on the ones close to those people. The Indian Agent and Father Mackey told my mother that if she did not send her children to the residential school, they would get them anyway. So my mother signed a document saying that she would give them for one year. After a year, they told her that the fine print in those papers gave the school custody of the children until they reached the age of sixteen. My mom suffered loneliness when we were sent to the residential school.[21]

Bill stated that his experience in the residential school caused him to raise social barriers against other people, including family members, for a long time:

> For many years, I did not let anybody get close to me so that I could be hurt. I blame the residential school for that. There is a specific event that is stuck in my memory and broke my sense of trust toward others for a long time. Once, one of the nuns was giving me a bath ... I was a little

kid and I was splashing water ... you know, like little kids do. So she put my head under the water and held it there for a while. I got extremely scared. From that day on, I swore I'd never allow anybody to get too close to me. For many years, I could not even hug my own daughter without getting uncomfortable. I cried many times because of that.[22]

After successfully healing, Bill said that he relearned to let family members and friends get close. His diffidence is, and was, common among survivors. It has played a significant part in the development of their social skills and sense of place in the world.[23]

Mi'kmaw survivors learned to parent according to the model of domination and punishment that they experienced in the Shubenacadie School. Jenny, the daughter of a former student, recalled her childhood memories: "My mother was violent because she came from the residential school. She was full of anger and cold."[24]

When discussing her parenting choices, Regina highlighted how effective the residential school's harsh methods were in altering the fabric of Mi'kmaw family life:

> I brought up my kids in a regimental fashion, just like I was raised in the residential school. I had to give them some structure. And that's the only one that I knew. That's a by-product of the residential school ... Not everything was bad. Some of it was good. I knew where my children were at all times. But I was very strict and old-fashioned. The switches used to hang above my door, and they got it if they misbehaved. As a single parent, there was no other way that I knew to raise them effectively.[25]

Knockwood (2015, 160) talks about some Mi'kmaw children who "looked on the school as a refuge from homes where they were abused, frequently by parents who had themselves attended the school and learned physical punishment as a method of child-rearing." This pattern of parent-child relationship extended to multiple generations of Mi'kmaq. With time, this cycle of abuse became the norm or, at least, a frequent aspect of many Mi'kmaw household dynamics. Haig-Brown (1988, 92) remarks that in response to such a rearing model, Indigenous children "began to defy parents and expect punishment as a means of enforcing the rules."

Aside from the absence of parental models, another by-product of the Catholic education imparted in the Shubenacadie School was a lack of parenting skills. Marital relationships were not an appropriate topic of instruction in the school's Catholic curriculum. Combined with the denial of experiential training in the households from which the children had been taken away, the lack of exposure to family planning and relationship building produced many young adults unable to manage marital life and parenthood. Once again, Regina's words clearly illustrate this point:

> I did not have a teen life because I was in the residential school. Not only was I torn away from my mom and my grandparents but also from our extended families. I was almost sixteen when I left the school. Coming out of the school, many boys and girls were searching for that love, and they got in with the wrong people. A lot of girls, like me, had children. We mistook love with having sex with a man, that you're pleasing a man and they are going to love you for what you did for them. A year after I got out of the residential school, I got pregnant. I did not know where babies came from or anything because the nuns never taught us anything about that ... A lot of people got married very young. They did not know how to parent. So they would desert their children, leave them with their grandparents, and take off. Those children were brought up by somebody else, or their children were sent to the residential school, too, when they were of age. That's why they say the school had an intergenerational impact. And the garbage that the survivors took out of the residential school ... We never had any healing process ... We took it right into our teen life and marriage life. We passed it on to our children, and our children passed it on to their children. So there are three generations that had an impact from that residential school syndrome.[26]

As these cases show, for many former students, surviving the school has resulted in (1) a lack of two fundamental components of individual development, namely, marital and parental skills, (2) a failure to establish healthy relationships with one's children, whom are inevitably also negatively affected, and (3) the subsequent disruption of family and community ties. Such challenges have contributed significantly to shaping many survivors' identities, self-esteem levels, and emotional distance from others.

The recurrent appearance of social problems in the narratives of the survivors and intergenerational survivors provides tangible evidence of the dark legacy of the residential school. For many Mi'kmaw survivors and their family members, their direct and indirect experiences of the residential school are inseparable from many of the struggles and challenges in their own lives. Consequently, speaking about the school means making automatic, and often exclusive, reference to such struggles and challenges.

"Survivor" as a Way of Empowerment

It is along these lines, focusing on cultural disruption as well as psychological and social problems, that the connection between surviving the school, on the one hand, and a supratribal identity and a sense of shared destiny as Indigenous peoples, on the other hand, can be understood. Hazel Hertzberg (1971, 15), for instance, states that the use of the English language in educational institutions was the single most important factor in stimulating pan-Indianism across North America. Adding to this point, Sally McBeth (1983, 126) says, "Boarding schools are not directly responsible for pan-Indian movements, but made possible the emergence of what appears to be an effective inter-tribal ethnic identity. They have come to represent an Indian way of life." These views certainly apply to the Mi'kmaw survivors' cases.

However, I argue that such a connection also surfaces due to another important aspect, namely, the sense of community and empowerment provided by the common fight of many Indigenous people across the country against the government and former educational institutions to obtain both recognition of their status as abused people and compensation for those abuses. The efforts toward recognition and compensation have become sources of political leverage providing many survivors with a sense of purpose. Discussing the residential school survivor, Niezen (2013, 7) remarks, "In its widest usage, it is a new identity concept that materialized out of a process of justice lobbying, litigation, and efforts toward collective healing and securing a new place in history."

The case of Nora Bernard is representative of this process of empowerment. Nora, who spent many years in the Shubenacadie School in the 1940s, was the main force behind the class action lawsuit on behalf of the Shubenacadie School survivors, which inspired dozens of other lawsuits related to residential schools nationwide. These legal actions were eventually conflated into the class action lawsuit of 2000, which threatened four religious denominations – Roman Catholic, Anglican, United, and Presbyterian – with bankruptcy (Paul 2006, 291). Tens of thousands of claims were filed.

Driven by the Assembly of First Nations, whose former chief Phil Fontaine is a residential school survivor, the litigation finally came to a resolution. On December 15, 2006, the courts across Canada approved a $4 billion settlement affecting more than eighty thousand living survivors. The compensation procedure was formally structured in September 2007.[27]

The Shubenacadie Indian Residential School Association has provided a sense of belonging to hundreds of Mi'kmaw survivors who relate to a community of Indigenous people sharing similar experiences. This sense of community – represented by the association, its meetings, and the legal struggles fought alongside Indigenous people from all over the country – has given many of these men and women a sense of empowerment and strength that goes beyond their individual destinies.

Similarly, the fight for institutional recognition of the abuses suffered in the residential schools has provided survivors with an alternative and much brighter perception of their Indigenous identity. Such a process has allowed survivors to savour some historic achievements. On June 11, 2008, Canada's then prime minister, Stephen Harper, recognized the responsibility of the government for the residential school policy. Speaking in the House of Commons in the presence of the then national chief, Phil Fontaine, and many survivors, Harper delivered a historic apology to all First Nations people who suffered as a consequence of residential school education. Chief Fontaine acknowledged the apology on behalf of all survivors and Indigenous people.[28]

Another opportunity for survivor empowerment was offered by the creation of the TRC, whose Indigenous advisory committee contained one Mi'kmaw survivor of the Shubenacadie School. The TRC was established as part of the Indian Residential Schools Settlement Agreement with the purpose of collecting the testimonies of survivors and thus giving them a voice in the shaping of the official memory of Indigenous residential schooling.[29]

Despite such honourable intentions, many have highlighted the TRC's limited capability and, as a consequence, its shortcomings. Building on the views of political scientists Taiaiake Alfred (2005, 152–54) and Matt James (2007, 139–41), political scientist Jeff Corntassel and philosopher Cindy Holder (2008, 472–73) question the authenticity of Canada's remorse and label the Canadian government's "Statement of Reconciliation" (Canada 1998), which was the basis for the TRC's creation, a quasi-apology. In their view, until compensation and proper restitution – which must include land and resources – take place, there can be no true reconciliation. Without restitution, the relationship between the settler state and Indigenous peoples remains skewed.

Brian Rice and Anna Snyder (2008) reiterate such a concept, thus highlighting the greater complexity of the relationship between the government and Indigenous people than is represented by the sole, although important, legacy of the residential school policy.[30] Similarly to Alfred (2005), Corntassel and Holder (2008), James (2007), and Rice and Snyder (2008, 52) point out that self-governance and land control are necessary aspects in any reconciliation attempt: "Today, Aboriginal communities face extensive systemic barriers. Despite gains made in self-administration and resource sharing, many government policies continue to limit the economic, social, and political development and empowerment of Aboriginal communities." Moreover, "dispossession of land has been a key factor underlying the pervasive impoverishment, ill-health, and social stress that Aboriginal communities experience across Canada. The Canadian government must make systemic changes in order to heal its relationship with Aboriginal peoples" (ibid., 53).

Aboriginal Health Foundation board member and Mi'kmaw leader Viola Robinson sums up this perspective well in her vision of the goals and outcomes of the TRC: "The residential schools' legacy comes from a deeper history that goes back to the taking of our land. Therefore, truth has to go deeper than residential schools or it will be superficial" (Rice and Snyder 2008, 49).

Such a statement, which highlights the link between residential schooling and the colonial experience of dispossession, also reveals a unifying element in the process of identity development that residential school survivors have undergone. Although it is true that residential schooling was experienced by a minority (albeit an important one) among Indigenous people, thus creating an overlaying identification paradigm distinguishing survivors from nonsurvivors, it is also true that all Indigenous people past and present have shared the experience of colonial dispossession in one way or another.

Linking residential schooling with colonial dispossession, particularly but not exclusively of land, allows survivors – whose experiences have mostly been characterized by forced disconnection from their cultural heritage, community life, and Indigenous identities – to realign their individual experiences with the broader Indigenous experience. The systemic changes that link reconciliation with restitution and self-governance, thereby providing a significant step toward the end of colonialism, become a shared goal of survivors and nonsurvivors alike. Such a goal contributes to forging a sense of reunification with Indigenous life and history in the survivors' perceptions of their place in the world.

Yet it is ironic that such a reunification must take place on grounds tainted by colonialism, anger, violence, and trauma (Green 2012; Capitaine, this volume). Furthermore, as cultural studies scholar Robyn Green (this volume) highlights, many current scholars – particularly Indigenous ones, including Taiaiake Alfred (2005), Glen Coulthard (2007, 2014), Leanne Simpson (2011), and Audra Simpson (2014) – refute reconciliation as a viable process by which to achieve improved Indigenous-settler relations. Rather, they point at the resurgence of Indigenous values and cultural practices as radical alternatives to the structural dimensions of colonial power, which are potentially reproduced by the settler state's current strategy of reconciliation and accommodation but not restitution. In this perspective, the achievement of a true decolonization process in the form of proper restitution and self-governance assumes an even greater scope as it becomes an alternative common ground upon which survivor and nonsurvivor trajectories of Indigenous identification can convene.

❦

Being a residential school survivor has become one way, and for many, the principal way, for former students to identify as First Nations people. Being a survivor means sharing a common history with other Mi'kmaw and Indigenous people, and this history replaces what is perceived as "lost Mi'kmaqness" or "lost Indianness," providing a somewhat stable sense of identity.

Although the "survivor" experience is one that is exclusive to those Indigenous who attended the residential school and, indirectly, to their family members, I illustrate through the examples of the Mi'kmaw people who attended the Shubenacadie Residential School how the legacy of the abuses suffered in the schools has resulted in psychological and social impairments aligned with those that often typify the lifestyle of many Indigenous people. In this sense, the survivors' much-desired reconnection with an Indigenous way of life, which was taken away by the schools, is often actualized in the form of personal failure and social deficiency, which are often perceived (albeit stereotypically and inaccurately) as markers of an "Indian way of life."

At the same time, however, I highlight how the survivors' struggles for recognition and compensation have both functioned as sources of healing and allowed them to reshape their Indigenous identities around empowerment and self-actualization. Together with the prospect of suitable restitution and self-governance proposed by some, this resilience offers the encouraging possibility that a dark chapter in the history of Canadian Indigenous peoples can be brought to a close.

Sadly, as Nora Bernard remarked, "You can heal, but some part of the residential school experience will stay in the back of your mind and never leave you."[31]

NOTES

1 An early photograph of the school, taken by Mi'kmaw survivor Elsie Charles Basque in 1930, appears on the Nova Scotia Museum's website at http://novascotia.ca/museum/ mikmaq/default.asp?section=image&page=40&id=818&period=&region=. More photographs of and information about the school are available in the museum's Mi'kmaq Portrait Collection at http://novascotia.ca/museum/mikmaq/default.asp and on the Legacy of Hope Foundation's website at http://www.wherearethechildren.ca.

2 I owe many thanks to Brieg Capitaine for pushing me to reflect on the scope and significance of the "survivor" category. Our recurring conversations on this topic resulted in enhanced clarity and the sharpening of my ideas.

3 Among the works discussing the experiences of Native Americans in the US boarding schools, see Adams (1995), Archuleta, Child, and Lomawaima (2000), Ellis (1996), and Lomawaima (1994).

4 Regina, interview with author, November 18, 2003. Unless indicated, all names of interviewees are pseudonyms.

5 Lisa, interview with author, February 18, 2004.

6 Nora Bernard, interview with author, November 3, 2003. Nora gave me permission to use her real name.

7 Aboriginal Rights Coalition to Honourable Tom Siddon, August 1992, Indian and Northern Affairs File E6575–18–2, vol. 4, cited in Milloy (1999, 299). The Aboriginal Rights Coalition was created in 1975 by the Catholic, Anglican, and United Churches (later joined by other church denominations) to coordinate their efforts in cases of Indigenous justice.

8 See also the video testimonies of Mi'kmaw survivors on the Legacy of Hope Foundation's website at http://www.wherearethechildren.ca.

9 Niezen (2013, 48) discusses the discomfort that many survivors experienced when recalling their traumatic experiences in the course of the compensation claims process started in 2007.

10 Nora Bernard, interview with author, November 3, 2003.

11 Philip, interview with author, November 14, 2003.

12 Leonard, interview with author, December 16, 2003.

13 Clyde, interview with author, April 11, 2004.

14 For discussions of European colonialism in Mi'kmaw territory, see Paul (2006), Prins (1996), and Poliandri (2011, 183–206).

15 Susan, interview with author, September 11, 2004.

16 Ibid.

17 Bill, interview with author, February 26, 2004.

18 Clara, interview with author, October 18, 2003.

19 Indigenous substance abuse, particularly alcoholism, has been the topic of innumerable scholarly works over many decades. See, among others, French (2000), Kunitz and Levy (1994), Mancall (1995), and Waddell and Everett (1980).

20 Regina, interview with author, November 18, 2003.

21 Nora Bernard, interview with author, November 3, 2003.

22 Bill, interview with author, February 26, 2004.

23 For a comparable discussion of the breakage of family bonds and the loss of parenting skills among the Cree as a result of residential school experiences, see Vanthuyne (Chapter 7 in this volume).

24 Jenny, interview with author, September 8, 2004.

25 Regina, interview with author, November 18, 2003.

26 Ibid.

27 For a detailed illustration of the Settlement Agreement and the compensation structure, see Niezen (2013, 43ff).

28 Video recordings and transcriptions of Stephen Harper's and Phil Fontaine's speeches are available at http://www.aadnc-aandc.gc.ca/eng/1100100015677/1100100015680 and http://www.aadnc-aandc.gc.ca/eng/1100100015697/1100100015700.

29 Niezen (2013, 99ff, 129ff, 152ff) discusses the sense of empowerment that many survivors have acquired as a result of telling their own stories in their own ways at the TRC events.

30 Rice and Snyder's (2008) essay is part of a collection published by the Aboriginal Healing Foundation of Canada. More than thirty authors, most of them Indigenous, contributed to this volume, whose purpose, as stated by the foundation's president in his preface (Erasmus 2008, xiii), was to inform and advise the TRC as it set out on its work.

31 Nora Bernard, interview with author, November 3, 2003.

REFERENCES

Adams, David W. 1995. *Education for Extinction: American Indians and the Boarding School Experience, 1875–1928.* Lawrence: University Press of Kansas.

Alfred, Taiaiake. 2005. *Wasáse: Indigenous Pathways of Action and Freedom.* Peterborough, ON: Broadview.

Archuleta, Margaret L., Brenda J. Child, and K. Tsianina Lomawaima, eds. 2000. *Away from Home: American Indian Boarding School Experiences, 1879–2000.* Phoenix, AZ: Heard Museum.

Bauer, Otto. 1907. "The Nation." Reprinted in *Mapping the Nation,* ed. Gopal Balakrishnan, 39–77. London: Verso, 2012.

Canada. 1998. "Statement of Reconciliation." In *Gathering Strength: Canada's Aboriginal Action Plan,* 2–3. Ottawa: Minister of Indian Affairs and Northern Development. http://www.ahf.ca/downloads/gathering-strength.pdf.

Corntassel, Jeff, and Cindy Holder. 2008. "Who's Sorry Now? Government Apologies, Truth Commissions and Indigenous Self-Determination in Australia, Canada, Guatemala, and Peru." *Human Rights Review* (Piscataway, New Jersey) 9 (4): 465–89. http://dx.doi.org/10.1007/s12142-008-0065-3.

Coulthard, Glen S. 2007. "Subjects of Empire: Indigenous Peoples and the 'Politics of Recognition' in Canada." *Contemporary Political Theory* 6 (4): 437–60. http://dx.doi.org/10.1057/palgrave.cpt.9300307.

–. 2014. *Red Skin, White Masks: Rejecting the Colonial Politics of Recognition*. Minneapolis: University of Minnesota Press.

Ellis, Clyde. 1996. *To Change Them Forever: Indian Education at the Rainy Mountain Boarding School, 1893–1920*. Norman: University of Oklahoma Press.

Erasmus, George. 2008. "Preface." In *From Truth to Reconciliation: Transforming the Legacy of Residential Schools*, ed. Marlene Brant Castellano, Linda Archibald, and Mike DeGagné, xiii. Ottawa: Aboriginal Healing Foundation. http://www.ahf. ca/downloads/from-truth-to-reconciliation-transforming-the-legacy-of-residential -schools.pdf.

French, Laurence. 2000. *Addictions and Native Americans*. Westport, CT: Praeger.

Green, Robyn. 2012. "Unsettling Cures: Exploring the Limits of the Indian Residential School Settlement Agreement." *Canadian Journal of Law and Society* 27 (1): 129–48. http://dx.doi.org/10.3138/cjls.27.1.129.

Haig-Brown, Celia. 1988. *Resistance and Renewal: Surviving the Indian Residential School*. Vancouver: Tillacum Library.

Hanrahan, Maura. 2008. "Resisting Colonialism in Nova Scotia: The Kesukwitk Mi'kmaq, Centralization, and Residential Schooling." *Native Studies Review* 17 (1): 25–44.

Hertzberg, Hazel W. 1971. *The Search for an American Indian Identity: Modern Pan-Indian Movements*. Syracuse, NY: Syracuse University Press.

James, Matt. 2007. "Wrestling with the Past: Apologies, Quasi-Apologies, and Non-Apologies in Canada." In *The Age of Apology: The West Faces Its Own Past*, ed. Gibney Mark, Rhoda Howard-Hassman, Jean-Marc Coicaud, and Niklaus Steiner, 137–53. Philadelphia: University of Pennsylvania Press.

Knockwood, Isabelle. 2015. *Out of the Depths: The Experiences of Mi'kmaw Children at the Indian Residential School at Shubenacadie, Nova Scotia*. 4th ed. Halifax, NS: Fernwood.

Kunitz, Stephen J., and Jerrold Levy. 1994. *Drinking Careers: A Twenty-Five-Year Study of Three Navajo Populations*. New Haven, CT: Yale University Press.

Lomawaima, K. Tsianina. 1994. *They Called It Prairie Light: The Story of Chilocco Indian School*. Lincoln: University of Nebraska Press.

Mancall, Peter C. 1995. *Deadly Medicine: Indians and Alcohol in Early America*. Ithaca, NY: Cornell University Press.

McBeth, Sally J. 1983. *Ethnic Identity and the Boarding School Experience of West-Central Oklahoma American Indians*. Washington, DC: University of America Press.

Miller, James R. 2004. *Lethal Legacy: Current Native Controversies in Canada*. Toronto: McClelland and Stewart.

Milloy, John S. 1999. *"A National Crime": The Canadian Government and the Residential School System, 1879 to 1986*. Winnipeg: University of Manitoba Press.

Niezen, Ronald. 2013. *Truth and Indignation: Canada's Truth and Reconciliation Commission on Indian Residential Schools*. Toronto: University of Toronto Press.

Paul, Daniel N. 2006. *We Were Not the Savages: Collision between European and Native American Civilizations*. 3rd ed. Halifax, NS: Fernwood.

Poliandri, Simone. 2011. *First Nations, Identity, and Reserve Life: The Mi'kmaq of Nova Scotia*. Lincoln: University of Nebraska Press.

Prins, Harald E.L. 1996. *The Mi'kmaq: Resistance, Accommodation, and Cultural Survival*. Fort Worth, TX: Harcourt Brace.

Rice, Brian, and Anna Snyder. 2008. "Reconciliation in the Context of a Settler Society: Healing the Legacy of Colonialism in Canada." In *From Truth to Reconciliation: Transforming the Legacy of Residential Schools*, ed. Marlene Brant Castellano, Linda

Archibald, and Mike DeGagné, 43–63. Ottawa: Aboriginal Healing Foundation. http://www.ahf.ca/downloads/from-truth-to-reconciliation-transforming-the-legacy-of-residential-schools.pdf.

Simpson, Audra. 2014. *Mohawk Interruptus: Political Life across the Borders of Settler States.* Durham, NC: Duke University Press. http://dx.doi.org/10.1215/9780822376781.

Simpson, Leanne. 2011. *Dancing on Our Turtle's Back: Stories of Nishnaabeg Re-creation, Resurgence, and a New Emergence.* Winnipeg, MB: Arbeiter Ring.

Smith, Maureen. 2001. "Forever Changed: Boarding School Narratives of American Indian Identity in the U.S. and Canada." *Indigenous Nations Studies Journal* 2 (2): 57–82.

Waddell, Jack O., and Michael W. Everett, eds. 1980. *Drinking Behavior among Southwestern Indians: An Anthropological Perspective.* Tucson: University of Arizona Press.

6

"National Memory" and Its Remainders: Labrador Inuit Counterhistories of Residential Schooling

ARIE MOLEMA

> Our obligation as a Commission ... is to ensure that a national memory is established for this country, so that we can assure ourselves that in fifty or one hundred years from now, our children's children – and their children – will be able to have a source of information and truth available to them so that this country will never forget what happened and will never be able to deny that it did happen.
>
> – Honourable Justice Murray Sinclair, chair of the Truth and Reconciliation Commission of Canada, Saskatoon National Event, June 22, 2012

TRUTH COMMISSIONS HAVE A powerful discursive toolbox at their disposal, wielding powerful tropes of "truth" and "reconciliation." At the events of the Truth and Reconciliation Commission of Canada, however, references to creating memory, even *national* memory, were also audible. The TRC held national events and commemorative activities across Canada and collected thousands of testimonies from former residential school students. Many of these are now public, having been mediatized via webcast and archived alongside historical records in the National Research Centre for Truth and Reconciliation at the University of Manitoba. Creating this repository of archives was, as the TRC saw it, a project of national memory-making. This undertaking to educate Canadians on the residential schools

– where, for over a hundred years,[1] generations of Indigenous children were often forcibly interned – was an exercise in corrective historiography aimed at amending a central omission in the way we remember Canada's past.

Unfortunately, making room for Indigenous memories of residential schools within official national memory is a complicated and deeply compromised project. Residential schools epitomize the colonial violence that European settlement brought to Turtle Island, a violence that is frequently denied and officially disavowed in contemporary Canada.[2] Our political institutions and educational curricula prompt us to remember Canadian history as a heritage of tolerance, sown from the peaceful settlement of wilderness and frontiers (Trigger 1986; Mackey 1999, 2012; Thobani 2007), humble toil from which has grown a society offering global economic competitiveness with a benevolently multicultural twist.

Instead, former students of residential schools presented to the TRC a starkly different vision of Canadian history, as they painfully and painstakingly testified to the endemic physical, psychological, and sexual abuse they had endured in the schools, along with a loss of languages and cultural traditions. The forcible transfer of children from one group to another – the very premise of Indian residential schooling – alone qualifies for consideration under Article 2 of the United Nations Convention on the Prevention and Punishment of Genocide, which Canada signed in 1949.[3] Yet only one-third of Canadians report familiarity with the Indian residential schools, according to a national benchmark survey commissioned by the TRC in 2008 (Environics Research Group 2008, i). Fewer still – one in twenty – describe themselves as very familiar with the schools and their intergenerational impacts (see also Gaver, this volume).

The TRC's vision of making "truth available ... so that this country will never forget what happened" is a laudable, urgent campaign for public education on the Indian residential schools. Framed as a project of national memory-making, however, it is less straightforward. "Forgetting," as historian Ernest Renan (1882, 11) memorably declared, "is a crucial factor in the creation of the nation," and national memory is as much about disavowals and implicit obligations to forget as it is about active remembrance (Bhabha 1990, 311). National memory in this chapter, then, is not an essentialized shared object but a fluid memoryscape (Yoneyama 1994) – a field of unequal power relations, where competing interpretations of the past battle unevenly to produce historical knowledge and sway collective memory (Foucault 1977; Trouillot 1995; Sturken 1997; Yoneyama 1999).

Building on these two points – that memory is formed through a dialectic of commemoration and disavowal and that national memory is more about contestation than consensus – I focus on a third problem of memory politics. A common denominator underlying both points above, I suggest, is that national memory is predicated on a politics of recognition, a concept that has generated an important body of theory on the predicament of Indigenous peoples within settler colonial polities (Taylor 1992; Povinelli 2002; Coulthard 2007; Cattelino 2010). Extending this conversation, I focus on the recognition, adjudication, and comparative valuation of memories amid the politics of remembering the Indian residential schools. To do so, I draw on twelve months of ethnographic fieldwork, including participant observation at the TRC's national events as well as fifty interviews conducted in Nunatsiavut with Labrador Inuit who are former students of residential schools but have been denied recognition and compensation under the Indian Residential Schools Settlement Agreement.

I discuss the limitations of the Settlement Agreement, highlighting Labrador's exclusion. I reflect on the politics of recognition whereby law, as an instrument of government, is empowered to adjudicate whose residential school memories count and which colonial injuries are deemed justiciable for redress and compensation from the state. I then contextualize the history of residential schooling in Labrador, underlining commonalities in experiences and memories of residential schools gleaned from the narratives former students shared with me. Finally, I present important differences in residential school experiences, demonstrating how particular families experienced a triple burden of loss in the form of forced community relocation and child welfare apprehensions *in addition* to residential schooling, compounding experiences of institutionalized family rupture. These differences trouble the homogenized category of the residential school survivor (see also Poliandri, this volume) and point to how the TRC's project of national memory-making may perversely produce foreclosures of memory. I conclude that these foreclosures produce lived, embodied consequences for Labrador Inuit: when triage is performed in the name of national memory, those whose memories are marginalized carry the burden of remembering and inhabiting the remainders of national memory's unacknowledged pasts.

Adjudicating Memory: Labrador and the Settlement Agreement

The Indian Residential Schools Settlement Agreement, implemented in 2007, as detailed in the Introduction to this volume, was the product of sustained Indigenous activism on multiple fronts over several decades. The negotiations to subsume the outstanding court cases into the agreement began on May 30, 2005, concluding with an agreement in principle between the parties on November 20, 2005. Among the items for negotiation was which institutions would be recognized as residential schools. A total of 130 were included, with the proviso that residential schools could later be added if they met eligibility criteria pursuant to Article 12 of the Settlement Agreement. Indigenous political organizations were party to these negotiations, including the Assembly of First Nations, along with Inuit representatives, Nunavut Tunngavik Incorporated, Inuvialuit Regional Corporation, and Makivik Corporation. The Métis National Council was not party to these negotiations,[4] nor were the Labrador Inuit.

The year 2005 was already a momentous one for Labrador Inuit, who were implementing their transition to self-government with the signing of the Labrador Inuit Land Claims Agreement after twenty-eight years of arduous negotiations with the federal and provincial governments. As a Nunatsiavut government official explained to me, the Labrador Inuit were not invited to the Settlement Agreement negotiations and, upon belatedly learning of their exclusion, requested that Nunavut Tunngavik express concerns on their behalf. The decision to approve excluded schools, however, does not belong jointly to all parties of the agreement: it rests with the discretion of Aboriginal Affairs and Northern Development Canada (2013), representing the federal government.

Contesting the exclusion, the Nunatsiavut government prepared a request pursuant to Article 12 of the Settlement Agreement, providing three volumes of historical documentation suggesting that – contrary to Canada's claim that residential schools attended by Labrador Inuit were operated exclusively by the province or religious organizations – the federal government played an active role in financing and administering these schools through capital expenditure agreements with the province and family allowance policies (White, Ottenheimer and Baker 2007a, 2007b, 2008). For Labrador Inuit, being left out is a familiar predicament: their status as Inuit "south of sixty"[5] and Newfoundland's late entry into Canadian Confederation have served as pretexts for the federal government to shrug off its constitutional responsibilities and fiduciary duty to the Indigenous peoples of the province (Tanner 1998; Hanrahan 2003). Although Aboriginal Affairs rejected Nunatsiavut's request for inclusion, former students in Labrador have initiated a class action against the federal government, which was certified by the Supreme Court of Newfoundland and Labrador in June 2010 and is currently before the courts.[6]

The exclusion of Labrador from the Settlement Agreement and the pending class action in response underscore the power of law, as an instrument of government, in authorizing the politics of recognition that surround the Indian residential schools. Law provides a window for the acknowledgment of some memories of institutional harm while invalidating others as ineligible for state redress. Discussing the Australian Aboriginal context, anthropologist Elizabeth Povinelli (2002, 182) asks,

> What is it ... that allows the law to incite national and subaltern memory on behalf of a new collective self-understanding in a way that makes the rewriting of history seem a recognition of and accounting for that history; that allows the (re)entrenchment of cultural discrimination as a technology of state power; and, as if these were not enough, makes this new technology of state power seem like a means of liberating subalterns from the state?

The law, adjudicating which and whose residential school memories are justiciable for national redress, wields a powerful role in underwriting eligibility criteria for national memory and acknowledgment, a point that is often overlooked in memory studies literature. Among over forty truth commissions, the Truth and Reconciliation Commission of Canada, the first to have emerged as part of a court settlement, is particularly well placed to shed light on this point.

Liberal legal ideology posits that legal decisions "are primarily dispassionate, objective, noncontextual judgments of social facts rather than the primary means by which social facts are produced" (Povinelli 2002, 230). Examining the Settlement Agreement not as legal judgment but as social production spotlights the unequal power relations that determined who had a right to be party to the settlement negotiations. It also underscores the ongoing authority of the federal government, channelled through Aboriginal Affairs, to include or reject additional residential schools. Upcoming court decisions on excluded schools may also rule in favour of the plaintiffs, but these rulings would not change the foundational power asymmetry that affirms the settler state as arbiter of Indigenous rights and recognition. These asymmetrical politics of recognition are authorized by Crown law, a vexed vehicle for Indigenous peoples, which has "repeatedly refused to challenge the racist origin of Canada's assumed sovereignty over [them] and their territories" (Coulthard 2007, 451). In settler polities, Crown law requires the recognition of Indigenous rights by the settler state, even while, perhaps less conspicuously, the state relies on Crown law to defend its own sovereignty and legitimacy.

Within the context of the TRC, the commissioners employed a progressive interpretation of their mandate and made overtures to groups excluded from the Settlement Agreement. As cultural studies scholar Robyn Green (2012, 142) notes, the TRC's inclusion of excluded groups provided a measure of symbolic recognition in the absence of material compensation. Labrador Inuit were invited to attend the TRC's national events in Inuvik in June 2011 and Halifax in October 2011, and the TRC conducted two Labrador regional hearings in Hopedale and Happy Valley–Goose Bay in September 2011.

Symbolic recognition may be of small comfort when legal recognition is denied. At the Halifax National Event, a group of over twenty Labrador Inuit dressed in traditional white, fur-trimmed *silapaks* (parkas) were invited to make a public expression of reconciliation. The Nunatsiavut government's minister of health, Patricia Kemuksigak, spoke on behalf of the delegation:

> We all need to stand together ... so that the Labrador experiences of residential schools are acknowledged, recognized, and we too have an apology of the injustices that happened in the residential schools. Our trauma, abuses, and losses in residential schools are real, true, and we need that acknowledgment ... We deal with intergenerational trauma daily. We have many issues ... family dysfunction, suicide, family violence, and poverty, just to name a few. I would also like for people to send prayers to Nunatsiavut and to the community of Hopedale, as on Wednesday we lost another young man to suicide, a sixteen-year-old boy from Hopedale. We all need your prayers and support.

The Labrador Inuit delegation closed its presentation with an Inuktitut language performance of the hymn "God Be with You till We Meet Again."

Some Inuit cried and were comforted by others onstage, and their mournful and often halting rendering of the hymn belied the hopeful promise of its lyrics. As Minister Kemuksigak instructed the audience, "This [hymn] is our traditional way to end events. We don't say goodbye. We say, 'till we meet again.'" The tearful recitation of the hymn performed a cry for recognition of memories that are not acknowledged, poignantly questioning the closure presumed in the Settlement Agreement. The social ills in Labrador Inuit communities that the minister itemized in her remarks stem directly from the residential schools, but critically, they also derive from interrelated episodes of colonial violence. In the following sections, I describe these interwoven histories, seeking to demonstrate how the very notion of national memory-making around residential schools that the TRC espoused may foreclose broader understandings of colonial history.

Memory and Its Loss: Residential Schooling in Labrador

Labrador Inuit experienced European colonization well before it reached the Inuit of other *nunaat* (homelands). In the late eighteenth century, missionaries from the predominantly German-speaking Moravian Church acquired extensive land grants from the British governor of Newfoundland and established permanent settlements in Labrador beginning in 1771. The Moravian mission, for its own trading interests, favoured Inuit seasonal migration for optimal resource harvesting. Moravian schooling of Inuit children was therefore initially limited to winter months when Inuit families were in residence at the Moravian mission stations. Full-year residential schooling did not emerge until the early twentieth century, with the establishment of boarding schools in Makkovik in 1902 and Nain in 1926 (Rowe 1964, 184).

The Moravian curriculum was mostly limited to basic arithmetic and literacy and was equivalent to only a Grade 3 education (Stern 2010, 28). Bible reading and harsh discipline were emphasized, and school maintenance relied on the daily chores of children (MacMillan 1951, 65; Flanagan 1984, 61–62). As one middle-aged woman said to me of her time at the Nain Boarding School,

> It was very stringent. It was still more like teaching us to be labourers rather than learning and education. There was no real focus on goals for the long term to see what we would like to have pursued. We were all

given chores. It was horrendous. It was like I said, focused really to teach us to be maids and labourers, eh?

Confederation in 1949 prompted the Province of Newfoundland to take a more directive role both in standardizing Labrador school curricula to approximate Canadian standards (Rowe 1964, 184–85) and in enforcing school attendance, assisted by the newly applied federal government policy of withholding family allowances from parents whose children were not enrolled for an entire school year. This joint federal-provincial policy separated Inuit families, impacting their ability to harvest subsistence resources and transmit cultural knowledge to their children.

Elsewhere in Labrador, the International Grenfell Association, a locally founded philanthropy with extensive international connections, had launched other residential schools from 1926, including the Yale School in North West River, the Lockwood School in Cartwright (replacing the Gordon Orphanage in nearby Muddy Bay), and a mission school and orphanage in St. Anthony, Newfoundland. Until the Yale School dorms closed in June 1980, finalizing the transition to day schooling, thousands of children in Labrador attended residential schools. Many children came from Labrador's north coast communities, where no high school education was available, and boarded at the Yale School. Other children from Labrador's south coast attended the Lockwood Boarding School in Cartwright. Children who attended came from Inuit, Settler (or Kablunângajuit, "half white"),[7] and Métis families. Some Innu attended residential schools, but more often they attended Catholic-run day schools, where they were subjected to extensive physical and sexual abuse (Samson 2003).

Perhaps the most common thread in narratives of residential school experiences is that residential school memory is paradoxically about the loss of memory itself, namely, the loss of Indigenous cultural memory, as part of the residential school system's avowed objective of assimilation, or "killing the Indian in the child." Former students in Labrador describe their loss of the Inuktitut language, Inuit values, family traditions, and parenting skills as a result of extensive time in residential school. The residential school system was also interwoven with the dispossession of Indigenous lands, which is central to the settler colonial project (Corntassel, Chaw-win-is, and T'lakwadzi 2009, 146). In Labrador, residential schooling was part of a broader colonial history that disrupted intergenerationally transmitted knowledge of the land and resource harvesting, alienating Inuit from the lifeways that had previously granted a measure of self-sufficiency and fostering relations of dependency that anthropologist Robert Paine (1977, 3) has termed "welfare colonialism." The following account of residential schooling from a middle-aged man brings these losses of cultural memory into connection:

> I'm waiting for the day when the federal government will step up to the plate and apologize for the injustice that we went through. There are people who have lost their language, their culture, their traditions. There are people who became alcoholics, who became drug addicts. There are friends that have committed suicide. And all of this stems from the residential schools, from what we went through. I've got cousins, I've got friends who have kids of their own. And they don't know how to parent. But they're trying very hard to be parents. They can't parent because they were never *taught* ... We were took away and we lost a lot of our values ... When they got home, you know, people were lost ... Some people were ashamed of their own parents because of the way they did things ... fixing up sealskins and drying fish and all the traditional things. They were ashamed of it when they got home because they got used to a different type of lifestyle. They got used to the *white* lifestyle that they were living at the time ... It was like they had to be retaught again how to be an Inuk.

Although losses of cultural memory formed a common thread in many former students' accounts of residential schools, there were also stark differences in their experiences of and trajectories through residential schooling. Some individuals and their families had experienced forced community relocations and apprehensions through the child welfare system, which, coupled with residential schooling, formed a triple burden of loss centred on institutionalized family rupture and child removal. I explore the interweaving of these memories in the following section of this chapter, suggesting that a politics of recognition was at play when the TRC made *residential school survivors* the protagonists of its project of national memory-making. Notably, not all former students have acquired access to this community of belonging (see also Poliandri, this volume) and find their memories unrecognized.

A Triple Burden of Loss: Residential Schools, Relocation, and the Child Welfare System

Although abuses and cultural losses were shared by many who attended residential schools, former students of the Yale School impressed upon me that children were differentially vulnerable to abuse and sexual predation within the community of North West River, where the residential school was housed. One middle-aged woman noted, "There was favouritism for some people, and there was really strict, even abusive, behaviours to some kids." One Inuk elder philosophized that for the school administrators, "it [was] easier to work with ... those who look more white than brown" and that fairer-skinned students were able to "learn a trade or be given the support to higher your education or to work through the system much more smoothly than others who are looked at as different." The disparities in residential school experience were most clearly described to me by a middle-aged woman:

> Some people went through the dorm, and they ... just didn't see the underbelly of life here. I guess you had to be a welfare kid or somebody that nobody cares about. [The worst abuses are] not going to happen to the ones that had *family*, and families that are vocal. But check with the little meek families! Check with the Eskimo families. Speak with somebody whose parents didn't know the language very well and that maybe not only didn't know the language very well but *drank* a lot! See how they're believed! Because today people are saying there's no racism in Labrador. Speak to a little brown person! They can tell you all about the racism.

Indian residential schools have often been characterized as total institutions (Goffman 1961, 11–12), since the schools were often located in isolated areas where students were incarcerated and subjected to intensive surveillance by school personnel (Kirmayer, Simpson, and Cargo 2003, S17). The Yale School operated somewhat differently, as the school was located in a community and divided between several buildings. The Senior Dorm housed older high school students, most of whom came from coastal communities in Labrador with no high schools of their own and who returned home for the summer at the end of the school year. Wood Cottage and later Todd House housed the Junior Dorm, which, along with the Infants' Home, held children who had been orphaned or were apprehended by the provincial Department of Social Services and were "year-rounders," as one middle-aged man put it, staying in the summer when other students returned home. One middle-aged woman reflected on the especial vulnerability of these children and shared the pain of having discovered years later that a family member was sexually abused while in residence at the Junior Dorm:

> I don't know very much about all the abuse that occurred in Todd House. But it was easier sometimes with those kids. They were young. They did not have *anyone* to advocate on their behalf. They were isolated, and if they weren't isolated, whoever was using them found a way for them to be isolated. Especially from their siblings. And although there were some victims that had brothers and sisters, somehow those brothers and sisters did not *know* because that deception was so deep. Their older siblings didn't know! And had their older siblings known, some of these would have stood up and done something. Oh yes! Just because we're Inuit doesn't mean that we're always quiet, meek, mild, nice, respectful. I know some of these people very, very well. Oh, they would have done something! As young as they were. They would've done. But they didn't know!

Residential school memory in Labrador encompasses a wide spectrum of experiences that hang uneasily together. A partnership between the International Grenfell Association and Carnegie Corporation made special grants available to more privileged students so that they could pursue higher education elsewhere in Canada and the United States. Some graduates continued on in technical schools, business schools, or nursing schools, attending institutions such as the Pratt Institute, Wentworth Institute, and Berea College (Wall 1960, 36; Curtis 1963, 56–57; Rowe 1964, 186). Conversely, as the previous interview excerpts suggest, children who had been orphaned or apprehended and who boarded year-round were disproportionately vulnerable to predation from members of the community and, oftentimes, to abuse by teachers – or "house parents," as they were locally called – as well as by other children.

These differences in experience point to a central tension in the ways that the residential school history is remembered. In the work of meaning-making, former students in Labrador revisit and rework memories of residential schooling (see also Woods, this volume). Transformations in memory accompany transformations in former students' own self-concept and subjectivity as *residential school survivors,* itself a moral project (see Vanthuyne, this volume). The new category of identification as a trauma survivor has emerged in the Indigenous community in dialogue with public discourse on the Holocaust experience, the Vietnam War, and the feminist movement against spousal and child abuse (Fassin and Rechtman 2009; Million 2013, 88–91; see also Capitaine, this volume). Although the creation of residential school survivors as a community of belonging can help to affirm individual experiences and coordinate collective political action (e.g., in the work of the Indian Residential Schools Survivor Society and the National Residential Schools Survivor Society), it also risks homogenizing residential school memory and privileging the memories of particular individuals over others. Some former students I interviewed in Labrador proudly identified as residential school survivors, whereas others did not. Some claimed that they resented the label and felt that it essentialized and narrowed down their fundamental humanity. Others felt the term had become too closely associated with local "poster children" for residential school survival and with a triumphalist model of sobriety and cultural recovery that was not equally attainable for all former students, particularly those who experienced residential schools, relocation, and child welfare apprehensions, a triple burden of loss I now discuss in more detail.

Many of the residential school year-rounders described earlier came from the most visibly racialized Inuit families – rather than Kablunângajuit families – and/or families who had experienced the forced community relocations of the 1950s. A female mental health professional helped me to understand that for particular families, traumatic memories of family rupture and child removal were compounded through the cumulative experiences of community relocations, child welfare apprehensions, and residential schooling:

> [You] have to remember, too, the ones who are having a really hard time, they've been in the welfare system since they were kids. So there's all that traumatic issues that they have. Like some of their parents was relocated from either Hebron, Nutak, or Okak. And they themselves have been in the child welfare system. And in the residential school. Like, they're dealing with three different things for now, plus their own stuff. So like, four different major traumatic issues.

The relocation of children for residential schooling coincided with another series of dislocations in twentieth-century Labrador. Although these dislocations did not explicitly target Indigenous child removal, like residential schooling they engendered dramatic ruptures in Inuit family life, sociality, and household economies. The most traumatic relocations, or evictions (Brice-Bennett 1994), in the living memory of Labrador Inuit were the forced closures of Hebron and Nutak in the late 1950s, yet the Moravian mission and the Hudson's Bay Company had closed several other Inuit communities in the late nineteenth and early twentieth centuries, treating them as little more than "commercial stepping-stones" (ibid., xx) in the company's efforts to dominate trade in coastal Labrador. With the closures of these communities, many Inuit regrouped in Hebron, which became the northernmost Inuit community in Labrador.

In the 1950s, the ultimate decline in fur trade prices and consequent collapse of the exchange economy and credit system led to an unprecedented wave of government involvement in Inuit affairs in newly confederated Labrador and elsewhere in Inuit Nunangat (Tester and Kulchyski 1994, 4).[8] In Labrador the Newfoundland provincial government largely disdained the Inuit harvesting economy and promoted an industrial development strategy based on centralization and wage employment, constructing the new military airbase in Goose Bay as well as radar sites that were to form part of the Cold War's Distant Early Warning Line. This agenda converged with the interests of the Moravian mission and the International Grenfell Association in reducing their operating expenses by concentrating Inuit in fewer communities (Brice-Bennett 1994, 66). These institutions collectively withdrew their services from Nutak and Hebron in 1956 and 1959, effectively forcing Inuit to relocate against their will to communities farther south in a chaotic resettlement scheme where promised housing was not immediately available. Whereas Nutak families were primarily relocated to Nain, the new northernmost community in Labrador, Hebron Inuit were resettled by quotas in Nain, Hopedale, and Makkovik, severing established networks and family ties (Brice-Bennett 2000, 11) as well as the intergenerational transmission of traditional knowledge. Host communities were not notified prior to these arrivals, and some resented Hebron Inuit for substantially increasing their population and placing strains on local resources. The relocation impoverished Hebron Inuit, rupturing families that had previously enjoyed a measure of self-sufficiency through resource harvesting in established economic networks, and engineered a dependence on welfare. These traumatic changes demoralized Hebron Inuit and sparked a dramatic rise in alcohol abuse, family violence, accidental deaths, and criminal offences that would further contribute to a breakdown in family relations (ibid.,

11–13). In a study commissioned by the Royal Commission on Aboriginal Peoples, Inuk elder Augusta Erving recounted how the Angajo Kaukatiget, the traditional council of Inuit elders, found its authority usurped by provincial and federal institutions like the Department of Social Services and the Royal Canadian Mounted Police: "It's almost like the justice is running their lives for them. And if they had problems with children, it's almost like Social Services is running their lives. You know, if you do this and smack your kid, I'm taking your kid from you. It's almost like they got to be on their back all the time" (quoted in Brice-Bennett 1994, 125).

Relocation remains a living intergenerational legacy, and many Inuit I interviewed told me that descendants of relocatees remain overrepresented in the justice and child welfare systems. One Nunatsiavut government official described to me the limitations and disappointments of land claims settlement and self-government negotiations with Canada, saying that "right now it's just like more gradual handing-over of small little pockets of responsibility, or small little pockets of money." She identified the need for devolution of the justice system, child welfare, and education, which remain controlled by the province but are critical to Labrador Inuit sovereignty. Under the current policies of the provincial Department of Child, Youth and Family Services, Inuit are dissuaded from fostering children who have been removed from other homes in their community because of the surveillance and adversarial practices of the department – despite a longstanding tradition of child fosterage among extended families. Many Labrador Inuit children are being raised by white foster families in the predominantly Pentecostal community of Roddickton, on the island of Newfoundland. Another Nunatsiavut government official characterized this policy as "setting up more residential schools" and as an "economic development opportunity" for Roddickton following the decline of its fishery and pulp and paper industry. The Labrador Inuit context therefore powerfully illustrates Gitxsan scholar and activist Cindy Blackstock's (e.g., 2008) longstanding contention that the apprehensions of Indigenous children by child welfare agencies merely replicate residential schooling in a different guise. The ongoing and interconnected legacies of residential schooling, relocations, and child welfare apprehensions for Labrador Inuit demonstrate that colonial policies of Indigenous child removal and family rupture greatly exceed the Settlement Agreement and the TRC's narrow window of recognition of Indian residential schools alone, troubling the project of creating a national memory of a history that is far from past.

The recounting of oral history by middle-aged and elderly Labrador Inuit interweaves memories of family ruptures and child removals through relocation, child welfare apprehensions, and residential schooling, a triple burden of loss that exceeds the scope of the TRC's project of national memory-making regarding residential schools. The TRC's mandate derived from the Settlement Agreement, with legally authorized parameters that adjudicated some memories of residential schools as eligible for state redress while invalidating other memories of colonial violence. In this way, projects of national memory-making leave behind residues, or remainders – and those whose memories are unacknowledged carry the burden of remembering and embodying these remainders of national memory's unacknowledged pasts.

Projects of national memory-making are fundamentally projects of symbolization that attempt to collectivize and unify disparate, individual memories. In philosopher Slavoj Žižek's (2000, 33) analysis of the Lacanian concept of the remainder, he argues that "every synthetic unity is based on an act of 'repression,' and therefore generates some indivisible remainder." This remainder becomes "the 'bone in the throat' – which resists this symbolic representation" (Žižek 2004, 390). In this case, it is Labrador Inuit themselves who must swallow the bone in the throat that holds their unrecognized memories. If the pervasive losses that Inuit have experienced through colonial violence create an "ethical injunction to remember" (Stevenson 2006), the corollary of that ethical injunction is the burden of remembering that which has not been recognized. For Labrador Inuit who have experienced compounded losses, remaking a world (Das et al. 2001) or even making the everyday inhabitable (Das 2007) in the wake of and alongside that violence is a daily and uncertain battle, as one middle-aged woman helped me to understand:

> The TRC is about truth. They think they're about reconciliation, but they *aren't*. They think because I speak the truth that I'm reconciled. I'm not. Because ... there's no because. It's simply I'm not. The government does not acknowledge that I was in a residential school. How do you reconcile *that*? The TRC thinks that because I speak the truth, I'm on the step to *healing*. No. It doesn't go like that! It takes a whole lot more than *talking*. I've tried talking for years. It still stays in there! Three o'clock in the

morning when everybody's asleep and I can't sleep. And I'm alone in this world. And the thoughts are going around in circles. That's not reconciliation. I don't think it ever will be because that time is past. This is still in me. And they think because I spoke that I'm on my way to healing! It's not gonna be healed because this is always in here!

Ultimately, then, I end where I began, by questioning the TRC's program to establish a national memory of Indian residential schools. As I demonstrate, national memory-making under the parameters imposed by the Settlement Agreement not only excludes the residential school memories of former students in Labrador and others from recognition and redress but also denies a range of other memories of forced family rupture and child removal that are the heritage of colonial policies. National memory-making, at the TRC and beyond, should not be limited to corrective historiography of the past. "To articulate the past historically," as philosopher Walter Benjamin (1955, 255) argues, does not mean to recognize it "the way it really was" but "to seize hold of a memory as it flashes up at a moment of danger." In other words, memory is to be used in a way that "allows historical knowledge to remain critically germane to present struggles for social change" (Yoneyama 1999, 30). Given the lived legacies of relocation, residential schooling, and child welfare apprehensions in Labrador alone, and the need to devolve education, justice, and child welfare systems to Nunatsiavut government sovereignty, there is much work to which the remainders of national memory can be applied.

NOTES

1 The TRC's timeline of Indian residential schools is 1831–1996. Other sources date the beginning at 1879, when the Davin Report made federal support of church-run residential schools a matter of official government policy. There were also sporadic and short-lived efforts to introduce residential schooling for Indigenous children as early as the 1620s through the Jesuit and Récollets orders in Nouvelle-France.

2 Exemplary in this regard are Prime Minister Stephen Harper's statement that Canada has "no history of colonialism" during a press conference at the G20 Pittsburgh Summit in September 2009, as well as the June 2008 official apology for the Indian residential school system, which avoids mention of colonialism and characterizes the schools as a "discrete historical problem of educational malpractice" (Henderson and Wakeham 2009, 2).

3 Recent research has also confirmed the existence of federally sanctioned nutritional experiments in six residential schools (Mosby 2013). The TRC determined that over four thousand children died in residential schools due to inadequate medical care and neglect (quoted in

Walker 2014), a number that is expected to rise when an account is made of the TRC's review of the extensive historical records on the residential schools that were withheld by the federal government until a court order in January 2013.

4 Numerous institutions attended by Métis were also excluded from the Settlement Agreement. For further information, see Chartrand, Logan, and Daniels (2006) and Métis National Council (2012). Another important category of exceptions from the agreement was the Indian day schools. Students did not board in these generally church-operated and federally funded institutions but were often subject to similar abuses. Legal actions are currently being pursued in both cases.

5 This phrase refers to the 60th parallel, north of which lie the other three Inuit *nunaat* (homelands): Nunavut, Nunavik, and the Inuvialuit Settlement Area.

6 *Anderson v. Canada* represents former students of five residential schools: Lockwood School in Cartwright, Yale School in North West River, Makkovik Boarding School in Makkovik, Nain Boarding School in Nain, and St. Anthony Orphanage and Boarding School in St. Anthony. The latter was situated on the island of Newfoundland but was attended by numerous Labrador Inuit children.

7 Ethnocultural identification in Labrador is very complex and beyond the scope of this chapter. Labrador Métis predominantly identified as Settlers until the late 1970s (see Kennedy 1997) and have more recently self-identified as Nunatu Kavummiut, or Southern Inuit. In Labrador, the term "Settler" is widely used to describe the descendants of European fishermen and trappers who settled in Labrador beginning in the nineteenth century. At least initially, they commonly intermarried with Inuit (but see Ben-Dor 1966; and Kennedy 1982) and were called Kablunângajuit ("half white") (Ben-Dor 1966, 10) or, as one middle-aged Inuk woman told me, those who "live like us but [are] not us."

8 Inuit Nunangat refers collectively to the four Inuit nunaat in Canada.

REFERENCES

Aboriginal Affairs and Northern Development Canada. 2013. "Statistics on the Implementation of the Indian Residential Schools Settlement Agreement." http://www.aadnc-aandc.gc.ca/eng/1315320539682/1315320692192.

Ben-Dor, Shmuel. 1966. *Makkovik: Eskimos and Settlers in a Labrador Community: A Contrastive Study in Adaptation*. St. John's, NL: Institute for Social and Economic Research, Memorial University of Newfoundland.

Benjamin, Walter. 1955. *Illuminations: Essays and Reflections*. Ed. Hannah Arendt. Reprint, New York: Schocken Books, 2007.

Bhabha, Homi K. 1990. "DissemiNation: Time, Narrative, and the Margins of the Modern Nation." In *Nation and Narration*, ed. Homi K. Bhabha, 291–322. New York: Routledge.

Blackstock, Cindy. 2008. "Reconciliation Means Not Saying Sorry Twice: Lessons from Child Welfare in Canada." In *From Truth to Reconciliation: Transforming the Legacy of Residential Schools*, ed. Marlene Brant Castellano, Linda Archibald, and Mike DeGagné, 163–78. Ottawa: Aboriginal Healing Foundation. http://www.ahf.ca/downloads/from-truth-to-reconciliation-transforming-the-legacy-of-residential-schools.pdf.

Brice-Bennett, Carol. 1994. *Dispossessed: The Eviction of Inuit from Hebron, Labrador*. Ottawa: Royal Commission on Aboriginal Peoples.

–. 2000. *Reconciling with Memories: A Record of the Reunion at Hebron 40 Years after Relocation*. Nain, NL: Labrador Inuit Association.

Cattelino, Jessica R. 2010. "The Double Bind of American Indian Need-Based Sovereignty." *Cultural Anthropology* 25 (2): 235–62. http://dx.doi.org/10.1111/j.1548-1360.2010. 01058.x.

Chartrand, Larry N., Tricia E. Logan, and Judy D. Daniels. 2006. *Métis History and Experience and Residential Schools in Canada*. Ottawa: Aboriginal Healing Foundation.

Corntassel, Jeff, Chaw-win-is, and T'lakwadzi. 2009. "Indigenous Storytelling, Truth-Telling, and Community Approaches to Reconciliation." *English Studies in Canada* 35 (1): 137–59. http://dx.doi.org/10.1353/esc.0.0163.

Coulthard, Glen S. 2007. "Subjects of Empire: Indigenous Peoples and the 'Politics of Recognition' in Canada." *Contemporary Political Theory* 6 (4): 437–60. http://dx.doi. org/10.1057/palgrave.cpt.9300307.

Curtis, Charles S. 1963. "It Should Be Told: The Grenfell Mission's Work for Education, Concluded." *Among the Deep Sea Fishers* (International Grenfell Association) 61 (2): 54–57.

Das, Veena. 2007. *Life and Words: Violence and the Descent into the Ordinary*. Berkeley: University of California Press.

Das, Veena, Arthur Kleinman, Margaret Lock, Mamphela Ramphele, and Pamela Reynolds, eds. 2001. *Remaking a World: Violence, Social Suffering, and Recovery*. Berkeley: University of California Press. http://dx.doi.org/10.1525/california/9780520223295.001.0001.

Environics Research Group. 2008. *IRSRC – 2008 National Benchmark Survey*. Prepared for Indian Residential Schools Resolution Canada and the Truth and Reconciliation Commission of Canada. Ottawa: Environics Research Group.

Fassin, Didier, and Richard Rechtman. 2009. *The Empire of Trauma: An Inquiry into the Condition of Victimhood*. Princeton, NJ: Princeton University Press.

Flanagan, Patrick. 1984. "Schooling, Souls and Social Class: The Labrador Inuit." MA thesis, University of New Brunswick.

Foucault, Michel. 1977. *Language, Counter-Memory, Practice: Selected Essays and Interviews by Michel Foucault*. Ed. Donald F. Bouchard. Ithaca, NY: Cornell University Press.

Goffman, Erving. 1961. *Asylums: Essays on the Social Situation of Mental Patients and Other Inmates*. New York: Penguin Books.

Green, Robyn. 2012. "Unsettling Cures: Exploring the Limits of the Indian Residential School Settlement Agreement." *Canadian Journal of Law and Society* 27 (1): 129–48. http://dx.doi.org/10.3138/cjls.27.1.129.

Hanrahan, Maura. 2003. *The Lasting Breach: The Omission of Aboriginal People from the Terms of Union between Newfoundland and Canada and Its Ongoing Impacts*. Prepared for the Royal Commission on Renewing and Strengthening Our Place in Canada. St. John's, NL: Government of Newfoundland and Labrador.

Henderson, Jennifer, and Pauline Wakeham. 2009. "Colonial Reckoning, National Reconciliation? Aboriginal Peoples and the Culture of Redress in Canada." *English Studies in Canada* 35 (1): 1–26. http://dx.doi.org/10.1353/esc.0.0168.

Kennedy, John C. 1982. *Holding the Line: Ethnic Boundaries in a Northern Labrador Community*. St. John's, NL: Institute of Social and Economic Research, Memorial University of Newfoundland.

–. 1997. "Labrador Metis Ethnogenesis." *Ethnos* 62 (3–4): 5–23. http://dx.doi.org/10.1080/00141844.1997.9981550.

Kirmayer, Laurence, Cori Simpson, and Margaret Cargo. 2003. "Healing Traditions: Culture, Community and Mental Health Promotion with Canadian Aboriginal Peoples." *Australasian Psychiatry* 11 (1), supplement: S15–S23. http://dx.doi.org/10.1046/j.1038-5282.2003.02010.x.

Mackey, Eva. 1999. *The House of Difference: Cultural Politics and National Identity in Canada*. Toronto: University of Toronto Press.

–. 2012. "Tricky Myths: Settler Pasts and Landscapes of Innocence." In *Settling and Unsettling Memories: Essays in Canadian Public History*, ed. Nicole Neatby and Peter Hodgins, 310–39. Toronto: University of Toronto Press.

MacMillan, Miriam. 1951. *I Married an Explorer*. Watford, UK: Mayflower.

Métis National Council. 2012. *Nobody's Children: A Métis Nation Residential School Dialogue, March 28–29, 2012*. Surrey, BC: Raincoast Ventures.

Million, Dian. 2013. *Therapeutic Nations: Healing in an Age of Indigenous Human Rights*. Tucson: University of Arizona Press.

Mosby, Ian. 2013. "Administering Colonial Science: Nutrition Research and Human Biomedical Experimentation in Aboriginal Communities and Residential Schools, 1942–1952." *Social History* 46 (91): 145–72.

Paine, Robert. 1977. "Introduction." In *The White Arctic: Anthropological Essays on Tutelage and Ethnicity*, ed. Robert Paine, 3–6. St. John's, NL: Institute of Social and Economic Research, Memorial University of Newfoundland.

Povinelli, Elizabeth A. 2002. *The Cunning of Recognition: Indigenous Alterities and the Making of Australian Multiculturalism*. Durham, NC: Duke University Press. http://dx.doi.org/10.1215/9780822383673.

Renan, Ernest. 1882. "What Is a Nation?" Reprinted in *Nation and Narration*, ed. Homi K. Bhabha, 8–22. New York: Routledge, 1990.

Rowe, Frederick W. 1964. *The Development of Education in Newfoundland*. Toronto: Ryerson.

Samson, Colin. 2003. "Sexual Abuse and Assimilation: Oblates, Teachers and the Innu of Labrador." *Sexualities* 6 (1): 46–53.

Stern, Pamela R. 2010. *Daily Life of the Inuit*. Santa Barbara, CA: Greenwood.

Stevenson, Lisa. 2006. "The Ethical Injunction to Remember." In *Critical Inuit Studies: An Anthology of Contemporary Arctic Ethnography*, ed. Pamela R. Stern and Lisa Stevenson, 168–83. Lincoln: University of Nebraska Press.

Sturken, Marita. 1997. *Tangled Memories: The Vietnam War, the AIDS Epidemic, and the Politics of Remembering*. Berkeley: University of California Press.

Tanner, Adrian. 1998. "The Aboriginal Peoples of Newfoundland and Labrador and Confederation." *Newfoundland Studies* 14 (2): 238–52.

Taylor, Charles. 1992. *Multiculturalism and "the Politics of Recognition."* Princeton, NJ: Princeton University Press.

Tester, Frank J., and Peter Kulchyski. 1994. *Tammarniit (Mistakes): Inuit Relocation in the Eastern Arctic, 1939–63*. Vancouver: UBC Press.

Thobani, Sunera. 2007. *Exalted Subjects: Studies in the Making of Race and Nation in Canada*. Toronto: University of Toronto Press.

Trigger, Bruce G. 1986. *Natives and Newcomers: Canada's "Heroic Age" Reconsidered*. Montreal and Kingston: McGill-Queen's University Press.

Trouillot, Michel-Rolph. 1995. *Silencing the Past: Power and the Production of History*. Boston: Beacon.

Walker, Connie. 2014. "New Documents May Shed Light on Residential School Deaths." *CBC News*, January 7. http://www.cbc.ca/news/aboriginal/new-documents -may-shed-light-on-residential-school-deaths-1.2487015.

Wall, William M. 1960. *The Wall Report: A Survey of Educational Problems in Selected Study Areas in Northern Newfoundland and Labrador*. Prepared for the Board of Directors of the International Grenfell Association. St.John's, NL: International Grenfell Association.

White, Ottenheimer and Baker (law firm). 2007a. *In the Matter of: A Submission to Canada Pursuant to Article Twelve of the Indian Residential Schools Settlement Agreement. Request by the Government of Nunatsiavut to Add Additional Schools to the List of Recognized Residential Schools in Schedule "F."* Prepared for the Residential Schools Settlement Agreement.

–. 2007b. *In the Matter of: A Submission to Canada Pursuant to Article Twelve of the Indian Residential Schools Settlement Agreement. Request by the Government of Nunatsiavut to Add Additional Schools to the List of Recognized Residential Schools in Schedule "F," Part II*. Prepared for the Residential Schools Settlement Agreement.

–. 2008. *In the Matter of: A Re-submission to Canada Pursuant to Article Twelve of the Indian Residential Schools Settlement Agreement. Re-submission by the Government of Nunatsiavut to Add Additional Schools to the List of Recognized Residential Schools in Schedule "F."* Prepared for the Residential Schools Settlement Agreement.

Yoneyama, Lisa. 1994. "Taming the Memoryscape: Hiroshima's Urban Renewal." In *Remapping Memory: The Politics of Timespace*, ed. Jonathan Boyarin, 99–136. Minneapolis: University of Minnesota Press.

–. 1999. *Hiroshima Traces: Time, Space, and the Dialectics of Memory*. Berkeley: University of California Press. http://dx.doi.org/10.1525/california/9780520085862.001.0001.

Žižek, Slavoj. 2000. *The Ticklish Subject: The Absent Centre of Political Ontology*. London: Verso.

–. 2004. "The Structure of Domination Today: A Lacanian View." *Studies in East European Thought* 56 (4): 383–403. http://dx.doi.org/10.1023/B:SOVI.0000043002.02424.ca.

7

Remembering Residential Schools, Accounting for Decolonization through Development: Conflicting Viewpoints

KARINE VANTHUYNE

ARTICULATED IN THE CONTEXT of state and church officials' denial of the abusive nature and disastrous long-lasting impacts of the Indian residential school system, survivors' public testimonies of forced residential schooling have tended to focus on neglect, mistreatment, and enduring forms of victimization. In the courtroom, since the first lawsuit alleging abuse was filed by a survivor in 1990, former students have presented accounts of utter isolation, cruel acts of aggression and humiliation by school staff, as well as lives crippled by substance abuse and family violence in the aftermath of residential schooling. The growing popularity, in Indigenous and non-Indigenous circles alike, of healing theories stressing self-revelation as the key to recovery from traumatic experiences (Chansonneuve 2005) has prompted survivors to focus on victimization at the schools in their testimonials. More recently, the non-Indigenous Canadian population's persistent lack of awareness and acknowledgment of the genocidal nature of the residential school system encouraged the Truth and Reconciliation Commission of Canada to make public statements dealing with "horrible, sorrowful, traumatizing experiences" (Niezen 2013, 59) at its national events (see also Capitaine, this volume). In so doing, the TRC hoped to rouse the larger Canadian population's indignation and therefore support for its policy recommendations to further address the historical injustices and legacies of the residential schools.

English-language and literature scholar Sam McKegney (2006, 34) notes that the framing of residential schools as sites of abuse and causes of ongoing trauma, although "politically expedient, historically valuable, and potentially effective in struggles towards healing," has created "a discursive climate that conditions how Survivors are expected (both by the public and by academics) to recall their residential school experiences." In this climate, accounts of the residential school system that stress positive experiences and outcomes tend to be criticized (e.g., Boldt 1990) or discouraged. Anthropologist Ronald Niezen (2013, 59) argues that at the TRC's events, survivors "who think of themselves as having suffered only minimally or not at all" may also come to think of themselves "as having nothing to say." As a result, Niezen (ibid., 155) claims, competing accounts of the residential school system are sidelined, preventing a fuller account of "the actual dynamics of residential institutions." Alternative narrative strategies employed by survivors to overcome residential school related traumas, I argue, are also marginalized.

I highlight the variety of narrative strategies that survivors employ to account for the residential school system and its aftermath, and I identify what may prompt the use of one narrative framework over another. Drawing on his work on a Coeur d'Alene family's narratives of "forced removal from homelands, mandated residential schools and forced adoption programs," anthropologist Aaron Denham (2008, 397) calls for distinguishing historical trauma from the historical-trauma response. This response, he argues, may or may not be composed of the dysfunction usually associated with historical trauma in the literature describing this condition within Indigenous populations. Notably, this response may also include expressions of resistance and resilience. In this case, I describe how forced residential schooling and the ratification of the 1975 James Bay and Northern Quebec Agreement (JBNQA) are alternately storied by members of the Cree Nation of Wemindji through a narrative of disculturation and irreparable loss or through a narrative of resistance and resilience. I then demonstrate that one of the main factors influencing what type of narrative is employed by the Cree I interviewed in Wemindji is how the residential school system and the JBNQA figure into these actors' views of their nation's colonial history, decolonization processes, and agenda for decolonization.

In Canada the history of Indigenous peoples' relationships with the Crown and the provincial and federal settler states has varied tremendously through time and space. It has included trade partnerships and military alliances, feuding and violent conquest, colonial policies of tutelage and assimilation, and the more recent recognition of some Indigenous and treaty rights as well as legislated self-government (Miller 1989; Sioui 1999; Dickason and Newbigging 2010). As I have found in Wemindji, these various historical experiences and processes, including forced residential schooling, are the objects of competing narratives, with Wemindji's growing integration into the Quebec and Canadian settler states being the object of diverging moral projects (Cole 2003). The concept of moral projects was proposed by anthropologist Jennifer Cole (ibid., 99) to highlight how "local visions of what makes a good, just community, and the ways in which these conceptions of community reciprocally engage peoples' notion of what constitutes a good life ... shape agents' selection, interpretation and use of particular narratives." According to Cole, most of the scholarly literature that has analyzed the complex interplay between collective representations of the past and singular remembrances in the social sciences has tended to ignore the agents that produce them, losing sight of a central question, What is at stake when one uses a particular narrative for recounting past events? Cole (ibid., 98) argues that "after all, our memories are part of a landscape of action and the broader moral and political projects and historical circumstances in which narratives are inevitably situated." To make this argument, Cole explains, is not to return to the well-rehearsed view that the past is reread through the interests of the present (Antze and Lambek 1996). This argument points instead to the need to consider how individual concerns and desires interact with wider socio-political formations in moulding individual recollections of pivotal historical events. I therefore show how competing moral and political views of the relatively recent integration of Wemindji into the Quebec and Canadian settler states following the JBNQA shape the way that forced residential schooling is accounted for in this community – either as the beginning of a history of disculturation and loss or as what has allowed the Cree "to take things over."

Settler Colonialism in Eeyou Istchee

The Eastern James Bay Cree (here, referred to as "the Cree") have lived in Eeyou Istchee, their homeland of 400,000 square kilometres, since the glaciers melted about nine thousand years ago (Dickason and Newbigging 2010). Although their interactions with "Whitemen," as the Cree call non-Indigenous people in English (Coon Come 2004, 156), started in 1668, when they first became involved in the fur trade of the Hudson's Bay Company, it was not until the 1930s that the Cree's economic and political autonomy was significantly challenged. As anthropologist Toby Morantz (2002, 25) argues, for close to three centuries, the Cree were able "to exploit, shape or negotiate the circumstances of the fur trade that impinged on their lives." They remained foremost subsistence hunters and maintained control of their economic and political strategies. The transfer of Hudson's Bay Company lands to Canada in 1870, from Canada to Ontario in 1897 and 1902, and from Canada to Quebec in 1898 and 1912 did not change this situation. It was instead the sudden drop in the international demand for furs during the Great Depression, combined with the severe shortage in animal resources, that left the Cree with few alternatives but to accept the growing interference of the Quebec and Canadian governments in their lives. Beginning in 1932, Quebec established beaver preserves in the James Bay region. These preserves excluded nonlocal trappers, who had been the main impetus for the depletion, and limited Cree harvests until beaver populations recovered (Morantz 2002; Feit 2005).

Drawing on extensive archival and ethnographic research, anthropologist Harvey Feit (2005) cogently argues that although it constituted a project of state governance, the beaver preserve acknowledged the Cree's governance, in addition to affirming an expectation that the lands they occupied would be used to protect a Cree way of life. However, I argue that notwithstanding their ongoing autonomy, the Cree became, through this co-management process, more and more visible to the Quebec and Canadian settler states and, as a result, more and more perceived by them as wards of the state to be subjected to the 1876 Indian Act. It was during this period that, in Eeyou Istchee Cree territory, band council elections (officially required by federal law since 1899) were first organized, medical services and family allowances started to be offered, and forced residential schooling (in effect since 1920) began to be enforced (Morantz 2002).

Whereas some Cree, as seen in the next section, view residential schooling as one of the darkest chapters of their lives, others credit it with having provided the very tools that made it possible for them to effectively challenge the further encroachment of their territory. In April 1971 the Quebec government announced its plan to construct a massive hydroelectric complex on La Grande River (Niezen 2009). It had not previously taken steps to consult with the Cree and Inuit populations that would be affected by it. Cree and Inuit leaders, who had met in residential schools, hired lawyers and researchers to launch a court challenge seeking an injunction to halt the project until Cree and Inuit territorial rights were recognized by the Government of Quebec. This led to the JBNQA, which, in essence, involves the extinction of some of the Cree and Inuit rights to their traditional territories in exchange for a guaranteed measure of financial and administrative autonomy on their lands. Specifically, this so-called modern treaty (Miller 2009), and the subsequent Cree-Naskapi Act of 1984, provided the Cree with regional autonomy in the administration of education, healthcare, and social services through the establishment of the Cree School Board and the Cree Board of Health and Social Services of James Bay.[1] It also created a land management regime according to which the Cree have exclusive rights over Category 1 lands (2 percent of their territory), sole rights to hunt and fish in Category 2 lands (20 percent of their territory), and exemption from provincial game regulations and guaranteed harvesting rights to some species in Category 3 lands (the remaining 78 percent). The JBNQA also implemented the Income Security Program for Cree hunters and trappers, which provides a guaranteed income for participants in the program who spend most of their time each year in the forest. Feit (1991) argues that although this program has allowed an increasing number of Cree to make hunting, fishing, and trapping their primary productive activity, it has more largely contributed to the consecration of subsistence hunting as a means of social reproduction and resistance against assimilation.

Generally acknowledged to have been signed under duress, as ongoing construction of the first phase of the hydroelectric complex overshadowed the court proceedings and the subsequent negotiations of the agreement, the JBNQA ended up being more favourable to the state's right to exploit natural resources on Cree territory than to the Cree's desire to protect their hunting way of life (Penn 1997; Scott 2005). On the one hand, clear-cutting practices were extensively damaging the hunting territories of the Cree in the southern third of the James Bay territory. The Cree were unable to submit forestry operations to the environmental review procedures established under the JBNQA. On the other hand, government obligations regarding the funding of the infrastructure, social services, and economic development of the communities were not implemented effectively. Starting in the 1980s, the new regional government of the Cree therefore engaged in legal and political action, as prospects for community empowerment in the context of a loss of control over regional development became increasingly grim (Grand Council of the Crees 1995; McRae 2001; Craik 2004). In response, the Quebec government did not follow up on a number of its obligations under the JBNQA, eventually leading to a new round of negotiations between Cree leaders and the Government of Quebec, which were concluded by a major treaty modification in 2002, entitled the New

Relationship Agreement (also known as "Paix des braves"). According to this agreement, the Quebec government would pay $3.5 billion over fifty years to the Cree in return for the Cree dropping their lawsuits over past violations and the failed implementation of the JBNQA (Scott 2005; Niezen 2009). Moreover, the agreement also granted them the right to benefit directly from future extractive development on their land through the payment of royalties to the Grand Council of the Cree, the regional government of the Eastern James Bay Cree created by the JBNQA. In so doing, Quebec explicitly recognized the existence of the Cree as a nation, on terms that the Cree themselves had been demanding. It acknowledged that the Cree Nation had the authority to have a say and an ongoing stake in development on the bounded expanse of its territorial homeland. The linchpin of the New Relationship Agreement was that the Cree consented to another major hydroelectric project, the EM1-A Rupert River Diversion.

Contrasting Narratives of Residential Schools and the JBNQA

During my ethnographic field research in the Cree Nation of Wemindji, I explored how the impacts of the Settlement Agreement, the JBNQA, and the New Relationship Agreement were accounted for in this community. Although the accounts I collected from individuals who consented to speak with me about the residential schools varied,[2] I found that, ultimately, the people I talked with, whether survivors, their family members, or community workers involved in either healing or redressing the legacy of residential schooling in Wemindji, followed one of two contrasting narratives or a combination of both. The first narrative is an account of disculturation and loss – of being stripped of one's family connections and core cultural markers. The second narrative is an account of skilful appropriation of Whitemen's tools in order "to take things over" and recover the self-reliance of one's people. In order to illustrate how the Cree mobilized these narratives to account for brutal and profound disruptions in their personal, family, and community lives, I have chosen to single out two life stories. In anthropology, life stories are collected and analyzed, following a subjectivist approach, to document how individuals give meaning to pivotal events in their lives (Mohia 2000). From this perspective, life stories are seen as the product of complex intersubjective dynamics, both external and internal. They stem from the social and political construction of subjects, such as being identified as Indian and forcefully sent to school or being identified as Cree and taught how to survive on the land. They also stem from the various ways that subjects understand themselves and construct their worlds, whether as victims of the loss of family bonds and core cultural markers or as skilful actors in their nation's decolonization processes. The life stories I present below thus enable us to see how individual life trajectories, cultural constructions of what constitutes a good life – Cole's (2003) moral projects – and larger social and political forces complexly interact to shape the way that key historical chapters such as the residential school system and the JBNQA are remembered and narrated.

Although a woman gives voice to the narrative of loss and a man gives voice to the narrative of resistance in the following section, it is important to note that I did not find that one narrative tended to be voiced more by one gender than another. Memories are definitely gendered (Hirsch and Smith 2002), but in the context of this research, the languages of victimization and resilience were equally spoken by both males and females – a phenomenon also noted by sociologist Brieg Capitaine (this volume).

"They Stripped Us"

Florence Peace Georgekish was born in November 1956 on Old Factory Island, Wemindji's original location. Florence's family moved to Moose Factory in 1959, along with numerous other families from the region. Increased employment opportunities on the western shore of James Bay, thanks to the Ontario Northland Railway, which was extended to reach the town of Moosonee in 1932, provoked a large exodus of Eastern James Bay Cree to that region in the 1950s (Morantz 2002). In 1962, at the age of six, Florence was sent to Bishop Horden Hall, a residential school run by the Anglican Church in Moose Factory. Like most of those I interviewed who recalled their time in residential schools as a very dark chapter of their lives, Florence remembered details of her first day at the school:

> I remember the first day I went to school. And I was anxious to go. I wanted to go. It looked nice. And when I did go, it wasn't what I expected. I remember going up those stairs and my parents standing at the bottom of the stairs ... They sent the girls this way and the boys that way and that was it. We never got to see anybody. We only saw each other from afar. We couldn't talk to each other. And they stripped you the first day. I remember my parents buying me this new outfit, but that was it. I have

never seen it again, gone. They took it. Everybody had the same uniforms. They stripped you, they put you in the shower ... I still remember that. It's very clear. To this day, it's still very clear, that very first day. And I never got to see my sister. She was about three years older than me. We never got to eat together. I think it's when our bond started to break.[3]

Even though her parents lived in town, Florence was allowed to see them and her siblings, who also attended Bishop Horden Hall, for only a month or so during the summer breaks. Florence attended that institution for eight years. Afterward, she was sent to a nonresidential high school in Sault Ste. Marie by the Department of Indian Affairs. When I asked Florence what she remembered most about residential school, she replied,

The military type routine. By six we were up. We had to make our beds, wash up, line up for Baptist. As you got older, too, you got chores. It was like that every day. The same routine. And then we went to school. Once we got at the residence for lunch, again line up ... And it was pretty strict for the first couple of years, and then, as time went on, I didn't see as much abuse.

Like all of those I interviewed who centred their accounts on the hardships they had suffered at residential schools, Florence did not mention any abuse that she had experienced herself. She did however describe what she was forced to witness as a bystander: "That first year that I was there, I've seen a girl who had wet her bed. She was forced to put her sheet on the top of her head in front of the whole group. Imagine what that did to her."

The other kinds of mistreatments that were recounted to me by other former residential school students in Wemindji included harsh punishments for being caught speaking Cree, not being notified when a sibling had passed away (and not having had the opportunity to attend the funeral as a result), and being bullied and beaten up by peers.

As quoted above, when Florence described her first day in school, she identified the breaking of family bonds as one of the lasting impacts of forced residential schooling in her family. When I asked her how attending Bishop Horden Hall had impacted her, she said, "To this day, that's what affects me a lot. There is not that closeness." Asked whether this lack of intimacy with her siblings had affected her relationship with her children, she said,

It goes from generation to the next. I hear some elders saying that a long time ago we used to always be hugging and kissing, but now you don't see it that much. There is no touch ... We've lost our parenting skills. I had to learn on my own to be good at upbringing children. I tried to bring my kids up the best way I could, but they still had problems. And like I said, that touching, that bonding, because you weren't able to get it, you lost it, so it's really hard to give it to your kids. I tried to give them as much as I could when they were small. But when I hug someone, I don't know how to say it, but I'm not at ease.

In addition to the breaking of family bonds and the loss of parenting skills, the enduring legacies of the residential school system in Wemindji outlined by the other former students, family members of former students, and community leaders I spoke to in the village included the loss of fluency in the Cree language and the interruption of the transmission of essential skills such as hunting and trapping, as well as alcohol and drug abuse.

In 1982 Florence's parents moved back to Wemindji. Radical increases in employment opportunities, improvements in infrastructure and social services, and the establishment of the Income Security Program for Cree hunters and trappers enticed numerous Eastern James Bay Cree families who had resettled in Moose Factory or Moosonee in the 1950s to move back to the region (Niezen 2009). At that time, Florence had already left home and was residing in Val d'Or. She returned to Wemindji only in the late 1980s, before moving with her husband to another Cree community of Eeyou Istchee, Waskaganish, in the early 1990s. When I asked her about the impact of the JBNQA in Wemindji, she did not focus much on how it had allowed her parents to "return to the bush," where they were able to make hunting, fishing, and trapping their primary productive activities, as I later learned in my interview with her. Instead, she replied,

I think this is when a lot of social issues came in. It happened so suddenly. I wasn't here, I was still in Ontario [finishing high school in Sault Ste. Marie] when it happened. But just from reading articles and stuff or talking to people, I think it happened too suddenly. They weren't able to adjust themselves to the new changes [with a lot of money coming in] ... and jobs ... people. The main focus is on the money ... I think people should learn to find the work they are interested in. It should be about what you like to do, not how much you can make. I worked so many years, till I was fifty-five ... It wasn't really how much you can have; it was just to get by. Now people are so materialistic. They got to have every new gadget.

Florence decried materialism as being a new, foreign value that an increasing number of residents in Wemindji embraced as a result of the sudden proliferation of employment opportunities that ensued following the ratification of the JBNQA. From her perspective, being materialistic means considering a higher income to be a priority over any other criteria when deciding what kind of employment activity to invest oneself in. According to Florence, such materialism has contributed to many social issues. She did not name the issues here, but later in our interview, she identified them as being drug and alcohol abuse, broken marriages, as well as child neglect.

As described above, Florence's primary memories of her time at Bishop Horden Hall included being stripped of the new outfit her parents had just bought her and the breaking of family bonds. Likewise, from her perspective, the JBNQA has damaged the Cree's connections to their ancestors and has "stripped" them of their traditional "outfit" and their particular ways of being in the world and relating to one another, provoking important social turmoil.

"We Took Things Over"

Fred Blackned was born inland in 1940, on his family's winter grounds near Little Pike Lake, a few kilometres from the Old Factory settlement. In 1946, at the age of six, he was sent to Toronto to be hospitalized. Since his parents had left Old Factory for their winter grounds and could not be reached when he was released, he was sent to Bishop Horden Hall, where he spent the rest of the winter. When he returned to Old Factory in 1947, he started to attend the summer school that Catholic (Oblate) missionaries had been running there since 1937 (Paul-Émile 1952). In that school, which was minimally funded by the federal government, the children were taught prayers, basic reading skills, and syllabics. Fred really enjoyed these classes, he explained to me in an interview, as he was eager to learn.[4] Even though forced residential schooling was first enforced in the region in the 1930s, Fred's parents did not let him attend Bishop Horden Hall for another few years. One of Fred's older brothers had passed away while at school, so they were afraid that their convalescent son would not be properly taken care of there. Fred's father also wanted to teach him how to survive on the land if he ever decided to make hunting, fishing, and trapping his primary sources of income. As Fred remembered,

> My father told me, "Keep that in mind all the time. Keep what you have learned, what you can do to survive [on the land] if something happens ... This is the Cree way of doing things. You are a Cree. You want to keep that, even if you will be out in another place, because if you ever come back, you will still be able to remember what you have learned ... the traditional way of life."

In 1953, at the age of thirteen, Fred left Old Factory for Bishop Horden Hall, which he attended for five years, until he turned eighteen in 1958. During his time in residential school, he returned to Old Factory only for a few weeks each summer. When I asked him what he recalled the most about his time at Bishop Horden Hall, Fred shared numerous anecdotes of how he had been able to reverse situations of intimidation by supervisors or older students to his advantage, as the following excerpt illustrates:

> There was one time that we were lining up, and I was in the line. I thought I was in the line, and then [the supervisor] came slowly and said, "I've told you to get in the line." I said, "I am in the line." Then he pulled me away from the lineup and started whining and said, "Either you decide to line up with the other students or you're gonna miss your meal." And I said, "Okay. Are you sure you want me to miss my meal? You would like that?" And then I walked up, and another guy came behind me, and he said, "I'm in. It's gonna be two of us now." And the [supervisor] was really afraid. He thought that we would beat him up or something. He said, "Get in the line." I said, "For supper?" [He replied,] "Yeah." [I said,] "Okay."

Among the Wemindji accounts of the residential school system that focused on more positive experiences, one common characteristic was an emphasis on the students' capacity to use skilful schemes in order to circumvent or defeat abusive policies, practices, or situations, such as the prohibition against speaking Cree, the impossibility of keeping in touch with siblings, or the bullying suffered from staff or older students.

When I asked Fred how he had been impacted by his stay at Bishop Horden Hall, he replied,

> I don't regret attending residential school. And I don't complain nothing about residential school. Whatever happened to me, it could have happened, the same thing, at home, if I had stayed with my parents. I could have been spanked by them or told, "Do this," even if I don't like it. So I always thought that, as a result of having attended residential school, I have learned something. If I didn't attend residential school, I would probably not be able to speak to you. I learned my English there. And whatever happened in residential school, I've always believed that was the way God wanted me to live in this world. I don't cry when I think about residential school. I've seen some cry and say that they didn't like it. But I have always said that God wanted me in residential school. It has helped me in many ways.

From my conversations with him before this interview, I knew that Fred had applied for the Common Experience Payment. When I asked why he had applied for this compensation program even though he "don't complain nothing about residential school," he answered,

> The only thing that I can say that I don't really accept – when I was in residential school, I was told to speak English. Even during the first stay I was there. I didn't know how to speak another language. One time, I tried to make something known, and there was no way I knew how to say that in English, so I had to speak in Cree. Some other person who worked in the residential school told me that I shouldn't do that. I shouldn't talk to somebody in Cree who doesn't understand Cree. And that didn't look too good to me. Give me a time to learn, you know, how to say things in English, before ordering me to speak it.

When he left Bishop Horden Hall in 1958, Fred was hoping to pursue his postsecondary education. It was not until 1963 that the Department of Indian Affairs agreed to send him to North Bay and then to Sudbury to complete his studies in vocational training schools. In the meantime, Fred helped his parents move from Old Factory to Wemindji in 1960. He then divided his time between working in Toronto in the summer and hunting and trapping with his father elsewhere in Ontario in the winter. At that time, the Quebec government had banned hunting and trapping on the eastern shore of James Bay, given the serious depletion of beaver populations in the region. Numerous Cree therefore went to Ontario to trap (Morantz 2002). Following his studies in Sudbury, Fred returned to Wemindji, where he worked as a carpenter until 1970, when he was elected as the chief of Wemindji's band council for three years. As he recalled,

> Right from the start, I got involved in putting the [James Bay and Northern Quebec] Agreement together. First, we had the agreement in principle ... signed on November 15, 1974. And then we worked from there. We had a lot of meetings with people [in the then eight Eastern James Bay Cree communities] to tell them ... "Listen, here we have a chance to take over something from the government, whatever they are doing to get things done in the community ... You're never gonna see that the government is doing things in your community, and you're never gonna see your community get better and better, unless *we* do it ... We have to take over the education from the government, take over the local government, take over health services, take over housing, build houses in our community, to run our community, our own office with our own equipment to maintain our roads" ... At that time, we didn't have running water in our community. I told them that we can have running water, you know.

For Fred Blackned, as for the other young Cree political leaders who participated in the negotiations of the JBNQA, this agreement was about guaranteeing some measure of financial and administrative control over their territory in a context they perceived as being characterized by the decreasing viability of their traditional subsistence – hunting, fishing, and trapping – as well as by their consequential increasing dependency on the federal government's assistance programs. In the 1970s a large number of Cree were collecting welfare payments (Feit 1991). For Fred and his fellow political leaders, the JBNQA would provide them with the means to build their villages, create local employment, and ensure that they would have a say in how exactly their villages would be developed and governed.

Competing Moral Projects of Self-Reliance and Reciprocity

Florence and Fred provided quite different accounts of their experiences in residential school and of the impacts of forced schooling and the JBNQA on their community. Whereas Florence stressed abuse, suffering, and tragic losses, Fred emphasized resistance to mistreatments and the acquisition of literacy skills in English that allowed him and his peers to "take things over." It is important to note that these differences do not mean that Fred disagreed with Florence that his people had been unjustly victimized in the residential school system. Although he "don't complain nothing about residential school" because "whatever happened to me, it could have happened, the same thing, at home," he did denounce the fact that he was forbidden to speak Cree: "Give me a time to learn, you know, how to say things in English, before ordering me to speak it."

I argue that, beyond the differing personal experiences at Bishop Horden Hall and their life trajectories afterward, the contrasts between Florence's and Fred's narratives are grounded in divergent, yet closely interconnected, moral projects that emphasize reciprocity. As explained earlier, moral projects, according to Cole (2003), refer to local perspectives of what a just community is and of how people should individually and collectively conduct themselves in order to attain that ideal. Drawing on extensive ethnographic fieldwork conducted in Whapmasgoostui, another Cree community of Eeyou Istchee, anthropologist Naomi Adelson (2000) suggests that for the Cree, conceptions of what constitutes a good life are anchored in ideals of *miyupimaatisiiun* (being alive well). As she explains, the Cree conceive of miyupimaatisiiun as being rooted in the practice of activities that distinguish them from Whitemen, such as "living in the bush and partaking in all that the bush life offers" (ibid., 108). In the accounts above, both Florence and Fred expressed ideas of who they were that referred to similar conceptions of miyupimaatisiiun. They both identified themselves as belonging to a group, a "we," that was fundamentally different from that of Whitemen. Like the Cree with whom Adelson spoke, Fred described this difference as his people's capacity "to survive on the land" – to hunt and trap for subsistence. Although Florence did not identify subsistence hunting and trapping as what characterized the Cree, she did refer to being non-materialistic – that is, to be working "just to get by" – as a key component of her people's identity. This view that the Cree have traditionally worked just enough to sustain themselves is, in fact, closely related to their conceptualization of hunting as a fundamentally reciprocal, noncumulative, subsistence activity. As Feit (1991) explains, from the Cree's point of view, animals give themselves to hunters so that humans may live, and hunters, in exchange, respect their souls, make proper use of their bodies, and share the gift of food with other humans. Fred and Florence thus shared a common notion of Cree identity as being based on a particular, essentially reciprocal, way of relating to their natural and social environments. Where Fred's and Florence's narratives diverged was in their assessment of their people's ability to remain who they essentially were/are in the context of the increasing integration of the Cree into Quebec and Canada's market economy since the ratification of the JBNQA.

Florence asserted that, with the ratification of the JBNQA and the increased employment opportunities that ensued, her people had become materialistic. She said that today people's "main focus is on [making] money" to purchase "every new gadget." In contrast, Fred said that, through the achievement of self-governance in education, health services, local infrastructure, and economic development thanks to the JBNQA, his people had regained their capacity to be self-reliant and thus to reciprocate. Despite agreeing on what it means to be Cree, Fred and Florence disagreed on what it had meant for their people to increasingly open their territory to Whitemen-led development. This disagreement undoubtedly had much to do with their personal life experiences. Fred had been able to continue to trap and hunt for subsistence while holding a salaried position at the band council. Florence rarely went out to the bush and had more recently witnessed the drying-up of the Rupert River near her new community, Waskaganish, and the impact of this change on traditional fishing practices.

Similar disagreements regarding the Cree's ability to maintain their cultural identity in the face of growing externally led development in their territory were expressed, reports anthropologist Brian Craik (2004), during the community consultations that preceded the ratification of the New Relationship Agreement. As Craik (ibid., 183) explains, not everyone agreed that consenting to another major hydroelectric project was a good thing:

> Those who opposed the agreement articulated a view of the Cree as stewards of the land and stated that the people should not accept the diversion of the [Rupert] river and more flooding ... They ... claimed that the proposed project would ruin the Cree way of life and that the land should be preserved for future generations. Those who promoted the agreement ... eschewed the vision of the Cree as stewards and spoke of this view as portraying them as janitors, taking care of the territory so that others could develop it. They claimed that the Cree way of life would continue,

as the harmful effects of the project would be relatively small ... and they pointed to the growing population of unemployed young Cree who need opportunities.

What is the impact of the increasing number of major hydroelectric dams, logging industries, and mines in Cree territory? Does it necessarily entail the demise of their traditional ways of relating to their environment? Does it signify the death of a cultural identity anchored in self-reliance and reciprocity? Whereas some do not see a contradiction between cultural autonomy and the ratification of agreements with extractive companies (Lapointe and Scott forthcoming) or forestry corporations (Feit 2004), others do. Such is the dilemma, I argue, that currently underlies contrasting narratives of forced residential schooling in Wemindji.

✒

Drawing on Jennifer Cole's (2003) work on moral projects and historical narratives, this chapter highlights how divergent views of First Nations colonial history and the decolonization process have shaped survivors' accounts of the residential school system. Two types of historical narratives of forced schooling were prevalent in Wemindji: one focused on mistreatments and the loss of close family relations, and the other focused on resistance to abuses and the useful acquisition of English literacy to "take things over." Both accounts are underlined by a common ideal of miyupimaatisiiun, or "being alive well," rooted in the conception of a specifically Cree (i.e., nonwhite) way of relating to the world. These accounts differ, however, in their assessment of the Cree still "being alive well" following abusive experiences in residential schools and the implementation of the JBNQA. Whereas the first account deplored that the Cree had lost their closeness and their cultural, nonmaterialistic way of relating to their social world, the second one emphasized that the Cree had skilfully managed to maintain their self-reliance. This disagreement echoes ongoing debates about the ability of the Cree to maintain their cultural identity in the face of growing externally led development in their homeland, such as hydroelectric dams, forestry industries, and mines.

As analyzed in detail by sociologist Eric Woods in this volume, there has been an important shift in representation of the residential school system on the national scene. From their initial representation as a humanitarian, even sacred, enterprise, residential schools have come to be seen as a terrible tragedy. However, like anthropologist Arie Molema and in contrast with anthropologist Simone Poliandri, both contributors to this volume, I demonstrate that this new dominant historical narrative has not necessarily taken root at the local level. Thanks to the new truth that systematic abuses were committed in the name of "civilization" in Canada through the residential school system, some survivors are acknowledging for the first time that they were molested while at school (Vanthuyne forthcoming). Nonetheless, when they provided accounts of their time in residential school, other Cree focused on more positive experiences and impacts. I believe they did so to highlight their people's capacity to resist past and ongoing colonial domination. Through restorying (Alfred and Corntassel 2005), they subverted a dominant narrative that positions Indigenous communities as essentially damaged.

ACKNOWLEDGMENTS

I foremost offer my most sincere gratitude to Fred Blackned, Jimmy Blackned, Florence Peace Georgekish, Mary Ruth Georgekish, Rodney Mark, Dorothy Stewart, Rev. Rod Brant Francis, Rev. Lisa Brant Francis, and all the other research participants in my project who have asked to remain anonymous. *Mishtamiikwehch*. I have learned so much from you all!

An earlier version of this chapter was presented at the conference "Native Residential Schools in Quebec: Legacies for Research," Université de Montréal, April 2013. I thank the conference audience and the anonymous reviewers of this chapter for their insightful comments. I also acknowledge my research assistants, Katherine Davis, Kristin Glenn, Halyna Mokrushyna, and Audrey Rousseau, for their valuable help, as well as the University of Ottawa for funding the research on which this chapter draws.

NOTES

1 The Inuit have negotiated separate arrangements in this domain (Rodon and Grey 2009).
2 Following anthropologist Veena Das's (2007, 6) work on narratives of mass violence in India, I acknowledge silence as another "narrative" strategy through which survivors "pick up the pieces and ... live in this very place of devastation." For a full discussion of this topic in the

context of the aftermath of Guatemala's genocide of 1981–83, see Vanthuyne (2014, esp. Chapters 2 and 5).

3 Florence Peace Georgekish, interview with author, Wemindji, July 16, 2012. All of Florence's quotations are from this interview.

4 Fred Blackned, interview with author, Wemindji, July 25, 2012. All of Fred's quotations are from this interview.

REFERENCES

Adelson, Naomi. 2000. *"Being Alive Well": Health and the Politics of Cree Well-Being.* Toronto: University of Toronto Press.

Alfred, Taiaiake, and Jeff Corntassel. 2005. "Being Indigenous: Resurgences against Contemporary Colonialism." *Government and Opposition* 40 (4): 597–614. http://dx.doi.org/10.1111/j.1477-7053.2005.00166.x.

Antze, Paul, and Michael Lambek. 1996. *Tense Past: Cultural Essays in Trauma and Memory.* New York: Routledge.

Boldt, Menno. 1990. "Review of *Indian School Days.*" *Canadian Literature* (124–25): 311–12.

Chansonneuve, Deborah. 2005. *Reclaiming Connections: Understanding Residential School Trauma among Aboriginal People.* Ottawa: Aboriginal Healing Foundation.

Cole, Jennifer. 2003. "Narratives and Moral Projects: Generational Memories of the Malagasy 1947 Rebellion." *Ethos* (Berkeley, California) 31 (1): 95–126. http://dx.doi.org/10.1525/eth.2003.31.1.95.

Coon Come, Matthew. 2004. "Survival in the Context of Mega-Resource Development: Experiences of the James Bay Crees and the First Nations of Canada." In *In the Way of Development: Indigenous Poeples, Life Projects and Globalization,* ed. Mario Blaser, Harvey A. Feit, and Glenn McRae, 153–64. London: Zed Books and International Development Research Centre.

Craik, Brian. 2004. "The Importance of Working Together: Exclusions, Conflicts and Participation in James Bay, Quebec." In *In the Way of Development: Indigenous Peoples, Life Projects and Globalization,* ed. Mario Blaser, Harvey A. Feit, and Glenn McRae, 166–86. London: Zed Books and International Development Research Centre.

Das, Veena. 2007. *Life and Words: Violence and the Descent into the Ordinary.* Berkeley: University of California Press.

Denham, Aaron R. 2008. "Rethinking Historical Trauma: Narratives of Resilience." *Transcultural Psychiatry* 45 (3): 391–414. http://dx.doi.org/10.1177/1363461508094673.

Dickason, Olive Patricia, and William Newbigging. 2010. *A Concise History of Canada's First Nations.* 2nd ed. Don Mills, ON: Oxford University Press.

Feit, Harvey A. 1991. "Gifts of the Land: Hunting Territories, Guaranteed Incomes and the Construction of Social Relations in James Bay Cree Society." *Senri Ethnological Studies* (30): 223–68.

–. 2004. "James Bay Crees' Life Projects and Politics: Histories of Place, Animal Partners and Enduring Relationships." In *In the Way of Development: Indigenous Poeples, Life Projects and Globalization,* ed. Mario Blaser, Harvey A. Feit, and Glenn McRae, 92–110. New York: Zed Books and International Development Research Centre.

–. 2005. "Re-cognizing Co-management as Co-governance: Histories and Visions of Conservation at James Bay." *Anthropologica* 47 (2): 267–88.

Grand Council of the Crees. 1995. *Sovereign Injustice: Forcible Inclusion of the James Bay Crees and Cree Territory into A Sovereign Québec*. Nemaska, QC: Grand Council of the Crees.

Hirsch, Marianne, and Valerie Smith. 2002. "Feminism and Cultural Memory: An Introduction." *Signs* (Chicago, Illinois) 28 (1): 1–19. http://dx.doi.org/10.1086/340890.

Lapointe, Ugo, and Colin Scott. Forthcoming. "A Balancing Act: Mining and Protected Areas in Wemindji." In *The Science and Politics of Protected Area Creation: Striking the Balance*, ed. Monica E. Mulrennan, Katherine Scott, and Colin Scott. Vancouver: UBC Press.

McKegney, Sam. 2006. "'I was at war – But it was a gentle war': The Power of the Positive in Rita Joe's Autobiography." *American Indian Culture and Research Journal* 30 (1): 33–52. http://dx.doi.org/10.17953/aicr.30.1.l411581221o4m664.

McRae, Glenn. 2001. *Protest Journeys: Vermont Encounters in a Campaign of Translocal Solidarity with the James Bay Crees, Interdisciplinary Arts and Sciences*. Cincinnati, OH: Union Institute, Graduate College.

Miller, J.R. 1989. *Skyscrapers Hide the Heavens: A History of Indian-White Relations in Canada*. Toronto: University of Toronto Press.

–. 2009. *Compact, Contract, Covenant: Aboriginal Treaty-Making in Canada*. Toronto: University of Toronto Press.

Mohia, Nadia. 2000. "Le récit de vie: Une approche anthropologique heuristique?" *L'Autre* 1 (2): 259–79. http://dx.doi.org/10.3917/lautr.002.0259.

Morantz, Toby Elaine. 2002. *The White Man's Gonna Getcha: The Colonial Challenge to the Crees in Quebec*. Montreal and Kingston: McGill-Queen's University Press.

Niezen, Ronald. 2009. *Defending the Land: Sovereignty and Forest Life in James Bay Cree Society*. 2nd ed. Upper Saddle River, NJ: Pearson Prentice Hall.

–. 2013. *Truth and Indignation: Canada's Truth and Reconciliation Commission on Indian Residential Schools*. Toronto: University of Toronto Press.

Paul-Émile, Soeur. 1952. *La baie James: Trois cents ans d'histoire militaire, économique, missionnaire*. Ottawa: Éditions de l'Université d'Ottawa.

Penn, Alan. 1997. "The James Bay and Northern Quebec Agreement: Natural Resources, Public Lands, and the Implementation of a Native Land Claim Settlement." In *For Seven Generations: An Information Legacy of the Royal Commission for Aboriginal Peoples*. CD-ROM. Ottawa: Libraxus.

Rodon, Thierry, and Minnie Grey. 2009. "The Long and Winding Road to Self-Government: The Nunavik and Nunatsiavut Experiences." In *Northern Exposure: Peoples, Powers, and Prospects for Canada's North*, ed. Frances Abele, Thomas Courchene, Leslie Seidle, and France St-Hilaire, 317–43. Montreal: Insititut de recherches sur les politiques publiques.

Scott, Colin. 2005. "Co-management and the Politics of Aboriginal Consent to Resource Development: The *Agreement Concerning a New Relationship between Le Gouvernement du Québec and the Crees of Québec* (2002)." In *Canada: The State of Federation 2003: Reconfiguring Aboriginal-State Relations*, ed. M. Murphy, 133–63. Montreal and Kingston: McGill-Queen's University Press.

Sioui, Georges E. 1999. *Pour une histoire amérindienne de l'Amérique*. Quebec City: Presses de l'Université Laval.

Vanthuyne, Karine. 2014. *La présence d'un passé de violences: Mémoires et identités autochtones dans le Guatemala de l'après-génocide*. Quebec City/Paris: Presses de l'Université Laval/Hermann.

–. Forthcoming. "From Giving Voice to Trauma to Negotiating Self-Determination in Eeyou Istchee." In *The Spiritual Burn Victims*, ed. Karl Hele and Marie-Pierre Bousquet. Montreal and Kingston: McGill-Queen's University Press.

Part 3

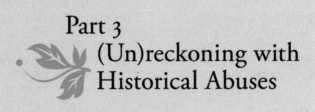

(Un)reckoning with Historical Abuses

8

The New Victims: Perpetrators before the Canadian Truth and Reconciliation Commission

JULA HUGHES

THE CANADIAN TRUTH and Reconciliation Commission was charged with creating a historical record of Indian residential schools and their legacy.[1] In its historical overview, the TRC states, "Indian Residential Schools date back to the 1870's. The policy behind the government funded, church-run schools attempted to 'kill the Indian in the child'" (TRC 2016a, para. 1). This policy goal was similar to other colonizing strategies that have been aptly described by prominent postcolonial scholar Homi Bhabha (1984, 126) as colonial mimicry, defined as "the desire for a reformed, recognizable Other, *as a subject of a difference that is almost the same, but not quite*" (emphasis in original).

Achieving a status balanced between difference and sameness was important to the colonial enterprise. If Indigenous children as subjects of colonization had been recognized as fully and equally human, neither the means nor the goals of Indian residential schools could have been maintained. If Indigenous parents had been recognized as possessing parental capacity, love, and responsibility equal to that of settler parents, Canadians would not have tolerated the forced removal of Indigenous children. At the same time, reforming the subject in the colonizer's image served to legitimize the colonial project. Emphasizing current difference and promoting a process by which this difference would be gradually narrowed cast residential schools in a benevolent light. Thus the ambivalence of mimicry was constitutive of the colonial enterprise. Less clear is what happens to colonial mimicry in the course of (ostensibly) decolonizing efforts such as national reconciliation measures.

By considering the treatment of perpetrator organizations and their staff by the TRC, I show that reconciliation processes are vulnerable to a kind of colonial mimicry of their own, a resort to making people and institutions almost, but not quite, the same. As in the case of Bhabha's colonial mimicry, the purpose of what I call conciliatory mimicry is to legitimate power and to maintain a comfortable balance between sameness and difference.

The TRC was established as part of a court-approved settlement known as the Indian Residential Schools Settlement Agreement (IRSSA 2006). The establishment of a truth and reconciliation commission had originally been recommended by the Royal Commission on Aboriginal Peoples (1996) in its final report, but the recommendation had remained unimplemented (AANDC 2009). The settlement was related to a certified national class action and was negotiated between former students, the federal government of Canada, churches that had run residential schools, and various Aboriginal organizations, including the Assembly of First Nations (Hughes 2012).

In related litigation, the TRC reiterated that its origin in the Settlement Agreement positioned it at some remove from the government and argued that this status gave it necessary independence from government.[2] In the same litigation, the federal Crown claimed that the TRC was not independent at all. Justice Goudge characterized the position of the government as follows: "Canada argues that to give effect to the Settlement Agreement, the TRC was created a federal department for all purposes by Order in Council. The Attorney General of Canada therefore has the exclusive conduct of any and all TRC litigation and since the Attorney General opposes the proceedings brought by the TRC, they cannot proceed."[3]

Ultimately, the Ontario Superior Court of Justice determined that the TRC was indeed separate from government.[4] This highlights the very contentious nature of the relationship between the TRC and those parties to the Settlement Agreement that represent perpetrator institutions, including the federal government but also the churches that operated the schools.

Beyond the contested, but nonetheless significant, independence of the TRC, its origin in a court settlement also means that compromises between victim plaintiffs and perpetrator defendants were reached in the course of negotiations. Some of these compromises severely limited the legal powers of the TRC.

Under the terms of the Settlement Agreement, the TRC lacked a power of subpoena and was thus unable to compel the attendance of alleged perpetrators of abuse in the residential school system, nor could it force institutional representatives of government and churches responsible for the administration and operation of schools to attend.[5] The mandatory co-operation of perpetrator institutions was limited to funding and document production. Despite assurances, even this limited involvement was slow and contentious. At one time, the TRC's research director accused the churches of dragging their feet, resulting in the director's resignation and an apology by the TRC's chair and chief commissioner, Justice Murray Sinclair (Hughes 2012). Subsequently, the TRC sought the direction of the Ontario Superior Court, resulting in an order for further production of government documentation and an expansive interpretation of relevant documents.[6]

Nonetheless, if the TRC was to achieve its mandate of creating a historical record of Indian residential schools and their legacy, it was crucial for the credibility of that historical record among Indigenous and non-Indigenous Canadians alike that individual perpetrators and perpetrator organizations and institutions contribute to the TRC's truth-seeking endeavour. Otherwise, the truth that emerged from the process would be significantly deficient (Hughes 2013, 281). This concern is separate from the concern that the absence of perpetrators has resulted in a lack of public justice for survivors.

Based on this documentary review, I argue that the TRC responded to the difficulty of its limited legal powers by casting individual employees of the residential school system not as perpetrators but as a different class of victims and by casting institutional defendants not as perpetrator organizations but as co-sponsors of the TRC.[7] This reframing found almost universal acceptance among the respondent churches and was somewhat successful in attracting both individual and institutional participation.[8] However, it arguably altered the content of their contributions by selectively producing victim narratives and by narrowing the conceptual gaps between victims and perpetrators.

The Reframing Efforts of the TRC

The reframing efforts of the TRC are most apparent when we compare the language used to speak to survivors with that used to speak to perpetrator organizations and their staff. Speaking about survivors of residential schools, Chief Commissioner Sinclair and others repeatedly pointed to the urgency of the TRC's work given their age: "We recognize that many Survivors are elderly and that we need to move forward as quickly as possible to receive statements from anyone affected by the legacy of residential schools" (TRC 2009, para. 1).

In a letter to the defendant churches, Sinclair used very similar language regarding former staff: "Sadly, the number of former staff is rapidly declining. To ensure their voices are heard, we must work quickly to reach out to those who are still with us" (TRC 2011).

In the same vein, both former staff and survivors were given identical assurance about the statement-gathering process: "Your statements, documents and photographs are very important and can help Canadians understand what the schools were like, what happened inside them and how the experience affected people for generations to come. Those that lived, attended and worked at the schools will finally be given a voice through the statement gathering process" (TRC 2016c).

As part of the invitation letter, former staff members were assured of support analogous to supports available to survivors: "Interviews will take place in a safe supportive environment in a location that is convenient for the participant and in the language of their choice. Health supports will be provided if requested" (TRC 2011).

These communications suggest a stance that is at least unusual for a truth commission dealing with a perpetrator and/or bystander population, namely, the characterization of staff not as perpetrators and/or bystanders to the systematic physical, emotional, and sexual abuse of the residential school system but as co-victims of the residential school "experience":

> Residential school staff can provide us with a unique insight into the operation of the schools, the relationship between students and staff, and the day to day challenges of working in difficult circumstances. A better understanding of the experiences of former staff will help us to prepare a more comprehensive history of the residential school system and legacy which in turn will contribute to our final report and recommendations. (TRC 2011)

In its interim report, the TRC (2012, para. 4) went so far as to assert, "Over the past two years, the Commission has made it a priority to take every opportunity to hear directly from the people most affected by the residential school system: the students and staff who worked in the schools."

Thus, students and staff are passive victims of the system rather than abusers or bystanders to abuse. This observation is not to suggest that dichotomizing victims and perpetrators is invariably more "true" than acknowledging that the categories may be complex and may overlap (Borer 2003). However, there is a very large empirical and moral gap between, on the one hand, adults who work in difficult institutional circumstances while holding power over children and enjoying the legal freedom of resignation at a time of their choosing and, on the other hand, children who are forcibly removed from their family under a discriminatory law and held at an institution in inhumane conditions. Conciliatory mimicry obscures the size of the gap while supporting the pre-existing power structures of government and churches vis-à-vis Indigenous Canadians.

Reporting on the TRC: Church Publications

At its inception, the TRC did not attract high attention in the mainstream media.[9] And although later trends showed increased coverage, the most consistently extensive coverage was on the Aboriginal Peoples Television Network, which is dedicated to Indigenous news and entertainment, and in the church media, particularly those related to churches that are parties to the Settlement Agreement. For this study, it is assumed that church media align with the prevailing interests and attitudes of church leadership and members, making church media particularly fertile ground for analysis.

The three main churches involved in the Settlement Agreement are the Roman Catholic, Anglican, and United Churches. Each of the churches has a publication that reports on matters related to the denomination it represents, and each has provided some coverage of the TRC.

The Anglican Journal

The Canadian Anglican Church publishes the *Anglican Journal*.[10] From the early days of the TRC, the *Journal* reported on the Anglican Church's relationship with the TRC. In February 2008 the *Journal* cited Bob Watts, the then interim executive director of the TRC, in saying, "It was also important to hear how the churches, including the Anglican Church of Canada, have been affected and changed by the sad legacy of residential schools" (Sison 2008, para. 2). Even in this very first report, we see the TRC casting the church not as a perpetrator organization but as a body affected and changed.[11]

The *Journal* reported Archbishop Terence Finlay's response in early 2009, when the work of the TRC appeared threatened by the resignation of its first chief commissioner:

> "I need to tell you now on behalf of the Anglican Church, we're in this
> for the long haul, regardless of what happens with the TRC," he said. "We
> also believe that the healing of Canada is crucially important. For the
> injustice that was caused by the residential schools eats at the psyche and
> the soul of our country. What a glorious thing it would be if we could
> move together to restore a sense of empowerment, a sense of identity, a
> sense of the great gifts that each nation brings and offers." (Williams 2009,
> para. 7)

It is clear from the Settlement Agreement that the Anglican Church is a defendant to the class action and that it acknowledges, as part of the agreement, its responsibility for what is described in the first recital as "harms and abuses committed against ... children" (IRSSA 2006). However, if it was to complete its mandate, the TRC required the assistance of the churches to access documentation held in church archives as well as to find former school workers.

In April 2011 the TRC approached the Anglican Church to assist in identifying and contacting school workers. The *Journal* reported, "Justice Murray Sinclair, TRC chair, has sought the help of the Anglican Church of Canada in identifying former staff members who may wish to speak with the TRC" (Sison 2011b, para 3). The church hierarchy cooperated:

> The primate, Archbishop Fred Hiltz, plans to send out a letter to surviving
> residential school employees encouraging them to share their stories with
> the TRC.
>
> The Anglican General Synod Archives has identified about 2,000 people
> who worked in about three dozen residential schools and hostels admin-
> istered by the church on behalf of the federal government between 1820
> and 1969. The schools were mostly in the northern regions of central and
> western Canada. The Presbyterian, Roman Catholic and United churches
> also administered residential schools. (Ibid., paras. 4–5)

Congruent with the approach of the TRC, the *Journal* reported on the activities of the church with the TRC as a co-sponsor and contributor rather than as a perpetrator and adversary. For example, the *Journal* noted that the Great Synod Archives of the Anglican Church played a major role in the work of the TRC. However, discovered in the archives were not, as one might have suspected, the church's records of perpetrating ethnocide but instead stories about congregational generosity toward residential school children:

> Anglican parishes across Canada may not be aware that in the 1920s some of them sponsored students at the Indian residential schools through a monthly cash donation that went towards the purchase of clothing and supplies, members of the Canadian house of bishops were told at their spring meeting.
>
> This little-known fact was recently discovered by the General Synod Archives, which is playing a major role in gathering and sharing documents related to Anglican-run Indian residential schools across Canada. Documents have shown that members of the Women's Auxiliary or other groups, many of them from southern parishes, gave about $30 a year for a student who they only knew by name. (Sison 2009)

One item in the *Journal* that uniformly condemned residential schools and starkly portrayed the hardships of residential school students without any reference to redeeming narratives was an article that reported on experiences of a student in the school at Shubenacadie in Nova Scotia. The article began, "Isabelle Knockwood was just four years old when she was sent to the Shubenacadie Residential School, which was run by the Roman Catholic Church from 1930 to 1966" (Sison 2011c, para. 1).[12]

It is difficult to miss the irony that this article reports on a school not run by the Anglican Church. In a similar vein, an article reporting on a prison visit by the TRC commissioners told us that at the Kenora jail, "aboriginal inmates make up 92 per cent of the prison population." Against this stark figure, the *Journal* reported that the schools in the Kenora region were run by the Catholic and Presbyterian Churches as well as by the Catholic Order of the Oblates (Anglican Church of Canada 2012, para. 1).

The *Journal* also emphasized that the experience of residential schools was not uniformly bleak. In this context, it drew on the experience of one of its bishops, herself a residential school survivor:

"My experience (at residential school) was more good than bad," said Bishop Mamakwa, who attended the Poplar Hill School in northwestern Ontario, which was administered by the Mennonite-associated Northern Gospel Light Mission ...

"The good thing about it was learning about the Bible. We had Bible teaching every day, and we learned a lot of hymns. We also learned practical stuff like sewing, knitting, cooking and home nursing," said Bishop Mamakwa.

The bad part, which Bishop Mamakwa said she only came to grips with later on in life, was "we were made to feel that our identity was not good." (Sison 2011a)

Even from this brief excerpt, one cannot help but be disconcerted by the balance of good and evil asserted here. What followed was a description of residential school life that reflected the reports of many other students: isolation, deprivation of language and cultural identity, prohibitions against wearing clothing brought from home, and routine breaches of student privacy. It is difficult to imagine that absent the kind of normative framework offered by the church, a victim of this kind of abuse would assert that attending the school was, on balance, a good experience.

Occasionally, the institutional and personal perpetrator stories became interwoven. One of the diocesan bishops of the Anglican Church, David Ashdown, who self-identified as former residential school staff, was reported in the *Journal* as commenting,

"Part of the story is the untold story of staff. We all know that there was abuse; no one is denying that. But there were a number of staff who tried to do something about it, and a number of them got fired by the very church that's now ignoring their existence," he said.

Bishop Ashdown, who once worked as a residential school staff, said that "there were staff who, on very meager income, spent their money trying to provide for students' needs. Some physically risked their lives." He lamented that those staff, who are now in their late 50s and 60s, "are considered pariahs and are told, "you can come and sit at the hearing but you won't be allowed to speak." He added, "They are absolutely shattered ... their stories are being shunted aside, as well as those students who found their experience to be a positive one." Bishop Ashdown said "the whole story needs to be told" or the church runs the risk of "replacing one injustice for another." (Sison 2009)

In this entanglement of the personal and the institutional perpetrators, the power relationships play out starkly. It becomes apparent that the same institution that invited the participation of its former employees in response to the TRC's request for assistance was internally seen as marginalizing the same staff by not allowing them to speak. It was also remembered as the institutional employer that had acted as a powerful enforcer of the methods of the residential school regime: abuse and underresourcing.

The Catholic Register

The *Catholic Register* is the oldest Canadian Catholic weekly. Like the *Anglican Journal,* it now maintains an active web presence. Compared with the *Journal,* its outlook is generally more socially conservative, consistent with the overall political position of the Catholic Church in Canada.[13]

The position of the Catholic Church on residential schools is more complicated than that of the Anglican Church. The latter has shown no difficulty breaking with the past and articulating a vision of its role in the TRC process almost entirely removed from its history as a perpetrator organization. The Anglican attempt at a clean break with history has not been matched on the part of the Catholic Church. Although the Catholic Church operated three-quarters of all residential schools, it was the last of the perpetrator churches to issue an official apology.[14] To this day, the Catholic Church has difficulty articulating a position that steps away from the colonial missionary tradition, and it unapologetically continues to pursue Christianization of Indigenous Canadians, despite demands by Chief Commissioner Sinclair at the time of the TRC hearings that the churches "would have to tell people that they don't have to be Christian if they really want reconciliation" (Swan 2011a, para. 4). The *Register* reported Archbishop Lavoie's response to Sinclair:

> Lavoie, archbishop of Keewatin-Le Pas, isn't quite ready to give up the evangelical mandate of the Church. He believes a well-rounded Catholicism can be part of native culture – just as it is part of other cultures. But that doesn't mean the Church is going to force Catholicism on anybody, he said.

"People are going to choose whatever they're going to choose," said Lavoie. "They have to be free to do that."

"Why would I advise somebody to let go of something that could be a great help to them?" (Ibid., para. 7)

In the same breath as acknowledging Indigenous people's freedom of choice regarding their spirituality and religion, the archbishop positioned himself not as a representative of a perpetrator institution seeking reconciliation but as a spiritual adviser of the very people with whom he ostensibly wished to reconcile. In what followed, it becomes apparent that this repositioning was entirely without self-awareness: "For many of the people recovering from abuse at the schools there has been a rediscovery of faith that begins with recovery from alcohol abuse with a 12-step program, followed by embracing native spirituality and finally a discovery of an authentic Catholic identity" (Swan 2011a, para. 8). Particularly, the last reported statement indicated a continued commitment to a colonial narrative of progress from Indigenous (alcoholic) identity to Indigenous spirituality to Catholic religiosity, a progress that follows the well-trodden path of church-based Indigenous education in the residential schools.

In another article that is instructive, if invidious, the *Register* brought into proximity two different reconciliation narratives: a promise of church friendship with Indigenous people and two accounts of survivor apologies for intergenerational harm. The desire for friendship was expressed as follows:

Mackenzie diocese Bishop Murray Chatlain promised native people of the north the continued commitment of the church in friendship.

"Relationship and friendship are so important to maintain, but that takes courage," he said. "It takes courage to really hear what people have to say. That friendship we have is so important ... Together we have a chance to have new life." (Swan 2011b, paras. 7–8)

It is difficult to parse this quotation. Who had to have courage? The church? The survivors? Why was the church offering a continued commitment? Was the TRC not about discontinuing certain church practices? The rhetorical device of invoking the Christian metaphor of "new life" was deeply problematic, as it invoked the colonial pattern of Christianization. The ambiguity of the quotation removed the church as perpetrator from view and replaced it with a continued missionary narrative of reconciliation.

This promise of church friendship was immediately followed by the first of two accounts of survivor apologies, which was attributed to a named, but otherwise curiously unidentified, participant:

> A focus on the next generation dominated much of the testimony from Survivors speaking in the circle of reconciliation in the Sir Alexander Mackenzie School gym. Terri Brown asked the children of residential school Survivors to stand so she could address them directly.
>
> "I want to say, we love you," said Brown. "Whatever we did to you, we did it because we didn't know any better." (Swan 2011b, paras. 9–10)

Even though the report did not make it clear who Terri Brown was, her position at this event was actually important. She was a member of the TRC's Indian Residential School Survivors Committee. This ten-member committee served as an advisory body to the TRC (2016b). Thus, Brown acted as a representative of the commission in this talking circle. The attribution of responsibility as reported shows the distortion: victims of residential schools took responsibility for the harms the schools caused, and the TRC's representative offered an apology to the second-generation victims. Left out of the report, one suspects, was the explication of the causal link between the victimization of children and their subsequent difficulties in parenting their own children. This link was clearer in the subsequent narrative.

The second of the two accounts of survivor apologies introduced us to another perspective, one where the victim minimized some of the harms that were prominent in the claims of the class action and emphasized his personal responsibility for the intergenerational effects of the residential schools. The only mention in the article of a specific act of abuse was therefore one perpetrated by a residential school victim:

> Survivor Earnie Bernhardt brought his three daughters forward to apologize directly to them for abuse he inflicted on their mother and his subsequent split from the family.
>
> "Everybody talks about the loss of language and culture. Sure that's important. But what I missed was the love of my mother and my father. I didn't learn any of that from them. I had to learn for myself, the hard way," he said.

Bernhardt faced his three daughters and pleaded with them not to make the mistakes he had made.

"You can forgive me on your own time," he said. (Swan 2011b, paras. 11–14)

Nowhere in the article was there a mention of any concrete act of abuse or discrimination perpetrated by the church or its staff. Acts of intergenerational violence were foregrounded. They supported a view of the Indigenous parent as in need of amelioration and support, a view that had once justified the residential schools.

A third strategy of conciliatory mimicry employed by the church and endorsed by the TRC was to emphasize that the experience of residential schools may not have been universally bleak. We have already seen this strategy illustrated in the *Anglican Journal* through the testimony of an Anglican diocesan bishop. In a similar vein, the *Register* reported that Archbishop Gerard Pettipas, chair of the Catholic group of parties to the settlement, had indicated his commitment to attend all national events. In this context, he was quoted as follows: "We expect many of these stories will deal with difficult issues from this dark chapter in our country's history," the archbishop said. "However, we believe former students and staff may also have more positive accounts to relate" (Gyapong 2010, para. 5).

The *Register* also reported on the TRC from a perspective of greater distance than that taken by the *Anglican Journal*. It described the TRC, which was funded out of the court settlement, as a "federally funded commission" (Swan 2011b, para. 4). The schools themselves were described as "government-mandated residential schools" (Swan 2007, para. 3). The most hard-hitting article I was able to find in the *Register* regarding the harms of residential schools is one where the role of the church was relegated to a sterile boilerplate text at the very end (Swan 2012),[15] with the body of the article speaking to the governmental role. The article began, "The bitter history of Canada's attempt to wipe out aboriginal culture through a system of Church-run schools has come to Canada's largest and most invisible Native community – and it's biggest city" (ibid., para. 1). In the article, the president of the Native Friendship Centre in Toronto described the impact of the residential schools: "Our people are on the edge. Our people are facing extinction" (ibid., para. 4). Nothing in the article suggested that the church's ambitions for reconciliation included social responsibility or even an acknowledgment of concrete acts of wrongdoing.

The Catholic Church was a late and reluctant participant in the Settlement Agreement (Wilson 2004). It continued to be a somewhat reluctant party to reconciliation efforts despite the reframing efforts of the TRC.

The United Church Observer

The final church publication under consideration is the *United Church Observer*. The *Observer* is a monthly magazine with an active web presence. The TRC had closer linkages to the United Church than to the other churches. Marie Wilson, one of the three TRC commissioners, spoke to the United Church General Council (the church's annual general meeting) shortly after her appointment. The *Observer* reported on the connection between Commissioner Wilson and the church:

> Rev. James Scott, the United Church's senior adviser for residential schools, introduced Marie Wilson by pointing out that she is an active United Church person from Yellowknife. As she began her remarks, Wilson told Council she had "a familiar feeling of home" in the meeting room, adding, "In a way, I feel I know all of you." (Wilson 2009, para. 8)

Locating herself in the United Church, Wilson (2009, para. 9) went on to develop the message that the TRC was grounded in the church's sponsorship of the process:

> In her address, Wilson credited the United Church with helping to sustain the momentum that led to the federal apology last year and the establishment of a truth and reconciliation process. She outlined the Commission's plan for the next five years and offered Council her thoughts on how individual church members can help make truth and reconciliation a reality for all Canadians. "Talk to each other. Make sure you are not alone. Open your circles."

Commissioner Wilson thus framed the involvement of the church in terms of its role in the settlement process rather than its role as a perpetrator organization. The United Church, like its Anglican counterpart, drew a clear line between its past involvement and its new and improved self-image as a partner of the TRC. This had the conceptual advantage that it could fully embrace the invitation of the TRC to participate as a co-sponsor in the reconciliation effort, but not everyone was prepared to let the organization off the hook so easily. For example, the *Observer* ran articles about Kevin Annett, an activist and former United Church minister in Port Alberni (where a residential school run by the United Church was located), decrying him as a headline-grabbing filmmaker and self-styled crusader (Milne 2008). Annett had accused the church and governmental leaders of mass killings of children, an accusation the church emphatically denied. What is interesting about the Annett articles is not that there was disagreement over the scope of violence or the level of abuse but rather the striking contrast between the church's self-imagining as a benevolent co-sponsor of the TRC in almost all articles covering the residential schools and its strong defensive tone in response to a vocal critic making specific allegations of wrongdoing.

The tension between the new and improved self-image of the church and its engagement with its colonizing past was also apparent in the discussion about any ongoing or new missionary work, particularly as it related to new immigrants:

> [A United Church minister] suggests that United Church people might be unsure about reaching out to newcomers because they're afraid of being paternalistic like their forebears, some of whom took part in harmful mission projects like the residential school system. "But I'm not talking about converting people or asking them to be what they're not," he says, adding that a good place to start might be with Methodist immigrants who may not be aware that the United Church is the face of Methodism in Canada. (Rideout 2010, para. 16)

Australian postcolonialism scholar Lorenzo Veracini (2008) has argued that liberal democracies built on colonial pasts such as Canada and Australia must deny their founding violence to legitimize their current governments. It appears that the denial of concrete acts of founding violence is important not only to governments but also to other large institutions. What is different is that Christian theology offers a framework of reconciliation in traditional redemption stories. Unlike governments, churches can draw on established theological and philosophical frameworks for addressing past wrongdoing and reconciliation through contrition and ultimately forgiveness and redemption. There were two problems with applying these established frameworks in the context of the TRC: One, at least in the Catholic tradition, the church acts as a necessary intermediary between sinner and God in confession and between God and sinner in absolution. There is an institutional role, but the role did not readily fit the TRC context. Two, reconciliation and redemption are not offered to institutions but to individuals. They are not responses to systemic wrongdoing but to individual transgressions of religious laws. Both conceptual difficulties were put into sharp relief in one of the TRC's treasured success stories, that of Florence Kaefer. As a young woman, Florence Kaefer was a teacher at Norway House Residential School. There, she taught a five-year-old boy named Edward Gamblin. Gamblin later became a musician, and Kaefer reconnected with him upon hearing a recording of his song "Survivor's Voice." Kaefer and Gamblin became personal friends after Kaefer sought his forgiveness. Gamblin died of complications from a stage accident in 2010 at age sixty-two. The *Observer* published an article about Kaefer and Gamblin with a photograph of Kaefer backlit by church windows and in a saintly posture. The article highlighted Gamblin's difficult family background:

> The first truth of Gamblin's experience is that, unlike many others, he was not ripped from a happy home and spirited away. His life before residential school was already sad and ugly, and residential school was, in some ways, an escape. "My biological parents were both alcoholic. They had their own agenda, and I guess children weren't part of the agenda," he says matter-of-factly. Gamblin went to a foster home and later to the residential school in Norway House. (Wright 2009, para. 6)

The article acknowledged the physical, sexual, and cultural abuse Gamblin had suffered at the hands of school staff, but Kaefer was entirely exonerated. She described herself as naive: Gamblin related that students would keep the abuse secret from good teachers lest they be reassigned.

The article is interesting for the story it told but maybe more interesting for the story it failed to tell. We did not learn whether Gamblin's biological parents were themselves residential school survivors. No connection was made between Gamblin's hard life and the ongoing discriminatory practices of Canadian settler society. And no mention was made of any institutional effort for outreach on behalf of the United Church. Instead, the article emphasized individual responsibility.

Throughout the TRC documents, it is apparent that the TRC undercut the victim-perpetrator dichotomy in order to invite contributions from groups otherwise recognized as perpetrators. These groups included staff who had once worked in residential schools as well as the churches that had run the schools. Although there are many examples of perpetrator groups seeking recognition as victims, the TRC's reframing of perpetrator organizations as institutional sponsors and school staff as persons affected by Indian residential schools appears to be a unique instance of such a reframing by an institution charged with determining the truth about incidents of historical mass trauma.

Through this reframing, the TRC simultaneously captured some important truths about the realities of workers and institutions and distorted the nature of its inquiry. These truths included the revealing of an often young, typically isolated, underresourced, and underqualified workforce struggling with overcrowding, lack of essential supplies, poor facilities, and remote locations.[16] They also showed that individual efforts to interact with students in a humane and caring fashion were inadequate to the task of transforming residential schools.

The discourse became distorted because the institutional participants appeared as co-sponsors of the TRC rather than as perpetrator organizations and because the individual workers were highly unlikely to own up to abuse they may have perpetrated or witnessed as nonintervening bystanders. This distortion shows that the reconciliation process may obscure the difference in moral status between survivors, individual perpetrators and bystanders, and perpetrator institutions, rendering them almost, but not quite, the same. This variant of Bhabha's (1984) colonial mimicry – conciliatory mimicry – serves to legitimate and maintain institutional and structural differences in power, voice, and resources.

All three church publications under consideration utilized strategies of conciliatory mimicry in their reporting of the work of the TRC. Three strategies emerged, all of which operated both to suggest sameness and to maintain difference. The first strategy was to historicize the need for change. Under this strategy, the churches were no longer the perpetrator institutions that ran the residential schools but instead functioned as sponsors of the TRC, spiritual advisers to First Nations peoples, and positive forces in the lives of survivors. The relationship of victims and perpetrators was transformed into a common survivorship of a troubled past. The second strategy was to externalize negative experiences. Concrete examples of wrongdoing and abuse were attributed to schools run by another church, or the focus was on student-to-student abuse or intergenerational abusive effects. The third strategy was to muddy the moral waters by emphasizing some positive aspects of the residential school system or particular experiences in residential schools. For example, some articles narrowed the difference between residential schools and settler public schools by emphasizing the learning that went on in the schools and by noting that students had some good, even heroic, teachers. Like colonial mimicry, conciliatory mimicry is inherently unstable. Stories historicizing the perpetrator role of the churches are in tension with ongoing evangelical efforts. Stories emphasizing positive experiences require that trivial or inconsequential goods should be attributed equivalent or greater weight than serious and ongoing harm. Stories externalizing harm are difficult to reconcile with the institutional role of the churches as defendants in the class action. If the fault lay elsewhere, why did the churches accept responsibility?

Finally, the depiction of the reconciliation process of the TRC in church publications completely failed to capture the systemic and institutional impacts of the residential school system as part of a broader set of colonizing policies, and it did not offer any direction for the social-reform dimensions of reconciliation (Wale 2013). Indigenous material exclusion, political underrepresentation, and economic and human insecurity all remained largely hidden from view. Kim Wale (ibid., 7) has argued that "reconciliation becomes difficult when social divisions are the result of unequal power relations that are being perpetuated in society." Instead, settler victimhood is rendered visible and even dominant in a context that would appear to have demanded the opposite. Observations of these kinds of moral inversions are not novel. In the Australian context, Anne Curthoys (2009, 3) notes that "the contest over the past is perhaps not between positive and negative versions, but between those which place white Australians as victims, struggling heroically against adversity, and those which place them as aggressors, bringing adversity upon others." She goes on to suggest that "the self-chosen white victim finds it extremely difficult to recognise what he or she has done to others ... Reconciliation ... consequently remains unachievable in a society profoundly unsettled by *ressentiment*, and desperately seeking to hold onto foundational myths and sentiment which find little support elsewhere" (ibid., 18).

The mandate of establishing a historical record for Canadians of residential schools and their impacts required the TRC to develop a rich account.

It is desirable and even necessary that such an account should make simple dichotomies of perpetrator and victim identities more complex. However, if the work of the TRC is to contribute to lasting reconciliation between Indigenous and non-Indigenous Canadians, this complexity should not be used to obscure the history of individual and systemic instances of abuse. This review of church media suggests that this is one lesson in reconciliation we have yet to learn.

NOTES

1 I gratefully acknowledge the research assistance of Ms. Leah Ferguson.
2 *Fontaine v. Canada (Attorney General)*, 2013 ONSC 684, 114 OR (3d) 263 (CanLII), para.42.
3 Ibid., para. 40.
4 Ibid., paras. 45–47.
5 Anthropologist Ronald Niezen (2013) argues that a negative experience with the Independent Assessment Process had a greater impact on the TRC than commonly thought. He notes that in this process, priests and nuns felt as though they had been falsely accused because of the monetary incentive for former students to make these allegations. This circumstance has resulted in a sense of bitterness.
   According to Niezen (2013), because of these negative experiences at the compensation hearings, there has been an unwillingness on the part of most of those closely involved in running the schools to testify before the TRC.
   In my view, perpetrators, be they individuals or organizations, require a reason to participate, without which they are liable to stay away. In the absence of a coercive power vested in the TRC, it had to look for incentives. Whatever the true cause of the relative rarity of perpetrator participation, Niezen (2013) has observed similar victim identifications on the part of school staff. He notes that one priest referred to himself as abused: "Today I have been abused with all the accusations" (ibid., 52). Niezen notes that this priest's use of the word "abused" in reference to himself was contrary to the manner in which the term was otherwise used in the Independent Assessment Process hearings. (ibid., 53). By including himself in the category of the abused, the priest was calling into question the entire regime of compensation. Niezen also gives the example of certain priests arguing that they deserved financial compensation for the harms they had consequently suffered.
6 *Fontaine v. Canada (Attorney General)*, 2013 ONSC 684, 114 OR (3d) 263 (CanLII).
7 Attempts by perpetrator groups to reframe themselves as victims are common enough. See Mitten (1992), Lefranc, Mathieu, and Siméant (2008), and Baudinière (2008). What is different about the reframing described in this chapter is that the institution put in charge of discovering the truth actively contributed to the recharacterization.
8 The success was limited as regards individual staff contributions, as some staff noted negative experiences with the prior Independent Assessment Process (see Niezen 2013).
9 For the time period of January 1, 2008, to November 30, 2013, a search of the Infomart database of Canadian newspapers shows close to a thousand entries for the combined terms "truth and reconciliation commission" and "residential." This level of reporting is consistent with average reporting about a provincial board of inquiry (e.g., the Charbonneau Inquiry) but is much less than the reporting of news-dominating stories such as the resignation of

Nigel Wright as Prime Minister Stephen Harper's chief of staff in May 2013 and the scandals surrounding Toronto mayor Rob Ford until he left office in 2014. Perhaps more troublesome, the release of the TRC's (2012) interim report received only very modest coverage, with Infomart showing only five wire stories and only thirty-one newspaper stories.

10 The *Anglican Journal* is published ten times annually and maintains an active web presence. See http://www.anglicanjournal.com/about-us/our-story.

11 Sociologist Eric Woods (this volume) argues that this reframing was anticipated by the Anglican Church as early as the 1970s as the former church partners in the residential schools underwent a rapid volte-face; almost overnight, the civilizing mission was replaced with a mission to defend Indigenous culture.

12 Isabelle Knockwood is an important author on Indian residential schools. Her book *Out of the Depths: The Experiences of Mi'kmaw Children at the Indian Residential School at Shubenacadie, Nova Scotia* (2001) is one of the leading first-person narratives on the residential schools.

13 A history of the *Catholic Register* can be found at http://www.catholicregister.org/history.

14 Pope Benedict expressed sorrow for the residential schools in a press release of the Holy See on April 29, 2004. See http://press.vatican.va/content/salastampa/it/bollettino/pubblico/2009/04/29/0287/00674.html. The Missionary Oblates of Mary Immaculate offered an apology on July 24, 1991. See http://www.cccb.ca/site/images/stories/pdf/oblate_apology_english.pdf. The position of the Catholic Church in its official statements and in litigation related to Indian residential schools has typically been to emphasize local control and responsibility and to characterize the church as an unincorporated volunteer organization that cannot be sued, on the one hand, and as a state entity with immunity, on the other hand.

15 The article closed, "The four Churches that ran residential schools (about 60 per cent of them were Catholic, 30 per cent Anglican and the remainder United or Presbyterian) have representatives at The Meeting Place. The Church representatives are there to listen to Survivor stories and offer words of reconciliation. About 150,000 Indigenous children were placed in residential schools between 1870 and 1990. For most of their history the schools were designed to assimilate the children into white society by erasing their language and spiritual customs and equipping them with trades and farming skills" (Swan 2012).

16 These "ordinary" truths are important if we are to learn from the residential school experience, as Niezen (this volume) correctly points out.

REFERENCES

Aboriginal Affairs and Northern Development Canada (AANDC). 2009. *Backgrounder – Indian Residential Schools Truth and Reconciliation Commission*. Ottawa: Aboriginal Affairs and Northern Development Canada.

Anglican Church of Canada. 2012. "TRC to Gather Statements from Aboriginal Inmates." *Anglican Journal,* August 8. http://www.anglicanjournal.com/articles/trc-to-gather-statements-from-aboriginal-inmates-11014.

Baudinière, Caroline. 2008. "Une mobilisation de victimes illégitimes: Quand les épurés français de la Seconde Guerre mondiale s'engagent à l'extrême droite." *Raisons politiques* 2 (30): 21–39.

Bhabha, Homi. 1984. "Of Mimicry and Man: The Ambivalence of Colonial Discourse." *October 28, Discipleship: A Special Issue on Psychoanalysis* (Spring): 125–33.

Borer, Tristan Anne. 2003. "A Taxonomy of Victims and Perpetrators: Human Rights and Reconciliation in South Africa." *Human Rights Quarterly* 25 (4): 1088–116. http://dx.doi.org/10.1353/hrq.2003.0039.

Curthoys, Anne. 2009. "Expulsion, Exodus and Exile in White Australian Historical Mythology." *Journal of Australian Studies* 23 (61): 1–19.

Gyapong, Deborah. 2010. "Catholic Groups Welcome Start of Truth and Reconciliation Process." *Catholic Register,* June 16. http://www.catholicregister.org/item/8544-catholic-groups-welcome-start-of-truth-and-reconciliation-process.

Hughes, Jula. 2012. "Instructive Past: Lessons from the Royal Commission on Aboriginal Peoples for the Canadian Truth and Reconciliation Commission on Indian Residential Schools." *Canadian Journal of Law and Society* 27 (1): 101–27. http://dx.doi.org/10.3138/cjls.27.1.101.

–. 2013. "Home Truths about Truth Commission Processes: How Victim-Centred Truth and Perpetrator-Focused Adversarial Processes Mutually Challenge Assumptions of Justice and Truth." In *The Nature of Inquisitorial Processes in Administrative Regimes: Global Perspectives,* ed. Laverne Jacobs and Sasha Baglay, 271–92. Farnham, UK: Ashgate.

Indian Residential Schools Settlement Agreement (IRSSA). 2006. "Schedule N." In *Indian Residential Schools Settlement Agreement.* Ottawa: Government of Canada. http://www.trc.ca/websites/trcinstitution/File/pdfs/SCHEDULE_N_EN.pdf.

Knockwood, Isabelle. 2001. *Out of the Depths: The Experiences of Mi'kmaw Children at the Indian Residential School at Shubenacadie, Nova Scotia.* 3rd ed. Lockeport, NS: Roseway.

Lefranc, Sandrine, Lilian Mathieu, and Johanna Siméant. 2008. "Les victimes écrivent leur Histoire: Introduction." *Raisons politiques* 2 (30): 5–19.

Milne, Mike. 2008. "Reconciled to Hard Truths." *United Church Observer,* May. http://ucobserver.org/justice/2008/05/hard_truths.

Mitten, Richard. 1992. *The Politics of the Antisemitic Prejudice: The Waldheim Phenomenon in Austria.* Boulder, CO: Westview.

Niezen, Ronald. 2013. *Truth and Indignation: Canada's Truth and Reconciliation Commission on Indian Residential Schools.* Toronto: University of Toronto Press.

Rideout, Samantha. 2010. "Feature: Global Flair." *United Church Observer,* October. http://www.ucobserver.org/faith/2010/10/global_flair/.

Royal Commission on Aboriginal Peoples. 1996. *Report of the Royal Commission on Aboriginal Peoples.* Ottawa: Royal Commission on Aboriginal Peoples.

Sison, Marites N. 2008. "Truth Commission 'Needs to' Hear from Churches." *Anglican Journal,* February 1. http://www.anglicanjournal.com/articles/truth-commission-needs-to-hear-fromchurches-7694.

–. 2009. "Anglican Parishes Sponsored Residential School Students, Bishops Told." *Anglican Journal,* April 23. http://www.anglicanjournal.com/articles/anglican-parishes-sponsored-residential-school-students-bishops-told-8460.

–. 2011a. "Mixed Experiences at Indian Residential School." *Anglican Journal,* July 14. http://www.anglicanjournal.com/articles/mixed-experiences-at-mennonite-associated-residential-school-9923.

–. 2011b. "Residential Schools Staff Urged to Share Stories." *Anglican Journal,* April 18. http://www.anglicanjournal.com/articles/residential-schools-staff-urged-to-share-stories-9694.

–. 2011c. "Residential School Survivors Speak Out." *Anglican Journal*, October 29. http://www.anglicanjournal.com/articles/residential-school-Survivors-speak-out-10179.

Swan, Michael. 2007. "Government Still Balks at Issuing Apology for Residential School Abuses." *Catholic Register*, May 13. http://www.catholicregister.org/item/8414-government-still-balks-at-issuing-apology-for-residential-school-abuses.

–. 2011a. "Church Wants to Be Part of Recovering Native Identity." *Catholic Register*, July 4. http://www.catholicregister.org/item/5766-church-wants-to-be-part-of-recovering-native-identity.

–. 2011b. "Tears Flow as Native People Relive Years of Abuse." *Catholic Register*, June 29. http://www.catholicregister.org/item/5757-tears-flow-as-native-people-relive-years-of-abuse.

–. 2012. "TRC Commission Brings Native Issues to Heart of Toronto." *Catholic Register*, June 1. http://www.catholicregister.org/home/canada/item/14618-trc-commission-brings-native-issues-to-heart-of-toronto.

Truth and Reconciliation Commission of Canada (TRC). 2009. "A Message from the Acting Executive Director." *Newsletter*, Spring. http://www.trc.ca/websites/trcinstitution/File/pdfs/TRC_News_Spring09.pdf.

–. 2011. "Letter from the Honourable Mr. Justice Murray Sinclair, Chair, Truth and Reconciliation Commission, to Ms. Henriette Thompson, Director, Anglican Church of Canada." January 27. http://www.anglican.ca/wp-content/uploads/2010/11/SinclairlettertoIRSstaff.pdf.

–. 2012. *Interim Report*. Winnipeg, MB: Truth and Reconciliation Commission of Canada.

–. 2016a. "Historical Overview." In *About the Commission: Indian Residential Schools Truth and Reconciliation Commission*. http://www.trc.ca/websites/trcinstitution/index.php?p=39.

–. 2016b. *Meet the Members of the Indian Residential School Survivor Committee (IRSSC)*. http://www.trc.ca/websites/trcinstitution/index.php?p=6.

–. 2016c. "Your Statement Is Important." In *Statement Gathering Frequently Asked Questions*. http://www.trc.ca/websites/trcinstitution/File/pdfs/SG%20and%20FAQ_en.pdf.

Veracini, Lorenzo. 2008. "Settler Collective, Founding Violence and Disavowal: The Settler Colonial Situation." *Journal of Intercultural Studies* (Melbourne, Australia) 29 (4): 363–79. http://dx.doi.org/10.1080/07256860802372246.

Wale, Kim. 2013. *Confronting Exclusion: Time for Radical Reconciliation – South African Reconciliation Barometer Survey: 2013 Report*. Cape Town: Institute for Justice and Reconciliation.

Williams, Leigh Anne. 2009. "Reconciliation Has Begun, Participants in Residential Schools Conference Say." *Anglican Journal*, January 23. http://www.anglicanjournal.com/articles/reconciliation-has-begun-participants-in-residential-schools-conference-say-8318.

Wilson, David. 2004. "How the Residential Schools Deal Got Done." *United Church Observer*, January. http://www.ucobserver.org/justice/2004/01/how_the_residential_schools_deal_got_done.

–. 2009. "Truth and Reconciliation Take Centre-Stage on Day Two of General Council." *United Church Observer*, August. http://www.ucobserver.org/faith/2009/08/general_council_truth.

Wright, Richard. 2009. "'I Remember You. You Were My Teacher.'" *United Church Observer*, May. http://ucobserver.org/justice/2009/05/residential_school_teacher.

9

Residential Schools in Canada: Why the Message Is Not Getting Across

CHERYL GAVER

A POST ON AN INDIGENOUS friend's Facebook page contained three photos: (1) "The Holocaust – Never Forget," (2) "9–11 – Never Forget," and (3) "Colonialist Slave Trade – Get over It." Why, despite the recent public acknowledgment that Indian residential schools were a tragedy, are so many Euro-Canadians unable to understand the devastations that occurred in them?[1] This question emerged while I was engaged in researching the relationship between Indigenous and Euro-Canadian Anglicans in Canada's North, defined here as Northwest Territories and Yukon.[2] I discovered a more complex and nuanced relationship between Indigenous and Euro-Canadian Anglicans in Canada's North during the residential school era than is generally recognized, a historical relationship that shaped and continues to shape a more complex and nuanced relationship in the present. My research also revealed that many Euro-Canadians – and not just in Canada's Anglican North – are still unable to grasp what was "so bad" about Canadian residential schools and why those schools had such a profoundly negative impact on so many Indigenous people. Here, I concentrate on three factors, among the many that exist, that help explain why the message is not getting across: (1) ignorance and indifference, (2) personal knowledge, and (3) worldviews-in-collision.

The Anglican Church of Canada

The Anglican Church of Canada (ACC) operated approximately thirty-six residential schools across Canada over the years (ACC 2016b), but in 1967 the ACC began reassessing its dealings with Indigenous peoples in Canada (see Woods 2016, Chapter 4). A report presented to its General Synod called for forgiveness of Christian participation "in the perpetuation of injustices to Indians" (ACC 1967) and for the inclusion of Indigenous peoples in policy-making bodies and processes within the ACC as well as in federal and provincial governments. The ACC also commissioned sociologist Charles Hendry to study its relationship with Indigenous peoples. The Hendry Report, tabled in 1969, identified a situation where people "already buffeted by drastic social change and disorganization [had been] placed in an administrative straitjacket by an authoritarian or paternalistic government and deprived of the power and desire for independent action ... The system was paternalism – a harsh and also stingy paternalism" (Hendry 1969, 27). Among its many recommendations, the report called for the ACC to move from paternalism to partnership (ibid., 79ff). Its recommendations were accepted.

By 1970 the ACC had withdrawn from the residential school program. In 1972, for the first time, an Indigenous person, Rev. Ernie Willie, was added to the ACC's national staff (Barry 1993). In 1973 the Subcommittee on Native Affairs was established (Carlson 1995, 32), eventually evolving into the Anglican Council of Indigenous Peoples, with its own Indigenous bishop. Over the years, the council has organized national Native convocations, sought input and direction from Indigenous Anglican leaders for restructuring the national church, and extended its own "hand of partnership" to those who would help it to "build a truly Anglican Indigenous Church in Canada" (ACC 2016c). In 1991 the Residential Schools Advisory Group for Healing and Reconciliation was created to make and administer grants from the Anglican Healing Fund (ACC 2016a).

The ACC also established theological training schools to increase the number of Indigenous clergy in Canada, supported initiatives for preserving or reclaiming Indigenous cultures, and passed resolutions on Indigenous issues such as land claims (Gaver 2011, 182–86). In 1993, at the Second Native Convocation, the ACC's primate, Rt. Rev. Michael Peers, offered a formal apology to Indigenous peoples for the ACC's attitudes and actions, including its role in residential schools.

"Best Left as Indians"

My research began with the following question: Regardless of what was officially happening, had the ACC been successful in moving from paternalism to partnership with its Aboriginal members at the congregational level? This question was explored by focusing on the ACC in Canada's North. Research began with the assumption that conflict resolution and reconciliation initiatives within Anglican congregations in Canada's North would be examined, with the residential school issue as the window onto the relationship.

Preliminary research turned up literature stressing the profoundly negative impact of residential schools on Indigenous children and implying that residential schools throughout Canada were generally similar in their operation and their impact. Ethnographer Agnes Grant (1996, 87) has gone so far as to conclude that residential schools cannot be understood except from within the context of colonialism,[3] which has been characterized by (1) displacement of Indigenous peoples by European expansion, (2) isolation and containment of Indigenous peoples, (3) forced assimilation of Indigenous societies, (4) increasing political and economic domination of Aboriginal affairs by the colonizers, and (5) development of a racist ideology portraying Indigenous peoples as backward, savage, uncivilized, and child-like. Grant's conclusion led me to regard residential schools as both the products of colonialism (since they were established by missionaries) and its agents (since missionaries shaped Indigenous students).

The preliminary research was followed up with fieldtrips to Canada's North between 2006 and 2008. Findings from the first fieldtrip led to a fundamental shift in direction for my research. Interviews with both Indigenous and Euro-Canadian participants revealed that the situation in the North differed significantly from what I had expected based on readings (e.g., Grant 1996; Miller 2003; Milloy 2003). Had my research missed those who had been most negatively affected by residential schools? Were people in Canada's North at an early stage in the process of memory transformation (see Woods, this volume)? Such questions led to a more focused approach to (ethno)historical research. Eventually, and contrary to those policies and practices geared to deliberately killing the Indianness, as one Indigenous woman had phrased it (Barry 1993; see also Woods, this volume), I discovered a northern narrative that historian Kenneth Coates (1991) describes as "best left as Indians."

This northern narrative revealed a marked government *disinterest in assimilation* until the mid-twentieth century; church and residential school acceptance of, and at times promotion of, at least some Indigenous traditions; and a recognition by Euro-Canadians that their own survival frequently depended on the traditional skills of Indigenous hunters and fishermen. Several factors for such a government policy reflected the realities of northern geography and climate. Assimilation in the South often included a focus on farming but, in the North, farming is not an option except in the southernmost regions of the territories. Euro-Canadians tend to prefer southern climates to the North, where temperatures of minus forty degrees Celsius are not uncommon in the winter, which means that few Euro-Canadians have immigrated to Canada's North, except under special circumstances such as the Klondike Gold Rush of 1897–98. Even today, a high percentage of the population is Indigenous, and in some parts of Canada's North, Indigenous people are still the majority of the population. Furthermore, the North has a low population, which tends to make it and its issues a lower priority for the Canadian government compared with other parts of the country. In fact, and with the exception of the Gold Rush, it was not until the Second World War that the federal government took a more active role in the North (see Coates 1986, 132) and, after the Second World War, in northern education (Devitt 1965; Milloy 2003, 242–43).

Archival research revealed that Anglican residential schools in the Northwest Territories differed from what was generally presented by the media. At least one teacher at the St. Peter's Residential School in Hay River had crib notes with common phrases in an Indigenous language, and some Indigenous parents actually worked at the school.[4] Furthermore, and for at least part of its existence, the St. Peter's School included an Indigenous language in its curriculum (Johns 1971), the principal's wife taught Slavi to at least one student, and students who could act as interpreters were identified (ibid.). Some students attending residential schools had Indigenous mothers but non-Indigenous fathers (ACC Archives, see Note 4); in fact, Canadian anthropologist Richard Slobodin (1966, 13ff) noted that the term "Métis" was little known and seldom applied among northern peoples.[5] The St. Peter's School also trained adult Indigenous Christians for the ministry. Although they might have been treated like children, they also stood up for their own rights. Sarah Simon, for example, argued with one principal who tried to force Indigenous children to speak only English and won the right for them to speak their own languages (Carlson and Dumont 1997, 22). Several residential schools had worship services in at least two languages. At Shingle Point Residential School, teachers and students socialized to some extent and, on at least one occasion, sang "Eskimo and English carols."[6] A few interviewees also mentioned services in different languages in the schools. Since farming was generally impossible in most northern residential schools, youth were sometimes encouraged to use traditional trapping skills. In both Shingle Point and Coppermine, the residential school even had Indigenous staff who were responsible for teaching youth traditional skills, with boys taught to hunt caribou and other game and girls taught traditional cooking and sewing (Coates and Morrison 1988, 141–42; Sperry 2005, 135).

During my first fieldtrip, I also discovered that no lawsuits claiming abuse had been filed against the Diocese of the Arctic and that many clergy – including the Diocesan bishop, who had even attended a residential school – were Indigenous. On other trips, I learned that many Indigenous Christians had been converted by Indigenous – not Euro-Canadian – missionaries, who had considerable sensitivity toward traditional cultures (Gaver 2011). Such discoveries led to the unravelling of my original hypothesis, built on the assumption that relationships between Indigenous peoples and Euro-Canadians in residential schools had *always* been marked by a profoundly negative colonialism.[7] Further research uncovered that too often, Euro-Canadian participants did not grasp the negative impact of residential schools on Indigenous individuals, families, and communities. Exploring why this was the case led to two realizations: (1) relationships between Indigenous peoples and Euro-Canadians in Canada's Anglican North were, and are, more complex and nuanced than generally perceived; and (2) worldviews-in-collision shaped those relationships (the focal point of my thesis).

Ignorance and Indifference

Despite media coverage, workshops, and events sponsored by denominations or individual congregations, many non-Indigenous people know little about Canadian residential schools or why the issue is "such a big deal." Some people are simply not interested and never will be. They do not attend events dealing with residential school history or reconciliation initiatives.[8] Yet their lack of direct involvement does not prevent them from forming opinions, as can be seen from comments that appeared upon the publication of various Toronto newspaper articles:

> Natalie: "the record of what really happened might contrast with the overblown accounts of what supposedly happened that the 'truth and reconciliation' commission has been nurturing. Don't get me wrong, I do believe there were incidents of abuse, but I don't believe that [the]

government of the day started up these schools to abuse kids and commit 'genocide' on them." (Perkel 2013)

t_j: "How many times does the RoC [rest of Canadians] have to apologize before the majority of FN's [First Nations] get their collective heads in 'today'; $25k per residential school Survivor was a huge apology. Enough is enough; for anyone who doesn't want to change and do anything for themselves, let them suffer the consequences. The RoC is tired of babysitting for nothing." (King 2013)

onlyatoms: "The biggest crime that's being committed relating to the rez schools situation is the way children are being treated today. Can't native parents be positive and try to help their children to be better? Right now the children are all dragged down by parents feeding them pain. Stop telling your kids about the schools and start telling them about how great their life could be." (Milroy 2013)

atoms: "This is wasteful busy work. The govt has much higher priority items to be spending and working on." (Smith 2013)

Even those who know about the residential school issue have difficulty appreciating the scope of the tragedy or impact of residential schools on communities. Not every Indigenous person was abused physically or sexually in the schools, nor, as mentioned above, have lawsuits been filed against the ACC in the Northwest Territories. Such facts allowed research participants like Darien,[9] a Euro-Canadian clergy, to regard abuses they had heard about as exceptions to the norm, possibly committed by perverts who deserved to be punished, or as once-acceptable practices that are no longer tolerated, such as spanking. Such people, often sympathetic to the suffering of Indigenous people, tend to see residential schools as an "Indigenous problem" – nothing more. One priest asked why I wanted to interview members of his predominantly non-Indigenous congregation. Another said that his church had no Indigenous members, so meeting with his congregation was unnecessary. Even when I did meet parishioners following services, many Euro-Canadians told me they had nothing to contribute but directed me toward Indigenous members whom they believed did.

This insistence that residential schools are an Indigenous problem was reflected in the inability of some Euro-Canadian participants to see a link between the schools and the church. For example, I asked about reconciliation initiatives, leaving it up to respondents to interpret what "reconciliation" meant. Erica responded by asking, "Does that mean we have done something wrong? The Church has done something wrong so we have to apologize?" (Gaver's notes).[10] At one service, a letter was read in which the bishop asked those present for donations to help with Anglican schools in Africa. There was nothing unusual about his request; historically, Christians have often assumed responsibility for providing education, particularly in the absence of government programs.[11] However, nothing in the letter indicated that the bishop saw a similarity between Anglican schools for "poor children in Africa" and Anglican residential schools for "poor 'Indian' children in Canada." As might be expected, non-Indigenous congregants seemed to be interested, but the Indigenous congregants present were noticeably silent.

Personal Knowledge and Experiences

Personal knowledge, based on a variety of personal experiences, also contributes to Euro-Canadian inability to understand the residential school issue. No research participant questioned that perpetrators of physical and sexual abuse should be punished or that victims of abuse should be helped; however, many also asserted, based on their personal knowledge, that not everyone who attended residential schools was abused and insisted that some students had positive experiences.

Negative experiences with Indigenous people made it difficult for some Euro-Canadians, such as Alistair and Gary, to appreciate the residential school issue. Alistair, a fifth-generation northerner, saw himself as a victim of reverse discrimination. His personal experiences with the affirmative action programs of the Government of the Northwest Territories had left a bitter taste in his mouth and likely contributed to his feeling that the residential school issue was "a big crock" (Gaver's notes). Before moving north, newcomer Gary, a Euro-Canadian clergy, had talked with his Indigenous friends in the South, who had told him of their positive experiences in residential schools. When mentioning such experiences to northern Indigenous parishioners in his church – many of whom had suffered abuse and trauma at the residential schools *they* had attended – Gary alienated them. Struggling with the amount of anger he found among Indigenous parishioners, he eventually moved back south: "We have tried to apologize. We have a healing fund. We have tried to extend ourselves to conducting services which would be pleasing to them. But I live with the sense that I haven't been forgiven, and I wonder, how many times do I need to say that before it matters?" (Gaver 2011, 319).

Having Indigenous friends who recalled positive experiences in residential schools left a number of Euro-Canadian research participants confused about the whole issue. In Yellowknife, Euro-Canadian participants frequently asked me whether residential schools had been as bad as described in the media precisely because *their* Indigenous friends told a different story. Frank accepted media accounts as true *elsewhere but not in the North*. From his conversations with Indigenous people, he knew there had been "a lot of loneliness" (Gaver 2011, 163), but he had also been told how much Indigenous people had gained. Moriah, likewise, recounted how some elders had told her that "they knew they wanted to go and they were happy they went" (ibid., 162). Sam, Arthur, and other Euro-Canadian Anglican clergy emphasized that Indigenous children were *not* taken away by force; parents *had wanted* their children to go to the residential schools (ibid., 168).

Much of this was confirmed by Indigenous research participants. Nowyook said that his experiences of residential schools were "very different from the residential schools that I was hearing people talk about in the south" (Gaver 2011, 180). Kudloo said that her parents sent their son to residential school when he proved to be unruly (ibid., 168). Kavik refused to be interviewed because her experiences at the two hostels she had attended had been positive. She had not experienced any abuse and "wasn't forced to go either" (Gaver notes). Kiawak had attended residential school at his grandfather's urging (Gaver 2011, 167) and spoke angrily about the attention being given to negative stories about residential schools and the negative depiction of residential school staff, some of whom he considered to be "like Mother Teresa" (ibid., 162). Kiawak felt that the emerging residential school narrative was deficient if it focused only on the negative and ignored the positive.

Such stories and testimonies reaffirm what ethno-historical research had uncovered: the "best left as Indian" approach meant that the goal of education in northern residential schools was to help Indigenous people "meet the impact of civilization" (Marsh 1967, 7), not to bring about assimilation and cultural genocide. Such evidence does not mean that colonialism was non-existent; the question of how Indigenous people have been shaped by that colonialism and whether Indigenous perspectives reflect colonial mimicry (see Hughes, Chapter 8 in this volume) still needs to be asked. What the research does demonstrate, however, is that residential school history is more complex and nuanced than generally acknowledged or publicized. This very complexity can make it difficult for Euro-Canadians to appreciate the scope of the tragedy. Erica, for example, knew of one residential school with worship services "in three languages: English, Gwich'in and Inuit" (Gaver 2011, 124). Sam, a Euro-Canadian Anglican missionary, had hired Indigenous elders to teach students traditional skills in one residential school, and he had expected graduates to work as translators. Arthur, another Euro-Canadian Anglican missionary, who had been a colleague of Bishop Isaac Stringer (1866–1934), knew that Stringer had wanted to build schools in every northern community but that fiscal constraints – not genocidal intentions – had led to his establishing residential schools (ibid., 118). Such knowledge contradicted media accounts and made it difficult for its holders to grasp how disruptive residential schools had been for Indigenous communities.

Others, like Erica and Janna, who had lived in the Northwest Territories for decades, remembered what life had been like when they had first moved north; those memories shaped their views about residential schools. Erica spoke about a time before radio, telephones, and air travel, when long-distance communications – including her own long-distance relationship with her future husband – were a challenge (Gaver 2011, 178). Janna talked about the "early days" when even getting water in the winter was a dangerous activity and wondered whether those condemning residential schools believed "that everything has been like it is now" or were "judging [past] actions by today's values" (ibid., 204; Gaver's notes). Knowing this broader picture made it difficult for old-timers to even see what *could have been traumatic* for those Indigenous children attending residential schools and for their families.

Old-timers were more likely to talk about changing socio-cultural norms that they had experienced over the years. Several Euro-Canadian participants mentioned spanking – in fact, most Euro-Canadians of a certain age (including me) had been spanked as youngsters and never considered it to be a form of abuse. At least one research participant wondered whether the residential school tragedy reflected changing socio-cultural norms and whether our society should be held accountable for past actions that had been acceptable at the time. Other non-Indigenous participants – most of British descent – described their own boarding school experiences. Sylvie felt Indigenous children had been *lucky* to be forcibly removed from their homes, because at least they knew their parents had been unable to stop authorities from taking them away. Her own experience of her parents sending her away during the London Blitz in the Second World War had convinced her that she was unwanted and unloved (Gaver 2011, 281). Brandon, on learning about abuse in one residential school similar to what he had experienced in his British boarding school, essentially asked, "What was so bad about that?" and felt Indigenous people should simply "move on" (Gaver's notes). Other participants who had attended church-run residential schools in other parts of the world had similar queries about residential schools being "so bad." Lana, an Indigenous woman from Africa, brought a photo album to the interview to talk about her positive experiences in an African boarding school, and Raj sought me out at a party to talk about his experiences in a Presbyterian residential school in another country.

Given such personal experiences or relationships with former students who had talked about the residential schools' positive aspects, it is not surprising that many non-Indigenous people have difficulty appreciating the negative impact of residential schools on Canadian Indigenous peoples. It also raises a question: Even when Indigenous children were not taken away from their parents by force, even when few cases of physical and sexual assault occurred (at least in Anglican residential schools of the Northwest Territories), and even when children were allowed – and at times encouraged – to hold onto their own language and aspects of their culture, why are so many social problems involving Indigenous people traced back to the residential schools? (e.g., see Chansonneuve 2005; Kirmayer et al. 2007; Barlow 2009; and Kral 2012). As one research participant wondered, "I think that there's a whole story that is not really heard" (Gaver 2011, 281). Such questions led my research project in a new direction.

Colliding Worldviews

One clue as to what a part of this whole story might be emerged in 2003, when the government and churches were faced with thousands of individual and class action lawsuits, as well as Alternative Dispute Resolution cases (Nagy 2014, 206).[12] If they were found guilty and liable for huge payouts, several churches faced the possibility of bankruptcy.[13] The 2003 version of the Indian Residential Schools Settlement Agreement, which was significantly different from the 2006 official version (IRSSA 2006), set a cap on the amount churches would have to pay. In that agreement, the ACC was liable for $25 million. Individual congregations were pushed to contribute to this $25 million. At one 2003 congregational presentation on the issue, one Indigenous representative stated that many Indigenous peoples were so upset with the Settlement Agreement that they might withdraw from the Alternative Dispute Resolution Process. Euro-Canadian representatives seemed surprised. What emerged from the discussion was how differently the two groups perceived the residential school issue itself, as well as the agreement. The Euro-Canadian perspective was judiciary: Indigenous people were the plaintiffs, and the government and the churches were the defendants. There was no question that both the government and the churches would have to pay, but the ACC risked going bankrupt. The agreement was seen as a pact between the defendants that would guarantee the survival of the ACC; there was no need for the plaintiffs to be involved. "Why would they be?" was the answer given by one clergy. The Indigenous perspective, as I understood it, was relational: the relationship between Indigenous peoples, the government, and the churches had been damaged because of the schools. This had led to a large number of Indigenous children, families, and communities being hurt. The healing of individuals, families, and communities was important, but so too was the need to heal the relationship among the three parties. By excluding Indigenous representatives from part of the 2003 agreement's negotiations, the government and the churches had demonstrated that nothing had really changed: once again, Indigenous peoples were being silenced and marginalized (Gaver 2011, 278; St. Cuthbert's 2003). Good intentions may have existed – the ACC was committed to reconciliation and indemnifying those who had been hurt – but such miscommunication contributed to further hurt and indicated the need to reimagine (or rethink) the whole issue. Political scientist Rosemary Nagy (2014, 206) points out similar dichotomies in the Presbyterian and United Churches: Rev. Stephen Kendall (Presbyterian) spoke of the need to find "a new way of thinking," and Rev. James Scott (United Church) spoke of the shift in perspective from "viewing the lawsuits purely as a 'legal problem to be dealt with' to seeing them as signs of a 'broken relationship that needs mending.'"

How had differences in perceptions contributed to the residential school tragedy? Nowyook said,

> My parents were ... brought up in a life where, when something has to
> be done, it has to be done ... I think that's the way they felt when the
> authorities said they had to send their kids to school. That was something

they had to agree to. There was no other way around it. Even if they didn't want to send us to school, that was out of the question at that time. (Gaver 2011, 152)

Akpalapik explained that her parents held priests in such fear, the same kind of fear they had of their own shamans, that they would never think of opposing them or rejecting their suggestions (Gaver 2011, 295). Accepting situations as "simply the way things are" may have been normative for some Indigenous cultures. Could their responses have been misinterpreted by Euro-Canadian missionaries? Sam insisted that he had given parents the freedom to choose whether to send their children to residential schools (ibid., 168), but did these parents understand that they had this choice? (For a discussion on another type of fear that may also have played a role, see Gaudet and Martin, this volume.)

Alice recounted that an Indigenous friend had asked her to corroborate that she had been abused in the residential school both had attended. Alice declined because she had not seen any abuse, to which her friend replied, "But we had chores to do." What her friend saw as abuse, however, Alice saw as being "part of living as a family; you've got to learn to help in the home" (Gaver 2011, 166). Abuses in residential schools certainly did occur – even according to Euro-Canadian perceptions – and racism certainly existed, but *how much more abuse unknowingly and unintentionally occurred because of unrecognized cultural differences?* Legal scholar Jula Hughes (this volume) states that if (Euro)Canadians had recognized Indigenous parents as having the same parenting capacities as themselves, they "would not have tolerated the forced removal of Indigenous children." However, several research participants reminded me that, in the past, parents – particularly those of British descent – tended to believe that "children should be seen, not heard" and that, particularly among the wealthier class, parents actually sent their children away to boarding schools (Gaver 2011, 333).[14] Anne, one older participant, wondered whether some residential schools had actually been established as places of privilege (ibid., 283–84). Since many of the missionaries in Canada's North did come from Great Britain, might such attitudes have reflected British cultural norms rather than an inability to recognize Indigenous parents as being capable of raising their own children? Since some of the children sent to northern residential schools were of mixed ancestry – their precise numbers are unknown – might the experiences and impacts of residential schools in the North reflect cultural conflicts within families between patriarchal Euro-Canadian values and nonpatriarchal Indigenous backgrounds?

This question is not simply a matter of power differentials, although power is certainly part of the picture. The question of dealing with differences in perceptions and miscommunications in residential school history leads to today's question of *how to accommodate differences without privileging one group over another*. Jessica, an employee of the Northwest Territories government, asked, "How do we organize meetings? Set the agenda? Run the meetings? Who decides? Each decision is based on what we think is 'normal' – but normal according to whom? The Dene? Inuit? Dogrib? Slavey?" (Gaver 2011, 271–72). "We have not paid significant attention to differences in worldviews. So many of our interactions with Indigenous people end up being an interaction of two worldviews" (Gaver's notes). Jessica and a few other Euro-Canadian participants who interacted regularly with Indigenous people in Canada's North seem to have found a part of the whole story that is generally ignored by the media: worldviews-in-collision.

Worldviews are the lenses or filters through which people perceive, interpret, and organize reality. They shape people's views about what is and what ought to be; they shape "patterns and forms of thought, attitudes, time, emotions" (Naugle 2002, 246). Worldviews are essentially *invisible* to both those inside and those outside the society until they come into contact (or conflict) with those holding other worldviews (Guédon and Gaver 2010).

It seems obvious and even simplistic to say that cultures are different, that people from different cultures look at life differently, and that languages reflect these differences. What is not obvious is just how profound these differences are or what happens when people holding radically differing perceptions of the world come into contact with one another at any level. Discussion about cultural genocide in residential schools has often focused on *visible* aspects of culture, such as getting one's hair cut, being forced to wear Euro-Canadian clothing, and being forbidden to speak one's language. Healing and reconciliation initiatives likewise focus on *visible* aspects, such as promoting traditional hair styles and clothing as well as revitalizing traditional languages. Missing from the discussion are the *invisible* and *intangible* dimensions that impacted students in subtle ways, even when schools or staff were respectful of Indigenous cultures.

Differences in worldviews shape so much of what a people take for granted as normal. Why follow a solar calendar of twelve months in the year instead of a lunar one or divide time into seven-day weeks (or in some other way, as did the Dene)? Why have a school year run from September to June? Why categorize items based on genetic makeup rather than on usage? Why define family through mother and father rather than through a mother and mother's brother? Why have surnames? Why give children their father's surname instead of their mother's (or why not name parents after children, as some Dene did)? Why do English and French languages emphasize substance and precision rather than processes and ambiguities (Pinxten, van Dooren, and Harvey 1983, 3–4)? For Euro-Canadians with our Euro-Canadian worldview, the answer would likely be, "That's the way things are done." For Indigenous peoples with their differing worldviews, however, the answer may be, "That's what would never be done." The impact for residential school children, according to Lakota scholar Martin Brokenleg (2012), was a denigration of Indigenous cultures, whether intended or not.

Brokenleg (2012) identifies one basic difference between Western and Indigenous worldviews: the Western worldview (including our Euro-Canadian worldview) is, to a large extent, mono-oriented, unlike the Indigenous worldview. Although simplistic in reducing both Western and Indigenous worldviews to the singular, Brokenleg's categories are still a useful introduction to the topic. According to Brokenleg, Western cultures, strongly influenced by Western Christianity and Greek philosophy, emphasize that there is *one* God and *one* truth or *one* way to follow that God; that governments are hierarchical, with *one* leader at the top; and that businesses tend to be hierarchical, with *one* CEO at the top. Colonialism (however defined), with its emphasis on the superiority of Western culture over other cultures, is another example of the Western worldview. Indigenous worldviews are generally quite different. The Dene (Athapaskan) do not have a single supreme deity or religious dogma; individuals are free to find their own religious paths. No Dene word exists for "chief" because the Dene are a culture in which, traditionally, no single individual has official power over others (Guédon 2005).[15]

Unlike what happened in British boarding schools, in Canadian residential schools, faculty, staff, and students all came into contact with worldviews that were different from their own, with which they had to deal. Among the more obvious were different ways to understand what a family is, what education is, and what religion and the sacred are. A Euro-Canadian nuclear family of the era, for example, comprised a father as head of the family, a mother as his subordinate, and children as nonpersons, assumed to be incapable of making their own decisions and expected to obey without question. An Inuvialuit nuclear family also comprised a father, a mother, and children. Men and women, however, occupied complementary roles, and children were seen as persons and treated according to the kin connections associated with their names.[16] Children were recognized as persons capable of decision making, and parents were even named after their children. Parents could advise and encourage children but not force them to do anything. Athapaskans, in contrast, considered the extended family to be normative. One's kin group was generally matrilineal, with individuals belonging to their mother's side or clan. A clear distinction existed between the children of two brothers or two sisters and the children of a brother and a sister. In the first case, the children of two brothers, or the children of two sisters, and their respective partners would be regarded as siblings. In the second case, the children of a brother and the children of a sister and their respective partners would be regarded as potential mates. No wonder Janna, a Euro-Canadian research participant, believed that Indigenous children were quite bright, although their "relationships were getting horribly garbled" (Gaver 2011, 288). No wonder many Indigenous children came out of residential schools with a confused sense of identity.

The Euro-Canadian education system, grounded in principles of logic and rationality, tends to take a dichotomous approach to learning: things are either true or false, external "objective" knowledge is valued over internal "subjective" knowledge, and written sources have more weight than hearsay evidence. Precision is emphasized and ambiguity avoided. Education occurs within a formal, standardized structure, with students expected to conform to the demands of the system. Among both Inuvialuit and Athapaskan, in contrast, education is generally informal, often on a one-on-one basis, and fluid, being customized to each student's needs and capabilities. Knowledge is based on experience, not on true-or-false binary logic: something may be true *and* false at the same time, depending on the context. Personal experience is valued above, and differentiated from, book knowledge (Goulet 1998). One learns by watching and listening (Athapaskan) or watching and looking (Inuvialuit) rather than by being told or through trial and error (Euro-Canadian) (Gaver 2011, 342).

The different education systems reveal different concepts of power and religion. Within the standardized, "objective" Euro-Canadian educational system is a hidden ontology of an impersonal mechanistic universe (Luckert 1975, 5), where external entities (i.e., teacher, ruler, and God) have authority over the individual and where human beings have authority over the rest of creation. Those with authority have power over those with less or no authority. Those with power can use it to gratify their own desires or to help others. In the Inuvialuit worldview, in contrast, the universe is personal and dynamically alive, existing in relationship with human beings. Competition is encouraged, but so too is a formalized sharing of goods. Leaders are defined by their overall competence and number of relatives. The Athapaskan have a similar worldview: The universe is personal and dynamically alive, existing in relationship with human beings; it is not particularly hierarchical. Competitiveness and cooperation are both valued, and self-reliance is seen as the key to belonging to the community. The whole world, which includes what Euro-Canadians divide into "natural" and "supernatural," is essentially sacred. Human beings are part of nature, neither distinct from it nor superior to it. Communication and intelligence are gifts from the animal and spirit world (Gaver 2011, 344).

In Anglican northern residential schools, these different worldviews collided. It was, however, an unequal collision. Euro-Canadian faculty and staff had power (defined in Euro-Canadian terms) over Indigenous children. Perhaps more importantly, they were adults with a well-formed sense of cultural identity; children, depending on their age, often did not have that same strong sense of cultural identity. Many were able to deal with the alternate reality presented by the adults (e.g., Nowyook accepted "that's how the whites did it") without losing their own (Gaver's notes). Many, particularly if they had a European or Euro-Canadian parent, already had some familiarity with the Euro-Canadian worldview and could function within it.

Unfortunately, many were not familiar with Euro-Canadians and could not function. They could not accept the Euro-Canadian understanding of reality, with its emphasis on absolutes or on valuing humans above the rest of creation, which so contradicted the reality defined by their parents and their community. Nor could they continue to accept the understanding of reality defined by their parents and community, with its emphasis on ambiguities and on the interconnectedness of humans and the rest of creation, which so contradicted the reality defined by those in authority in the schools. Even when faculty and staff tried to respect and promote traditional cultures, the underlying message – the implicit teaching within the schools – was an undermining of traditional values and an increasing alienation from one's traditional culture. Too many Indigenous children were caught, as historian Kenneth Coates (1989) notes, "betwixt and between." What they were learning in the schools fractured their sense of normality, shattering at times their sense of reality itself.

Although worldviews-in-collision were very much part of the residential school life, they *continue* to be part of life in today's public schools and today's society. Small wonder that even quite recently, Indigenous bishop Mark MacDonald (2009) could speak of a "bifurcation of body and soul" that continues to plague Indigenous students in Canadian schools. Moving beyond the paternalism and colonialism of the residential school era requires more than just looking at power differentials; it requires seeing *everything* within the Western ontological system – in every discipline, from the humanities to the sciences – as a representation of a Western worldview rather than as an objective empirical truth. Until Euro-Canadians are willing to do so, they will not be able to grasp the devastation that many Indigenous people suffered *and continue to suffer* as a result of the Euro-Canadian residential and public school systems.

❧

My research originated with questions about the relationship between Indigenous and Euro-Canadian peoples in Canada's Anglican North in the era after residential schools. Nevertheless, the focus changed during the course of the project. One finding that emerged was how hard it is for Euro-Canadians to grasp the devastation that the residential schools caused to Indigenous peoples and communities.

This chapter explores three factors contributing to this difficulty: ignorance and indifference; personal knowledge; and, most importantly, worldviews-in-collision, which too often shattered children's constructs of reality, leaving them betwixt and between their traditional Indigenous and Euro-Canadian cultures. Yet might this conclusion itself be rooted in the Euro-Canadian worldview that one can live in only *one* world, with only *one* name, only *one* personality, and only *one* gender, rather than reflecting the reality of the Athapaskan, Inuvialuit, and many other worldviews held by Indigenous students and staff in the residential schools? Might even the concept of generic categories such as "Indigenous" and "Euro-Canadian" reflect a Euro-Canadian perspective and have little meaning for people who categorize others not in terms of abstract commonalities but in terms of one's relationship with them?

More could be written about, and more research is needed to better understand, each of the above factors.[17] Euro-Canadians live in shared spaces with Indigenous and other non-Indigenous people. How do we negotiate our differences in a way that is respectful of ourselves and others and that is cognizant of the impact of our actions on one another? As one participant in the research project asked, "In our efforts to make things better [*or develop economically?*], what unconscious, unrecognized, and unacknowledged values and worldviews might we bring to what we do? What are we doing now that's the same but we don't recognize it?" (Gaver 2011, 283).

Ultimately, many reasons exist for why Euro-Canadians do not grasp how devastating residential schools were for Indigenous peoples and communities. One important reason – which seems to be generally unrecognized by the dominant society – is that Euro-Canadians still do not realize just how different Indigenous societies are from their own.

NOTES

1 "Euro-Canadian" refers to "whites," and "non-Aboriginal" refers to "whites" and others (e.g., Chinese).
2 "Canada's North" generally also includes Nunavut.
3 The term "colonialism" has been defined in numerous ways, and numerous types of colonialism have been identified. This topic, however, is beyond the scope of this chapter. My research, using David Perley's (1993) characterization of colonialism expounded by Agnes Grant (1996, 87), focused primarily on colonialism in terms of paternalism and racism.
4 Anglican Church of Canada Archives (ACC Archives), Toronto, Ontario, Diocese of the Arctic Collection, Hay River Series, M71–4.
5 Cultural anthropologist A. Richard King (1967, 12) claims that there was a "relative meaninglessness of legalism in identifying Indian and non-Indian" and that the issue meant more to scholars than to many in the North.
6 *Arctic Mission,* 1929–48, 1933 issue, located in Diocese of the Arctic (D-Arctic), Yellowknife, Northwest Territories.
7 These discoveries did not lead me to reject colonialism as a component of the relationship between Indigenous and Euro-Canadian peoples but rather to reject Grant's (1996) conclusion that colonialism is the defining component of that relationship.
8 For example, St. Simon's Anglican Church in Oakville, Ontario, held two educational series on Indigenous issues in 2008 and 2009, but only those already involved in some way with Indigenous peoples or the issue attended the sessions at which I was present.
9 Names of participants in the research project have been changed in order to preserve anonymity.

10 "Gaver's notes" refers to interview quotations not included in my dissertation.

11 Matthew 25:31–46 and 28:19–20 are biblical imperatives for many Christian initiatives, including education. Many Canadian universities – including McGill, McMaster, Laval, and Ottawa – have religious beginnings.

12 Political scientist Rosemary Nagy (2014, 206) writes, "by the time of the IRSSA [Settlement Agreement], there were almost 15,000 individual claims ... 5,000 Alternative Dispute Resolution cases ... and 11 class action lawsuits." Among them was the *Baxter* class action, which represented 80,000 direct and intergenerational survivors and "ultimately claimed $100 billion in damages" (ibid., 205).

13 The Diocese of Cariboo ceased operations in 2001, and the "remaining parishes in the Southern Ontario Region of the Diocese of Keewatin" were transferred to the Diocese of Rupert's Land (ACC 2015).

14 The *Harry Potter* books and movies reveal how much a part of British culture boarding schools still are.

15 Marie-Françoise Guédon, personal communication with author, December 23, 2013.

16 In Inuit cultures, one's *atiq*, or "soul-name," determines one's relations. According to anthropologist Hugh Brody (1987, 139), "If I give my grandfather's *atiq* to my baby daughter, she *is* my grandfather" (emphasis in original; see also Gaver 2011, 330). People who have the same name are seen as being related; if one changed one's name, these relationships would also change.

17 Some scholars, such as Kristin Norget (2007), are exploring the relationship between the churches, Christian theology, and (de)colonialism. Others, such as Christine Elsey (2013), are looking at "the clash of meaning and being between colonial institutions and First Nations." A number of Indigenous scholars, including Brokenleg (2012), are exploring Indigenous Christianity. Even so, more needs to be done. What role did Christian theology play in how Christians interacted with Indigenous peoples? What lessons have been learned, or is the same narrative being played out in new forms today?

PARTICIPANTS IN RESEARCH PROJECT

Indigenous:	Akpalapik, Kavik, Kudloo, Nowyook
Mixed heritage:	Joanne, Kiawak
Non-Indigenous:	Alice, Alistair, Anne, Arthur, Brandon, Darien, Erica, Floyd, Frank, Gary, Janna, Jessica, Moriah, Sam, Sylvie, Tyler

REFERENCES

Anglican Church of Canada (ACC). 1967. "Report of General Synod Committee on Indian and Eskimo Affairs." August 1. http://www.anglican.ca/tr/newsarchive/pr16/.

–. 2015. "Dioceses and Ecclesiastical Provinces of the Anglican Church of Canada." http://www.anglican.ca/resources/dioceses/.

–. 2016a. "Anglican Healing Fund." http://www.anglican.ca/healingfund/.

–. 2016b. "Historical Sketch for Anglican Residential Schools." http://www.anglican.ca/tr/schools/.

–. 2016c. "A History of Our Work." http://www.anglican.ca/im/ahistory/.

Barlow, J. Kevin. 2009. *Residential Schools, Prisons, and HIV/AIDS among Aboriginal People in Canada: Exploring the Connections*. Ottawa: Aboriginal Healing Foundation.

Barry, Lisa, dir. 1993. *Dancing the Dream*. VHS. Toronto: Anglican Video for the Council for Native Ministries.

Brody, Hugh. 1987. *Living Arctic: Hunters of the Canadian North*. Vancouver: Douglas and McIntyre.

Brokenleg, Martin. 2012. "Culture in Education." Presentation to the Aboriginal Education Centre. http://www.prn.bc.ca/abed/wp-content/uploads/2012/03/CULTURE-IN-EDUCATION-Compatibility-Mode.pdf.

Carlson, Joyce. 1995. *Dancing the Dream: The First Nations and Church in Partnership*. Toronto: Anglican Book Centre.

Carlson, Joyce, and Alf Dumont. 1997. *Bridges in Spirituality: First Nations Christian Women Tell Their Stories*. Toronto: United Church Publishing House.

Chansonneuve, Deborah. 2005. *Reclaiming Connections: Understanding Residential School Trauma among Aboriginal People*. Ottawa: Aboriginal Healing Foundation.

Coates, Kenneth S. 1986. "A Very Imperfect Means of Education: Indian Day Schools in the Yukon Territory, 1890–1955." In *Indian Education in Canada*, vol. 1, *The Legacy*, ed. Jean Barman, Yvonne Hébert, and Don McCaskill, 132–49. Vancouver: UBC Press.

–. 1989. "'Betwixt and Between': The Anglican Church and the Children of the Carcross (Chooutla) Residential School, 1911–1954." In *Interpreting Canada's North: Selected Readings*, ed. Kenneth S. Coates and William R. Morrison, 150–68. Toronto: Copp Clark Pitman.

–. 1991. *Best Left as Indians: Native-White Relations in the Yukon Territory, 1840–1973*. Montreal and Kingston: McGill-Queen's University Press.

Coates, Kenneth S., and William R. Morrison. 1988. *Land of the Midnight Sun: A History of the Yukon*. Edmonton: Hurtig.

Devitt, W.G. 1965. "History of Education in the Northwest Territories." In *The Canadian Superintendent 1964: Education North of 60*, ed. Canadian Association of School Superintendents and Inspectors, Department of Northern Affairs and National Resources, 61–67. Toronto: Ryerson.

Elsey, Christine J. 2013. *The Poetics of Land and Identity among British Columbia Indigenous Peoples*. Halifax, NS: Fernwood.

Gaver, Cheryl. 2011. "Solitudes in Shared Spaces: Aboriginal and EuroCanadian Anglicans in the Yukon and the Northwest Territories in the Post–Residential School Era." PhD diss., University of Ottawa. http://www.ruor.uottawa.ca/handle/10393/19995.

Goulet, Jean-Guy. 1998. *Ways of Knowing: Experience, Knowledge, and Power among the Dene Tha*. Lincoln: University of Nebraska Press.

Grant, Agnes. 1996. *No End of Grief: Indian Residential Schools in Canada*. Winnipeg, MB: Pemmican.

Guédon, Marie-Françoise. 2005. *Le rêve et la forêt: Histoires de chamanes nabesna*. Quebec City: Presses de l'Université Laval.

Guédon, Marie-Françoise, and Cheryl Gaver. 2010. "Intangible Culture: Perspectives on the Immaterial Aspects of the Human World." Paper presented to the Canadian Museums Association National Conference, St. John's, Newfoundland and Labrador, May 10–15.

Hendry, Charles E. 1969. *Beyond Traplines: Does the Church Really Care? Towards an Assessment of the Work of the Anglican Church of Canada with Canada's Native Peoples*. Reprint, Toronto: Ryerson, 1998.

Indian Residential Schools Settlement Agreement (IRSSA). 2006. *Indian Residential Schools Settlement Agreement*. Ottawa: Government of Canada. http://www.residentialschool settlement.ca/irs%20settlement%20agreement-%20english.pdf.

Johns, Robert E. 1971. "St. Peter's Mission and Education in Hay River N.W.T. prior to 1950." Paper submitted to Fr. A. Renaud, located in Prince of Wales Heritage Centre, Yellowknife.

King, A. Richard. 1967. *The School at Mopass: A Problem of Identity*. Ed. George Spindler and Louise Spindler. New York: Holt, Rinehart and Winston.

King, Thomas. 2013. "'The Problem of Indian Administration,' Then and Now." *national Post*, October 16. http://news.nationalpost.com/full-comment/thomas-king-the -problem-of-indian-administration-then-and-now.

Kirmayer, Laurence J., Gregory M. Bass, Tara Holton, Ken Paul, Cori Simpson, and Caroline Tait. 2007. *Suicide among Aboriginal People in Canada*. Ottawa: Aboriginal Healing Foundation.

Kral, M.J. 2012. "Postcolonial Suicide among Inuit in Arctic Canada." *Culture, Medicine and Psychiatry* 36 (2): 326. http://dx.doi.org/10.1007/s11013-012-9260-4.

Luckert, Karl W. 1975. *The Navajo Hunter Tradition*. Tucson: University of Arizona Press.

MacDonald, Mark. 2009. "Self-Determination and Governance." Talk presented at St. Simon's Anglican Church, Oakville, Ontario, October 21.

Marsh, Donald Ben. 1967. *A History of the Work of the Anglican Church in the Area Now Known as the Diocese of the Arctic*. Yellowknife, NT: Diocese of the Arctic.

Miller, James R. 2003. *Shingwauk's Vision: A History of Native Residential Schools*. Toronto: University of Toronto Press.

Milloy, John S. 2003. *"A National Crime": The Canadian Government and the Residential School System, 1879 to 1986*. Winnipeg: University of Manitoba Press.

Milroy, Sarah. 2013. "A Stirring Exhibit Explores the Culture Fallout of Residential Schools." *Globe and Mail*, September 20. http://www.theglobeandmail.com/arts/art-and -architecture/a-stirring-exhibit-explores-the-cultural-fallout-of-residential-schools/ article14435382/comments/.

Nagy, Rosemary. 2014. "The Truth and Reconciliation Commission of Canada: Genesis and Design." *Canadian Journal of Law and Society* 29 (2): 199–217. http://dx.doi. org/10.1017/cls.2014.8.

Naugle, David K. 2002. *Worldview: The History of a Concept*. Grand Rapids, MI: William B. Eerdmans.

Norget, Kristin. 2007. "Decolonization and the Politics of Syncretism: The Catholic Church, Indigenous Theology and Cultural Autonomy in Oaxaca, Mexico." *International Education* 37 (1): http://trace.tennessee.edu/internationaleducation/vol37/iss1/5.

Perkel, Colin. 2013. "Harper Tories 'On the Side of Pedophiles and Sadists' by Hiding Information on Residential School Abuse, NDP Charges." *National Post*, October 22. http://news.nationalpost.com/news/canada/canadian-politics/harper-tories-on- side-of-pedophiles-and-sadists-by-hiding-information-on-residential-school-abuse- ndp-charges.

Perley, David G. 1993. "Aboriginal Education in Canada as Internal Colonialism." *Canadian Journal of Native Education* 20 (1): 118–28.

Pinxten, Rik, Ingrid van Dooren, and Frank Harvey. 1983. *The Anthropology of Space*. Philadelphia: University of Pennsylvania Press.

Slobodin, Richard. 1966. *Metis of the Mackenzie District*. Ottawa: Canadian Research Centre for Anthropology, Saint-Paul University.

Smith, Joanna. 2013. "Auditor General's Report 2013: Lack of Co-operation Threatens Indian Residential Schools Historical Record." *Toronto Star,* April 30. https://www.thestar.com/news/canada/2013/04/30/auditor_generals_report_2013_lack_of_cooperation_threatens_indian_residential_schools_agreement.html.

Sperry, John R. 2005. *Igloo Dwellers Were My Church.* Yellowknife, NT: Outcrop.

St. Cuthbert's. 2003. "Towards Healing, Reconciliation and New Life." Presentation to the Anglican Church of Canada, March 15.

Woods, Eric T. 2016. *A Cultural Sociology of Anglican Mission and the Indian Residential Schools in Canada: The Long Road to Apology.* New York: Palgrave Macmillan.

Epilogue

CHARLES R. MENZIES (GITXAAŁA)

> Colonialism is not simply content to impose its rule upon the
> present and the future of a dominated country. Colonialism is not
> satisfied merely with holding a people in its grip and emptying the
> native's brain of all form and content. By a kind of perverted logic,
> it turns to the past of the oppressed people, and distorts, disfigures,
> and destroys it. This work of devaluing pre-colonial history takes
> on a dialectical significance today.
>
> – Frantz Fanon, *The Wretched of the Earth*, 1963

FRANTZ FANON IDENTIFIES the critical relevance of a resurgent national
culture in the context of revolutionary struggles for political independence
from colonialism in Africa. Despite having been written more than sixty
years ago, these words were prescient and have immediacy today in Canada.
Indigenous peoples have been engaged in a permanent struggle for autonomy
practically since the first settlers arrived on our shores. The struggle has
waxed and waned. Over the twentieth century, the colonists appeared to
take the upper hand. However, a renewed and resurgent indigenism is re-
verberating throughout Canada. From the decentred politics of Idle No
More to legal victories and government apologies, history is being restoried
as Indigenous peoples compel settlers to take note.

Our history can no longer be ignored. The Truth and Reconciliation
Commission of Canada's findings were stark: Canada committed cultural

genocide through the systemic support of the Indian residential schools over the course of more than a century. These schools took children from their homes, maltreated them, abused them, and did all of that under a cultural framework of white supremacy and a political framework of colonialism. As Fanon (1963, 211) notes in regard to Africa, colonialism is an active process by which a people's sense of self, sense of dignity, and sense of self-worth are deliberately and directly diminished and attacked: "The effect consciously sought by colonialism was to drive into the natives' heads the idea that if the settlers were to leave, they would at once fall back into barbarism, degradation, and bestiality." There is no other way to comprehend the objectives, processes, and outcomes of Canada's residential school system.

The findings of the Truth and Reconciliation Commission (2015, 1) provide empirical evidence of the depravity of Canada's colonialism:

> For over a century, the central goals of Canada's Aboriginal policy were to eliminate Aboriginal governments; ignore Aboriginal rights; terminate the Treaties; and, through a process of assimilation, cause Aboriginal peoples to cease to exist as distinct legal, social, cultural, religious, and racial entities in Canada. The establishment and operation of residential schools were a central element of this policy, which can best be described as "cultural genocide."

Central to the displacement of Indigenous peoples from our lands was the program of silencing us and the attempt to take away our memory and knowledge of our land, of our history, and of our ability to enact jurisdiction over these same things. Residential schools played a part in the reconstruction of memories, histories, and stories that prioritized the assumed racial superiority of the colonizing elite. Fortunately, the policy was not as successful as its architects may have hoped.

This volume resonates with Fanon's call to pay attention to the role of culture, history, and Indigenous intellectuals. The editors deploy the idea of restorying, a process that questions the imposition of colonial narratives. This notion places the emphasis upon the active work of confronting colonial narratives. Although there are problems inherent to restorying, particularly if the practice remains locked in the arcane world of letters, the contributors to this volume offer up the possibility of a future beyond restorying. There is a call to action embedded at the heart of this volume. Here, too, we find an echo of Fanon's description of the Indigenous intellectual's path toward joining in the liberation struggle.

Fanon, in discussing the role of intellectuals in the struggle for political liberation, outlines three phases through which the Native intellectual must pass. I suggest that the non-Indigenous fellow-traveller intellectuals might well find themselves on a similar trajectory. Fanon's (1963, 222–23) phases are

1 "the period of unqualified assimilation ... [Here] the native intellectual gives proof that he is assimilated to the culture of the occupying power";
2 the period during which the intellectual "decides to recognize what he is ... But since the native is not a part of his people, since he only has exterior relations with his people, he is content to recall their life only. Past happenings of the bygone days of childhood will be brought up out of the depths of his memory; old legends will be reinterpreted in the light of borrowed estheticism and of a conception of the world which was discovered under other skies"; and
3 "the fighting phase," when "the native, after having tried to lose himself in the people and with the people, will on the contrary shake the people. Instead of according the people's lethargy an honoured place in his esteem, he turns himself into an awakener of the people."

Fanon (1963, 227) cautions the Indigenous intellectual that "it is not enough to try and get back to the people in that past out of which they have already emerged; rather we must join them in that fluctuating movement which they are just giving a shape to, and which, as soon as it has started, will be the signal for everything to be called into question."

This volume is located somewhere between Fanon's second and third phases. There are aspects of the chapters that reveal a self-awareness of one's place in the colonial moment (for both Indigenous and non-Indigenous authors). Some of the chapters are clearly placed in the fighting phase, linking experience, history, and an articulation of a possibility to finally reconcile the colonial state to the Indigenous nations (rather than the reverse). This undertaking constitutes a call to action that echoes Fanon but is rooted in our current Canadian context.

This call to action has a long history within anthropology as well. Kathleen Gough (1968), then a professor at Simon Fraser University, exhorted her colleagues in the late 1960s to join with the liberation struggles of her day as allies in struggle. For non-Indigenous intellectuals, Gough's call and Fanon's analysis remain relevant and pressing. It is important to understand the intellectual currents of the contemporary struggle if one is to see the importance of restorying and rejecting the colonial narrative. The chapters in this volume all achieve this end. But in and of itself, that is not enough. We must also take action.

"The colonized man who writes for his people ought to use the past with the intention of opening the future, as an invitation to action and a basis of hope" (Fanon 1963, 232). This volume draws from the past and goes beyond the disempowering stories of victimhood. The artful, poignant, and perceptive analyses presented here offer a modicum of hope for change. To ensure that we do not squander this possibility, we must all transform the ivory tower and join with the Indigenous struggle for liberation and autonomy.

REFERENCES

Fanon, Frantz. 1963. *The Wretched of the Earth: The Handbook for the Black Revolution That Is Changing the Shape of the World*. New York: Grove Weidenfeld.

Gough, Kathleen. 1968. "Anthropology and Imperialism." *Monthly Review* 19 (11): 12–27. http://dx.doi.org/10.14452/MR-019-11-1968-04_2.

Truth and Reconciliation Commission of Canada (TRC). 2015. *Honouring the Truth, Reconciling for the Future: Summary of the Final Report of the Truth and Reconciliation Commission of Canada*. Ottawa: Truth and Reconciliation Commission of Canada. http://www.trc.ca/websites/trcinstitution/File/2015/Findings/Exec_Summary_2015_05_31_web_o.pdf.

Acknowledgments

First and foremost, we would like to thank the survivors of forced residential schooling in Canada and their relatives. Their stories are the cornerstone and lifeblood of this volume. For their faith and dedication, a special thanks to our contributors, as well as to Darcy Cullen and Lesley Erickson at UBC Press. We are also deeply grateful to our three anonymous reviewers. Their incisive comments have greatly improved this book. Thank you also to our colleagues at the School of Sociological and Anthropological Studies at the University of Ottawa for their friendship and intellectual stimulation. And, of course, our most sincere gratitude to our respective companions (Nolwenn and Wren) and children (Eliot, Louis, Aurélia, and Arthur).

Brieg acknowledges the intellectual support of Ronald Niezen, Jeffrey C. Alexander, Michel Wieviorka, and Marie-Blanche Tahon; the financial support of the Social Sciences and Humanities Research Council of Canada; and the logistical support of the Institute of Canadian and Aboriginal Studies and the Centre for Interdisciplinary Research on Citizenship and Minorities (CIRCEM), both at the University of Ottawa.

Karine acknowledges the research assistance of Kristin Glenn, Audrey Rousseau, and Halyna Mokrushyna; the financial support of the University of Ottawa; and the highly valuable support of various writing groups organized by Françoise Moreau-Johnson at the University of Ottawa.

Contributors

Brieg Capitaine holds a PhD in sociology from the École des Hautes Études en Sciences Sociales (Paris) and completed a SSHRC postdoctoral fellowship at McGill University. He is a professor of sociology at the School of Sociological and Anthropological Studies at the University of Ottawa. He is also co-director of the participation and citizenship research axis at the Centre for Interdisciplinary Research on Citizenship and Minorities (CIRCEM) at the University of Ottawa. He has published many journal articles and book chapters on Indigenous movements, violence, racism, and the politics of recognition. He is co-editor (with Geoffrey Pleyers) of *Penser les mouvements sociaux des années 2010* (2016).

Janice Cindy Gaudet is working on her doctorate at the University of Ottawa. She is a Métis from a farming community in Saskatchewan. Her current research explores the evolving practice and legitimization of Indigenous theories, philosophies, and methodologies. She sits on the board of the Aboriginal Healing Foundation and is a student of traditional knowledge. Her publications include "Dismantling the Patriarchal Altar from Within," in *AlterNative: An International Journal of Indigenous Peoples* (2014), "Rethinking Participatory Research with Indigenous Peoples," in the journal *Native American and Indigenous Studies* (2014), and "Is There Hope?" a chapter co-authored with William Louttit in the anthology *Reconciliation and the Way Forward* (2014).

Cheryl Gaver received a doctorate in religious studies from the University of Ottawa, a master of arts in religion and culture from Wilfrid Laurier University, a certificate in Jewish-Christian relations from the Centre for the Study of Jewish-Christian Relations, Cambridge, England, and a master of divinity from Knox College, Toronto. Her primary focus is the intersection points between cultures, particularly how different cultures negotiate and accommodate differing worldviews. Her doctoral thesis explores the relationship between Indigenous and Euro-Canadian Anglicans in the Yukon and Northwest Territories in the era after the residential schools.

Robyn Green received a doctorate in Canadian studies from Carleton University in 2016. Focusing on concomitant discourses of investment and therapy in policy and legal documents, her doctoral research explores how Indigenous-settler reconciliation in Canada is frequently enacted to not only compensate Indigenous peoples but also generate material and affective "returns" for the settler state. Her publications have been featured in the *Canadian Journal of Law and Society* (2012) and, more recently, in Cynthia Sugars and Eleanor Ty's anthology *Canadian Literature and Cultural Memory* (2014).

Jula Hughes is an associate professor of law at the University of New Brunswick. Her main research areas are judicial ethics, particularly disqualification, and the application of criminal law to marginalized and vulnerable populations. She is the principal investigator on a project titled "Urban Aboriginal People and the Honour of the Crown," which explores the application of the duty to consult to urban and off-reserve Aboriginal populations. Her publications on the Truth and Reconciliation Commission of Canada include "Home Truths about Truth Commissions," in Sasha Baglay and Laverne Jacobs's anthology *The Nature of Inquisitorial Processes in Administrative Regimes* (2013), and "Instructive Past: Lessons from the Royal Commission on Aboriginal Peoples for the Canadian Truth and Reconciliation Commission on Indian Residential Schools," in the *Canadian Journal of Law and Society* (2012).

Lawrence Martin is also known as Wapistan, which means "marten" in the Cree language. He grew up in a small community called Moose River Crossing with his mom, sister, and grandparents. He is a musician and

Juno Award recipient, a traditional healer, and a grandfather. He has been an elected leader as grand chief of seven First Nations communities and has been a mayor of two towns in Ontario, Cochrane and Sioux Lookout, making him the first "Native" person to ever become the mayor of a municipality. He currently resides in Quebec near Ottawa, running his business, Dudem Incorporated, with his wife, Angela. They assist First Nations communities in developing their agreements with mining companies. His most recent of many music productions is called *Train of Life* (2014).

Charles R. Menzies is a professor in the Department of Anthropology at the University of British Columbia (UBC), Vancouver. In addition to producing anthropological films, his primary research interests are natural resource management (primarily fisheries-related), political economy, contemporary First Nations issues, maritime anthropology, and the archaeology of British Columbia's North Coast. He has conducted field research in and has produced films concerning the North Coast, including archaeological research; Brittany, France; and Donegal, Ireland. His current research project, "Laxyuup Gitxaała," combines archaeological and socio-cultural anthropology to document the traditional territory of the Gitxaała First Nation. Other projects include founding and directing the Ethnographic Film Unit at UBC, establishing the online journal *New Proposals,* and coordinating an ecological-anthropology research group at UBC called Forests and Oceans for the Future.

Arie Molema recently completed a doctorate in the Department of Anthropology at the University of Toronto. His dissertation explores the politics of memory, affect, and discourse at the Truth and Reconciliation Commission of Canada, focusing in particular on Labrador Inuit experiences based on research conducted in collaboration with the Nunatsiavut government's Department of Health and Social Development.

Ronald Niezen is the Katharine A. Pearson Chair in Civil Society and Public Policy in the Faculties of Law and Arts at McGill University. He holds a doctorate from Cambridge University. His books include *The Origins of Indigenism: Human Rights and the Politics of Difference* (2003), *Public Justice and the Anthropology of Law* (2010), and *Truth and Indignation: Canada's Truth and Reconciliation Commission on Indian Residential Schools* (2013).

Simone Poliandri is an assistant professor of anthropology at Bridgewater State University, Massachusetts, where he teaches social science and Native American studies. He earned a doctorate in anthropology at Brown University, Providence. He has worked with the Mi'kmaw people of the Canadian Maritimes since 2000 on issues of contemporary identity dynamics and, most recently, Indigenous nationhood and nation building. He has published an ethnography titled *First Nations, Identity, and Reserve Life: The Mi'kmaq of Nova Scotia* (2011) and is currently editing a collection on *Native American Nationalism and Nation-Rebuilding*, to be published by SUNY Press. He is an editorial board member for the series "Ethnographie Americane," published at the Sapienza University of Rome, Italy. He lives in Massachusetts with his wife and daughter.

Karine Vanthuyne is an associate professor at the School of Sociological and Anthropological Studies at the University of Ottawa. In 2003, she won the Association canadienne des sociologues et anthropologues de langue française's Prix d'excellence Georges-Henri Lévesque and, in 2008, the Association for Political and Legal Anthropology's Best Student Paper Prize. Her research on violence, memory, and transitional justice in Guatemala has appeared in various journals, including the *Political and Legal Anthropology Review* (2009), *Ethnologie Française* (2011), and the *Journal of Genocide Research* (2016). She is also the author of *La présence d'un passé de violences* (2014). Her current research focuses on memories of colonization, Indigenous peoples and self-determination, and mining in Canada and Guatemala.

Eric Taylor Woods is a lecturer in sociology at the University of East London and a faculty fellow in the Center for Cultural Sociology, Yale University. He is also a member of the editorial boards of the journals *Nations and Nationalism* and *Cultural Sociology*, as well as an adviser to the Association for the Study of Ethnicity and Nationalism. His doctoral dissertation was awarded by the London School of Economics and Political Science in 2012. His research lies at the intersection of cultural, historical, and political sociology, with interests in nationalism, empire, and the British missionary enterprise. His books include *A Cultural Sociology of Anglican Mission and the Indian Residential Schools in Canada: The Long Road to Apology* (2016) and *The Cultural Politics of Nationalism and Nation-Building: Ritual and Performance in the Forging of Nations* (co-edited with R. Tsang, 2013).

Index

commission model, 13, 22*n*4. *See also*
National Indian Brotherhood
assimilation: centralization policy, 117–18;
church role, 188, 195*n*15; cultural shaming, 80–81, 96; definition, 115; education policy criticisms, 36; elimination
through legislation, 79, 90*n*5, 116;
humanitarian policy, 33–34; residential
schooling goals, 4, 5, 36, 42. *See also*
colonialism; residential school system
Athapaskan peoples, 212, 213, 214
Atlantic National Event, 74–90, 90*n*1
Atlantic National Event Concept Paper,
82
Australia (reconciliation), 193
autonomy, 158–60, 167, 220–23

Baker, Emerance, 75, 78, 90*n*2
Basque, Elsie Charles (survivor), 131*n*1
Bauer, Otto, 114
Baxter class action lawsuit, 82, 216*n*12
Bealy, Joanne, 38
belonging. *See* community
Benedict (pope), 195*n*14
Benjamin, Walter, 150
Bergson, Henri, 17
Bernard, Nora (survivor), 18, 82, 118, 120,
124, 127, 131
Bernhardt, Earnie (survivor), 187–88
Bhabha, Homi, 177, 192
Bishop Horden Hall (Moose Factory
Indian Residential School – Anglican),
161–66
Blackned, Fred (survivor), 164–67
Blackstock, Cindy, 148
boarding schools (British), 206–7, 209,
216*n*14
Borrows, John, 79, 86
Brave Heart, Maria Yellow Horse, 71*n*30
Breaking the Silence (Assembly of First
Nations report), 5, 80
British empire. *See* colonialism
Brody, Hugh, 216*n*16
Brokenleg, Martin, 211, 216*n*17
Brown, Father J. W., 115
Brown, Terri, 187
Bryce, Peter (Bryce Report), 34, 35
Butera, Eloge (survivor), 65–66

calls to action (decolonization), 221–23
Canada (North): about, 200–1; defined,
198, 215*n*2; immigration, 201
Candau, Joël, 17
capacity, 70*n*8, 165, 168–69
Capitaine, Brieg, 9, 18, 86
Cardinal, Harold, 37–38
Carnegie Corporation, 145
Cartwright community (Lockwood
Boarding School), 142, 151*n*6
Catholic Church: apology, 7, 185–89,
195*n*14; church coalition, 118, 131*n*7;
conciliatory mimicry, 14–15; pedophilia,
viii; reconciliation perspective, 10, 14–15,
185–89, 195*nn*14–15; residential schools,
115–16, 164; sexual abuse, 41–42, vii–viii;
survivor protests, 119
Catholic Register, 185–89, 195*n*13
Cattel, Jacob J., 17
Cecilia Jeffrey Indian Residential School
(Presbyterian), 38–39
Center for Cultural Sociology, 31
Chatlain, Bishop Murray, 186
Chaw-win-is, 21
child welfare system, 137, 148
Chrisjohn, Roland, 77
Christianity and reconciliation, 185–86,
204, 216*n*11, 216*n*17
churches: coalitions, 118, 131*n*7; conciliatory mimicry, 14–15, 178, 181–93; friendship, 186; lawsuits, 127–28; publications,
181–91; reconciliation perspectives, 45,
177–94, 195*n*11, 204, 215*n*8, 216*n*11; residential school funding, 206; residential
school statistics, 195*n*15; residential
schooling role, 188, 195*n*15; student
sponsorships, 183; survivor protests, 119
Circle of Reconciliation, 85, 90*nn*7–8
Climo, Maria G., 17
Coates, Kenneth, 200, 214
Coeur d'Alene family (survivors), 156
Cole, Jennifer, 157, 161, 168
collective identity, 53, 55–59, 66–69, 113
collective memory, 16–18, 66–69, 149–50
colonial mimicry, 84, 177–78
colonialism: "best left as Indian" approach,
200, 205; characterizations, 200; civilizing mission, 32–33; vs coloniality, 15;

cultural genocide, 46; genocide, 65–66; goals, 177, 221; government policy, 136, 150*n*2; land dispossession, 87–89, 117–18, 129; legislation, 79, 90*n*5, 116; logic of elimination, 79, 90*n*5, 116; racism, 7, 78, 88, 117, 140, 144, 200, 209; reconciliation process, 193–94; religion and research, 216*n*17; restorying and end, 129–30, 220–23; shame as trickery, 96; terminology, 215*n*3; worldview collision, 211. *See also* assimilation

common experience, 114–15, 120

Common Experience Payment, 8–9, 10, 11, 19, 44, 166

community: belonging, 128, 143, 146, 168, 213; concepts, 157, 168; empowerment, 127–28; moral projects, 145, 157, 161, 167–70; relocation, 137, 146–48

compensation hearings, 194*n*5

conciliatory mimicry (churches), 14–15, 178, 181–93

constructivist theory, 32, 52

conversations: decolonization and renewal, 107; harmony, 98; personal accounts, 100–5; research method, 98; shame, 99–107; sharing, 98–99; truth-telling spaces, 95–96

Coppermine residential school, 202

Corntassel, Jeff, 14, 21, 128

Coulthard, Glen, 89, 130

countermemories, 17–19

Craik, Brian, 169–70

Cree nation: autonomy, 158–60, 167; community, 156–57, 160–67, 170; cultural identity, 20, 169–71; homelands, 157–60, 169–70; land rights, 159; language, 104, 105, 162–63, 166, 168; legends, 10, 105–7; parenting skills loss, 125, 132*n*23; residential school narratives, 10, 20; self-reliance, 20; shame and identity loss, 100–1; traditional ways of life, 165

Cree-Naskapi Act (1984), 159

Crosby, Réverend Doug, 7

Crown law, 140

cultural genocide: vs real genocide, 63–65; residential schools, 43, 44, 46, 203, 210, 221; survivance and love, 75, 90*n*2; terminology, 64, 71*n*29, 71*n*31

cultural identity. *See* Indigenous cultural identity

cultural shaming, 80–81

cultural trauma: before and after, 50–51; classification, 51, 52, 54; collective identity, 66–69; community relocation, 146–48; countermemories, 18; examples, 50–51; individual experience, 53; social theory, 51–53. *See also* historical trauma; intergenerational trauma

Curthoys, Anne, 193

Das, Veena, 171*n*2

Davin, Nicolas Flood (Indian Affairs), 33–34

day schools, 142, 151*n*4

decolonization: autonomy struggles, 220–23; calls to action, 221–23; empowerment, 104; knowledge production, 16; restitution, 128–30; restorying, 8, 16–21, 75, 82, 221–23; shame, 99, 107; social movements, 36; transitional justice, 10–15, 21*n*3

Dene nation worldview, 211

Denham, Aaron, 156

Denny, Andrew, 87

Duplessis Orphans, viii

economic development, 147, 148, 159–60, 163–64, 169–70

education systems: history curricula, 136; integrated, 35–36; public schools, 214; worldviews, 212–14

Elsey, Christine, 216*n*17

Elsipogtog protests, 88

EM1-A Rupert River Diversion, 160

empowerment, 104, 107, 127–31, 132*n*29. *See also* power relations

English language, 70*n*8, 116, 121, 127, 166, 168, 201, 211

Erving, Augusta, 148

ethnic groups: categories, 214–15; identification, 151*n*7; vertical mosaic, 30; worldviews, 210–11

Euro-Canadians: boarding school experiences, 206–7; education principles, 212–13; family, 211–12; immigration, 201; Indigenous relationship, 156–57,

Hudson's Bay Company, 147, 158
Hughes, Jula, 10, 14–15, 84, 209
human rights, 12, 65–66
human rights revolution, 30, viii–ix
hydroelectricity projects, 158–60, 169–70

"I" and "we/us," 56, 57
identity (as survivor), 18–19, 55–58, 66–69,
    113–15, 119–27, 131n2, 145–46
Income Security Program, 159, 163
Independent Assessment Process, 8–9, 10,
    11, 19, 179, 194n5, 194n8
Indian Act (1876), 79, 90n5, 116
Indian Affairs, 5, 33–34, 35, 90n8
Indian Association of Alberta, 37
Indian Residential School Settlement
    Agreement (IRSSA): about, 82, 138;
    Labrador Inuit exclusion, 137–41, ix;
    lawsuits, 6, 12, 82, 178, 216n12; non-
    recognized residential schools, 19, 63,
    137–41, 151n4, ix; reparation programs,
    8–9; truth sharing, 84; versions, 207
Indian Residential School Survivors
    Committee, 50, 53–61, 187
Indian residential school syndrome, 43
Indian Residential Schools Survivor
    Society, 146
Indigenous cultural identity: defence of,
    39–40; human rights, 12, 65–66; loss,
    100–5, 121–22, 141–49, 160–71, 184,
    213–14; memory, 116, 141–43; mi-
    yupimaatisiiun (being alive well), 168,
    170; parenting skills loss, 118, 124–27,
    142–43, 163, 187–88; purification rituals,
    63; reciprocity, 168–70; self-reliance,
    20; shame and loss, 100–5; teachings,
    76, 90n3, 105–7; traditional ways of
    life, 118, 165, 202, 206, 213–14. See also
    decolonization
Indigenous language: cultural loss, 56,
    70n4, 116, 142, 163; curriculum, 201,
    206; decolonization, 104; retention,
    121–22; social capacity, 55, 70n8; sup-
    pression and punishment, 53–54, 70n3,
    99, 113, 162, 166, 168; survivor stories,
    53–54, 55–56, 70n8, 70nn3–4, 99, 116
Indigenous peoples: activism, 37–38, 39,
    40, 138; autonomy, 36, 39, 158–60,

167, 220–23; "best left as Indian," 200,
    205; clergy, 199, 202; empowerment,
    104, 107, 127–31, 132n29; family, 212;
    homelands, 141, 151n5, 151n8, 157–60,
    169–70; intellectuals, 16, 221–23; land
    dispossession, 87–89, 117–18, 129; land
    rights, 158–60, 167; prison population,
    183; religion worldview, 213, 216n17;
    substance abuse, 123, 132n19
Indigenous-settler relations: anger, 89;
    colonialism, 215n7; community vs state,
    83; decolonization and religion, 216n17;
    fear, 102; historical, 156–57; reconcilia-
    tion perspectives, 198–215; restitution,
    128–30; shame, 85; social inclusion, 86;
    teamwork, 85; transitional justice, 8,
    10–21, 21n3. See also Euro-Canadians
individual experience vs collective identity,
    53, 55–59, 66–69
Infomart newspaper database, 194n9
Innu (survivor testimony), 63, 67
intergenerational trauma: categories, 69,
    115, 118–19; pain, 55; perpetrators, 60,
    71n28; psychoanalytic theories, 61–63;
    youth, 59, 61, 63, 67, 82. See also cultural
    trauma; family breakdown; historical
    trauma; shame
intermediary actors, 60, 61, 63, 71n29
International Grenfell Association, 142,
    145, 147
Inuit nation: community relocation,
    147–48, 151n8; council of elders, 148;
    education worldview, 212; family
    worldview, 212, 216n16; homelands, 138,
    141, 147, 151n5, 151n8; language loss, 142;
    power and religion worldview, 213, 214;
    racism, 146; Southern, 142, 151n7; treat-
    ies, 171n1; Western, 212, 216n16. See also
    Labrador Inuit
Inuit Nunangat, 147, 151n8
Inuktitut language, 142
Inuvialuit (Western Arctic Inuit), 212,
    216n16
Inuvialuit Regional Corporation, 138

James, Matt, 12–13, 14, 15, 16, 128
James Bay and Northern Quebec
    Agreement (JBNQA): impact, 20,

163–64; modification, 159–60; narratives, 156–57; negotiations, 167
Johnson, Lottie Mae (survivor), 86
Johnston, Basil (survivor), 40
Jung, Courtney, 11–12
justice (retributive vs restorative), 11, 21*n*3

Kablunângajuit (half white), 142, 146, 151*n*7
Kaefer, Florence, 191
Kahnesatake standoff, 88
KAIROS (ecumenical organization), 85–86
Kemuksigak, Patricia, 140–41
Kendall, Rev. Stephen, 208
King, A. Richard, 215*n*5
Knockwood, Isabelle (survivor and author): anger, 123; collective identity, 113, 115; land dispossession, 87–88; parenting skills loss, 125; residential schooling, 123, 183, 195*n*12
knowledge, 16, 84, 105–6, 212, x
Kovach, Margaret, 98

La Grande River hydroelectric complex, 158
Labrador Inuit: cultural memory loss, 141–43; exclusion from Settlement Agreement, 137–41; forced community relocation, 137; lawsuits, 139, 151*n*6; mixed heritage, 142, 146, 151*n*7; national event delegation, 140–41; residential schooling memory, 135–50. *See also* Inuit nation
Labrador Inuit Land Claims Agreement, 138
Labrador Métis nation, 142, 146, 151*n*7
land dispossession, 87–89, 117–18, 129
land rights, 158–60, 167
Lane, Jill, 18
language. *See* Indigenous language
Lavabre, Marie-Claire, 17
Lavoie, Archbishop, 185–86
law (power), 139–40
Law Commission of Canada, viii
Lawrence, Bonita, 89
lawsuits (survivors), 5–6, 82, 127–28, 139, 151*n*6, 207–8, 216*n*12

Leacock, Stephen, 33
legends and knowledge, 96, 105–7
Levy, Daniel, 17
liberal humanism, 84
life stories. *See* student experiences; survivor testimony
Lockwood Boarding School (Cartwright), 142, 151*n*6
logic of elimination (colonization), 79, 116
loss (triple burden), 144–49
love: absence, 81; anger, 89; community, 83–86; conceptualizations, 77–79; denial, 79–81; emotions, 89–90; familial, 74, 80; feminism, 78, 90*n*4; home, 86–87; Indigenous teachings, 76, 90*n*3; reconciliation, 20–21, 74–90; secondhand, 81; shame, 85; survivance, 75, 90, 90*n*2; unconditional, 76

Macauley, Thomas, 32–33
MacDonald, Mark, 214
Mackey, Eva, 7
Mackey, Father Jeremiah P., 115, 124
Maclean's magazine, 38
Makivik Corporation, 138
Makkovik Boarding School (Makkovik), 141, 151*n*6
Makkovik community (relocation to), 147
Maliseet territory, 87
Mamakwa, Bishop (survivor), 184
Mamdani, Mahmood, 13
mandatory schooling, 90*n*5, 102, 142
marital relationship skills loss, 126
Martin, Lawrence, 10, 100–5
Martin, Paul, 63–64, 71*n*29, 71*n*31
materialism, 164, 169
McKegney, Sam, 155–56
meaning and suffering, 31, 44, 55
Meawasige, Isabelle, 104
media coverage: church publications, 181–91; mainstream, 68, 181, 194*n*9
memory: concepts, 137; countermemories, 17–19; cultural, 116, 141–43; loss, 141–43; politics, 137; studies, 9, 16–17
Mennonites (Poplar Hill Residential School), 184
mental health protection, 62–63

Passamaquoddy territory, 87
paternalism to partnership, 190, 199–202, 215n3
Paul, Daniel, 115
Peace and Friendship Treaties, 87, 90n8
peacemaker myth, 83
pedophilia. *See* sexual abuse
Peers, Rt. Rev. Michael, 199
performance (survivor testimony), 66–68
Perley, David, 215n3
perpetrators: ambiguity, 60–61, 71n28; cultural trauma classification, 51, 52, 54; reframing as victims, 179, 192–94, 194n5, 194nn7–8
Perry, Adele, 100
Pettipas, Archbishop Gerard, 188
philanthropy (residential schools), 142, 145
Poliandri, Simone, 10, 18–19, 67
Political Agreement, 6
politics of recognition, 137, 139, 140, 143
Poplar Hill Residential School (Mennonite), 184
Porter, John, 30
Povinelli, Elizabeth, 139
power relations: law, 139–40; religion, 212–13; role in meaning, 31; symbolic, 16; transformation, 8, 16–21. *See also* empowerment
Presbyterian Church, 7, 195n15, 208
prisons (Kenora), 183
psychoanalytic theory (trauma), 61–63
public hearings, 53–66, 131n9, 194n5
public school system, 214
public sphere (residential school representation), 29–46, 54–55, 59, 65, 70n3, 136
purification rituals, 63

racism, 7, 78, 88, 117, 140, 144, 200, 209
real vs cultural genocide, 63–65
reciprocity, 168–70
reconciliation: approaches, 13–14; church perspective, 45, 177–94, 195n11, 204, 215n8, 216n11; differences, 210; education, 215n8; harmony, 97, 98; judicial vs relational perspectives, 208; love, 74–90; narratives, 186–88; process, 75, 177–94; redemption, 190–91; redress,

75–76; restitution, 13–14, 128–30; societal healing, 13; sports metaphor, 85. *See also* survivor testimony; Truth and Reconciliation Commission of Canada (TRC)
Red Paper, 37
redress/restitution, 5, 13–14, 21n2, 42–43, 75–76, 128–30
Regan, Paulette, 75, 82, 83
regional economic development, 147, 148, 159–60, 163–64, 169–70
religion and power, 212–13
Renan, Ernest, 136
reparation programs, 8–9, 10, 11
research: Indigenous-settler relations, 215, 216n17; methodology, 200; participants, 203–7, 215, 215n9 , 216
resentment and anger, 89, 123
residential school survivors. *See* student experiences; survivor testimony
residential school system: about, 4; absence of love, 79–81; abuse, 125, 144–45, 146, 155–56, 161–62, 209; assimilation intent, 33–34, 42; beginnings, 32–35, 150n1; church role, 188, 195n15; church statistics, 195n15; closure, 35–40; colonial dispossession link, 129; criticisms, 35–40; cultural genocide, 46, 64; curriculum, 141–42, 201–2, 206; end, 35–40; goals, 33–34, 42, 188, 195n15; government funding, 138, 150n1, 206; health report, 34; historical records, 150n3; Holocaust analogy, 64–65; "Indian residential school syndrome," 43; Indigenous curriculum, 201, 206; Indigenous problem, 68, 203–4; inquests/inquiries, 4–5, 38–39; institutional, 144; integrated system, 35–36; legacy, 117–19, 163, 187–88; living conditions, 35; mandatory schooling, 79, 90n5, 102, 142; meaning and suffering, 29–46; missing children and experimentation, 64, 90n6, 150n3; national memory, 135–50; nonrecognized (settlement agreement), 19, 63, 137–41, 151n4, ix; nutritional experiments, 90n6, 150n3; opinion polls, 68; philanthropy, 142, 145; public representation phases, 44–46;